move Up

Advanced
Student's Book
Simon Greenall

Editorial Consultants
Bridget Green Mukogawa Fort Wright Institute
James Hunter Gonzaga University English Language Center
Institute for Extended Learning, Community
Colleges of Spokane

MACMILLAN
HEINEMANN
English Language Teaching

Map of the Book

Lesson	Grammar and functions	Vocabulary	Skills and sounds
1 *English... At Home and Abroad* — Signs in English from around the world	Questions; basic rules	Words used in English from other languages	**Reading:** reading signs from around the world; reading and answering a questionnaire; reading for main ideas **Speaking:** talking about hopes and expectations for an English course; asking questions about **Move Up** Advanced **Writing:** writing questions about **Move Up** Advanced
2 *The Best Way to Learn* — Discussion about language learning styles	Tag questions; negative questions; imperative questions; suggestions and reply questions	Vocabulary to describe language errors and parts of speech	**Sounds:** intonation in tag questions; using a model dialogue for guided speaking practice **Listening:** listening for main ideas; inferring **Writing:** writing an essay *The Best Way to Learn English*
3 *Good Behavior* — Customs and rituals in different cultures	The definite and indefinite article	Gestures and movements of the body	**Speaking:** talking about ways of greeting and addressing people; using a model dialogue for guided speaking **Reading:** reading for main ideas; understanding text organization; focusing on topic sentences; inferring
4 *Social Customs, Past and Present* — Customs in different age groups			**Sounds:** /ði:/ and /θə/ **Listening:** listening for main ideas; interpreting information **Speaking:** talking about spare-time activities **Writing:** text organization in an informal letter; writing an informal letter about customs and rituals
5 *Passion Play* — Soccer in Mexico	Tense review: present tenses	Soccer and sports	**Speaking:** exchanging information on hobbies and leisure activities; a commentary of a sporting event **Reading:** reading for main ideas; linking ideas; dealing with unfamiliar words **Writing:** preparing a commentary of a sporting event
6 *Hobby or Obsession?* — Hobbies and leisure activities	Criticizing behavior and habits; agreeing and disagreeing	Sport and leisure activities	**Speaking:** talking about hobbies and leisure activities; a discussion about hobbies **Listening:** listening for main ideas; listening for specific information **Sounds:** stressed words in sentences of complaint **Writing:** writing a report of a discussion about hobbies
7 *Making Plans* — Arranging a day out in Boston	Tense review: talking about the future; making and responding to suggestions	People, places, and types of entertainment	**Listening:** identifying context and purpose; listening for specific information **Speaking:** planning a day out in Boston; making suggestions **Writing:** identifying the difference between formal and informal expressions; writing a formal business letter
8 *Twenty-four Hours in Your Town* — Planning a tourist guide to a town or region	Tense review: talking about the future	Features of city life	**Reading:** reading for specific information; evaluating a text **Sounds:** polite and friendly intonation **Speaking:** describing different aspects of a town or region **Writing:** making notes; writing a tourist guide for a town or region
Fluency 1 *Mind Your Manners!*	**Apologizing and thanking**		
Progress Check Lessons 1–8	Review	Learning vocabulary	**Sounds:** /ɔ:/ and /ɜ:/; /ə/; stressed words in sentences **Speaking:** talking about plans for a penpal's visit **Writing:** writing a letter giving advice about greeting people and arrangements for a visit
9 *Achievements...* — An extract from *Great Railway Journeys* by Lisa St. Aubin de Terán	Tense review: present perfect simple and continuous	Important life events	**Speaking:** talking about personal achievements and ambitions; exchanging information about biographies **Reading:** predicting; reading for main ideas; reading for specific information; evaluating a text; inferring **Writing:** writing questions to obtain biographical information
10 *...and Ambitions* — Personal achievements and ambitions	Tense review: present perfect simple and continuous	Important life events	**Sounds:** weak form /bɪn/ **Listening:** listening for specific information **Writing:** writing a biography for a newspaper article

Lesson	Grammar and functions	Vocabulary	Skills and sounds
11 *Nurse Coxall's Revenge* *Nurse Coxall's Revenge,* a short story	Tense review: past tenses	Words connected with medicine	**Speaking:** talking about truth and deception **Listening:** predicting the order of events; listening for man ideas; listening for specific information **Writing:** rewriting the story from a different point of view
12 *Trust Me—I'm a Doctor* The story of a doctor in the 19th century	Describing a series of events in the past	Words connected with medicine	**Sounds:** syllable stress **Reading:** reading for main ideas; inferring; dealing with unfamiliar words **Speaking:** talking about different jobs
13 *Wish You Were Here?* An extract from *The Lost Continent* by Bill Bryson	Adjectives	Adjectives describing places	**Speaking:** talking about features of a vacation; discussing holiday preferences **Writing:** writing statements about holiday preferences **Reading:** reading for main ideas; inferring; understanding a writer's style; distinguishing between fact and opinion
14 *Dream Vacation* Talking about vacations	Describing position	Geographical description	**Listening:** listening for specific information; inferring **Sounds:** linking sounds /j/, /w/ **Writing:** writing a description of a town or region using fact and opinion adjectives
15 *Spooky Stories* Four ghost stories from *True Ghost Stories of Our Time*	Participial (*-ing*) clauses	Words connected with the senses	**Reading:** reading for main ideas; reading for specific information; dealing with difficult vocabulary **Speaking:** talking about ghost stories
16 *Strange Sensations* A ghost story set in Utah	Verbs of sensation	Words connected with sounds	**Sounds:** pauses, stress, intonation for dramatic effect **Listening:** predicting; listening for specific information; inferring; dealing with difficult expressions **Speaking:** talking about a ghost story **Writing:** writing a ghost story; linking words *meanwhile, eventually, finally*
Fluency 2 *Family and Friends*	**Giving opinions; expressing emotions**		
Progress Check Lessons 9–16	Review	Positive and negative connotation; adjective suffixes	**Sounds:** /ɔɪ/ and /əʊ/; stressed words in sentences **Listening:** listening and taking notes **Speaking:** retelling a story
17 *First Day at School* An extract from *To Kill a Mockingbird* by Harper Lee	Talking about memories; *remember* + noun/-*ing*	Education and school	**Speaking:** talking about early schooldays **Reading:** predicting; reading for main ideas; dealing with unfamiliar words; inferring
18 *Memories of School* An interview with a teacher in the Sudan	*Used to* and *would* + infinitive; *be/get used to* + noun/-*ing*	Education and school	**Listening:** listening for specific information; inferring **Sounds:** /j/ in American and British English **Writing:** interpreting and writing a school report
19 *Law and Order* Strange laws around the world	Modal verbs: *must, have to, have got to, can't, must not*	Words connected with crime	**Sounds:** syllable stress **Reading:** reacting to a text; reading for main ideas; reading for specific information **Speaking:** talking about new laws **Writing:** writing new laws
20 *Guilty or Not Guilty* The legal system in the United States	Modal verbs: *don't need to/don't have to, didn't need to/didn't have to, should/shouldn't*	Words connected with law and order	**Listening:** listening for main ideas; listening for specific information **Reading:** reacting to a text; reading for main ideas **Writing:** writing a letter to a newspaper expressing an opinion; linking words and expressions for opinions
21 *Go West* Pioneers on the Oregon Trail	Clauses of purpose	Words from a passage about pioneers on the Oregon Trail	**Reading:** reacting to a text, reading for main ideas; dealing with unfamiliar words **Speaking:** talking about necessities for a journey **Writing:** writing about necessities for a journey

Lesson	Grammar and functions	Vocabulary	Skills and sounds
22 *Inventions* Strange inventions	Noun/adjective + *to* + infinitive	Household items and actions	**Speaking:** guessing the purpose of different inventions **Listening:** listening for main ideas; listening for specific information **Sounds:** assimilation of /t/ and /d/ in connected speech **Writing:** writing a product description
23 *Food, Glorious Food!* What your choice of food reveals about you	Conditionals (1): zero, first, and second conditionals; *if* and *when*	Food and drink	**Speaking:** talking about different ways of cooking and preparing food; talking about typical food and drink **Reading:** reading and answering a questionnaire; reading for main ideas **Listening:** listening for specific information; inferring **Sounds:** stressed words in sentences
24 *Meals on Wheels* Car engine cooking	Conditionals (2): *unless, even if, as long as, provided* (*that*), *or/otherwise*	Food and drink	**Reading:** predicting; reading for main ideas; reading for specific information **Speaking:** talking about car engine cooking **Writing:** writing advice on eating in different situations, such as picnics and barbecues
Fluency 3 *Home Visit*	**Expressing ability; making and responding to compliments; asking a favor**		
Progress Check *Lessons 17–24*	Review	*Remember, forget, try, stop, regret* + *-ing* or infinitive; opposite or negative meanings with prefixes	**Sounds:** /aʊ/, /oː/, and /ɔː/; different ways of pronouncing *-ough*; stressed words in connected speech **Listening:** listening and taking notes **Writing:** rewriting news stories
25 *Hi-tech Dreams or Nightmares?* A computerized home	The passive	Words connected with technology	**Reading:** predicting; reading for specific information; inferring **Writing:** writing a letter of complaint
26 *In Touch* New technology	Passive infinitive; passive gerund	Words connected with different methods of communication	**Listening:** listening for specific information; inferring **Sounds:** stress in compound nouns **Speaking:** a discussion about technology and communication **Writing:** writing a summary of a discussion
27 *The Amish* The Amish people of Pennsylvania	Relative clauses	New words from a passage about the Amish people	**Speaking:** talking about lifestyles; talking about changes in lifestyles **Reading:** reading for specific information; inferring
28 *Lifestyles* Living in California	Relative and participial clauses	Lifestyle in California	**Listening:** predicting; listening for specific information **Sounds:** pauses in restrictive and nonrestrictive relative clauses **Writing:** writing a diary entry for a day spent with an Amish family or in a Californian community
29 *Lucky Escapes* Talking about lucky escapes	Third conditional	Positive and negative feelings	**Speaking:** talking about lucky situations **Listening:** listening for main ideas; listening for specific information **Reading:** reading for specific information **Writing:** writing a summary
30 *Bad Luck!* Stories about bad luck	Expressing wishes and regrets	Opinions	**Reading:** predicting; reading for main ideas; understanding text organization **Sounds:** /s/ and /ʃ/; stressed words in sentences expressing wishes and regrets **Speaking:** talking about stories
31 *All-time Greats* The story of the song *The Girl From Ipanema*	Phrasal verbs	Types of music and words connected with music	**Speaking:** talking about different types of music; talking about national characteristics of music **Reading:** reading for main ideas; inferring; linking ideas

Lesson	Grammar and functions	Vocabulary	Skills and sounds
32 *What's Your Favorite?* Favorite music and books	Phrasal verbs	Words connected with music and books	**Sounds:** stressed words in sentences with phrasal verbs **Listening:** listening for main ideas and specific information **Writing:** completing a book review using attitude words or phrases; writing a review of a favorite piece of music or a book **Speaking:** talking about favorite music and books
Fluency 4 *Business Matters*	**Talking about ability**		
Progress Check Lessons 25–32	Review	Phrasal verbs	**Sounds:** /θ/ and /ð/; silent consonants; being aware of a speaker's attitude **Writing:** preparing for a game called *If Things Had Been Different* **Speaking:** playing *If Things Had Been Different*
33 *Spending Money* An extract from *Tender is the Night* by F. Scott Fitzgerald	Countable and uncountable nouns	Shopping items; new words from a story	**Speaking:** talking about shopping, discussing humorous sayings **Reading:** predicting; understanding the writer's style; reading for main ideas; reacting to a text **Sounds:** timing and intonation in jokes
34 *Born to Shop* Different shopping habits	Ways of expressing quantity	Words connected with money	**Speaking:** talking about words connected with money **Listening:** predicting; listening for main ideas; listening for specific information **Speaking:** talking about shopping habits **Writing:** writing a questionnaire about shopping habits
35 *Trends* How to survive in the 21st century	Future conditional and future perfect		**Reading:** predicting; reading for main ideas; dealing with difficult vocabulary; inferring **Speaking:** talking about future trends **Writing:** writing about future trends
36 *For Better or Worse* The outcome of people's plans for the future	Future in the past	Words connected with life plans	**Listening:** listening for main ideas and specific information **Sounds:** /t/ **Writing:** looking at words and phrases often used in discussions; writing a summary
37 *Davy Crockett* The story of Davy Crockett	Passive constructions with *say, believe*	Words connected with folk heroes	**Reading:** reading for main ideas; reading for specific information **Speaking:** talking about folk heroes and legends
38 *Folk Heroes and Legends* Some American folk heroes	Speculating about the past: *may have, might have, must have, can't have*	Words connected with folk heroes and legends	**Listening:** predicting; listening for specific information; listening and taking notes; inferring **Sounds:** stressed words in a dialogue **Writing:** writing a guide to folk heroes and legends
39 *Brand Image* Characteristics of different brands and products	Reported speech	Adjectives to describe different products	**Speaking:** talking about well-known brands and products **Listening:** predicting; listening for main ideas; listening for specific information **Sounds:** understanding different tones of voice
40 *The Real Thing?* Global advertising	Reporting verbs		**Speaking:** talking about advertising; using a model dialogue for guided speaking practice **Reading:** reading for main ideas; linking ideas; distinguishing between main ideas and examples **Listening:** predicting; understanding text organization **Writing:** complaining about an advertising claim
Fluency 5 *Beyond Words*	**Saying what you mean**		
Progress Check Lessons 33–40	Review	Idioms, slang, and informal language	**Sounds:** homophones; homographs **Speaking:** planning a stay in a foreign country

① English... At Home and Abroad

Questions: basic rules

VOCABULARY

1. Here are some words from other languages which are used in English. Are there any which you also use in your language? Are there any words which come from your language?

sushi pasta pizza salon samba alpha
sauna karate boutique mascara drama
panorama piñata delicatessen route
kindergarten delta concerto kebob
glasnost junta typhoon siesta piano
bungalow

2. Work in pairs. Say what the words in the box mean and where they come from.

3. Write down five English words which you often hear in your language.

READING AND SPEAKING

1. Look at the signs written in English from around the world. Read them and decide where you might see them. Choose from these places:

– in a hotel   – in a zoo   – in a laundromat
– in a restaurant   – in a street

2. Work in pairs. The English in the signs is grammatically correct but each sign has a different meaning from what it intends to say. Say what each sign intends to say and what it really says.

3. Which sign do you find the most amusing? Have you come across any similarly confusing signs in English or in your language?

The elevator is being fixed for the next day. During that time we regret that you will be unbearable.

Visitors are expected to complain at the office between the hours of 9 and 11 A.M. daily.

Please do not feed the animals. If you have any suitable food, please give it to the guard on duty.

Please leave your values at the front desk.

STOP – DRIVE SIDEWAYS →

Ladies are requested not to have children in the bar.

Our wines leave you nothing to hope for.

4. Here are some questions about using English at home and abroad. Read them and think about your answers to them.

1. Have you ever been to an English-speaking country?
2. Can you meet English-speaking people in your country?
3. Where can you hear English spoken or written in your town?
4. Have you ever spoken English with a native speaker?
5. How long have you been learning English?
6. What do you like most and least about learning English?
7. Do you ever use your own language during your English lessons?
8. Do you usually ask questions during your lessons?
9. Who speaks to you most often in English? Your teacher or your fellow students?
10. Are you looking forward to your Advanced-English course?

5. Work in pairs and talk about your answers to the questions.

I've been to the States a couple of times, and...

6. Work in groups of three or four and make a list of your hopes and expectations for your English lessons. Use these phrases:

We hope we'll... We'd like to... We expect we'll...
When you have finished, share your ideas with the rest of the class and make a class list. You could put your hopes and expectations on a wall poster to remind you.

GRAMMAR

> Questions: basic rules
> **Here are some rules for forming questions.**
> **You put the auxiliary verb before the subject in written questions and usually in spoken questions.**
> **You put the rest of the verb after the subject.**
> *Have you ever studied another foreign language?*
> **When a verb has no auxiliary, you use the auxiliary *do* in the question, followed by an infinitive without *to*.**
> *Do you write down every new word you come across?*
> **You don't use *do* in questions with modal verbs or the verb *be*.**
> *Can you guess what a word means from the context?*
> *Are you looking forward to working in groups?*
> **When you use a question word (*who, what, where, when, how*), you put an auxiliary verb before the subject.**
> *How long have you been in this class?*
> **When *who, what,* or *which* is the subject of the sentence, you don't use *do*.**
> *What helps you the most, your textbook or your dictionary?*

1. Read the rules for making questions in the grammar box. Find one more example of each rule in *Reading and Speaking* activity 4.

2. Work in pairs and think of questions that you could ask your fellow students. Work with another pair and ask your questions. Then tell the rest of the class some of the things you have found out about your partners.

SPEAKING AND WRITING

1. Look through *Move Up* Advanced. Write five questions about the book to ask your partner.

Where's the Grammar Review?

2. Work in pairs and exchange questions. Can you answer your partner's questions?

The Grammar Review is at the back of the book.

2 | *The Best Way to Learn*

Tag questions; negative questions;
imperative questions; suggestions; reply questions

SOUNDS AND SPEAKING

1. Read the dialogue and decide where Pat's sentences
a–g below should go.

PAT (1) ____

DON Yes. In fact, I speak French and Chinese.

PAT (2) ____

DON Yes, when I was seventeen, I took Chinese for a
couple of years.

PAT (3) ____

DON No, in fact, I've almost forgotten Chinese. It's
easy to forget a language if you don't practice.

PAT (4) ____

DON No, I practiced when I was in Canada.

PAT (5) ____

DON For the weekend?

PAT (6) ____

DON Is it? Yeah, I guess it is. But aren't you worried
about the cost?

PAT (7) ____

a. You speak French, don't you?
b. Well, why not? It's only a few hours from the
border, isn't it?
c. Chinese! You didn't learn Chinese at school,
did you?
d. I've got an idea. I'd love to go to Montreal,
wouldn't you?
e. You've never visited China, have you?
f. No, it'll be fun. And you'll have plenty of
opportunities to speak French, won't you?
g. And what about your French? You haven't forgotten
that too, have you?

2. 🔊 Now listen to the dialogue. Write R if you think
the intonation is rising on Pat's tag questions and F if
you think the intonation is falling. For more
information on the intonation of tag questions, see
the Grammar Review at the back of the book.

3. Work in pairs and act out the dialogue.

LISTENING

1. Look at these statements about learning a foreign
language and decide if you agree with them. Work in
pairs and compare your answers with your partner.

You forget a language if you don't use it.

You can learn a language outside the classroom.

The best way to learn a language is to go to the
country where it is spoken.

You should always use a dictionary if you don't
understand a word.

Don't worry about making mistakes; it's more
important to make yourself understood.

Learning grammar is very useful.

Listening, especially to native speakers, is the most
difficult skill to develop.

It's easier for children to learn a foreign language than
adults.

2. 🔊 Listen to Hannah, Mike, and Janet talking
about how they learned a foreign language.
Find out where and when they first started learning
the language.

3. Work in pairs. Put the name of the speaker by the
statements in 1 that you think they would agree with.

🔊 Now listen and check.

GRAMMAR

Tag questions
Tags after affirmative statements
*You speak French, **don't you**?*
*You'll have plenty of opportunities to speak French, **won't you**?*
Tags after negative statements
*You haven't forgotten that too, **have you**?*
*You didn't learn Chinese at school, **did you**?*
Negative questions
***Aren't you worried** about the cost?*
Imperative questions
***Take out** the garbage, **will you**?*
Reply questions
*It's only a few hours.   **Is it**? I didn't know that.*
*He doesn't like grammar.   **Doesn't he**? I thought he did.*
For more information, see the Grammar Review at the back of the book.

1. Look at the grammar box. How do you form the following?

   1. tag questions after affirmative statements
   2. tag questions after negative statements
   3. tag questions after imperatives
   4. negative questions
   5. reply questions

2. Complete the sentences with a suitable question word or tag.

   1. Shut up, ____ ?
   2. You haven't been waiting long, ____ ?
   3. He just finished, ____ ?
   4. That was great, ____ ?
   5. "We have to go."
      "Oh, ____ you stay longer?"
   6. "____ horrible weather?"
      "Yes, it is."
   7. "I didn't like the movie."
      "____ ? I did."
   8. "I'm tired."
      "____ ? You don't look tired."

3. Choose four statements from *Listening* activity 1 and rewrite them with tag questions.
Work in pairs and ask each other your questions.

WRITING AND VOCABULARY

1. This essay was written by a learner of English. It contains twenty-three mistakes. Mark the mistakes in the following ways.
– Underline any words which are wrong.
– Circle and arrow any words which are in the wrong position.
– Insert any words which are missing.
The first four have been done for you.

2. Work in pairs. Use these words to analyse the other mistakes in the essay.

punctuation spelling word order missing word wrong word preposition verb form noun adjective

Are there any mistakes which you often make?

3. Write an essay with the same title. When you have finished your first draft, read through it and check that you have avoided the types of mistakes mentioned in activity 2.

4. Work in pairs and exchange your essays. Do you both agree on the best way to learn English?

The Best Way to Learn English

Since many years, people have ʌ been trying to find the best way to learning a language (foreign). For me, the best way is to last a long time in the country, such as England or United States. Listening comprehension is extremely hardy and you needed to hear to English authentic. it is good to hear to the radio and wacth television in English. Gramer is important two, so you must spend long time to learn the rules. At last, the most important thing to do is seize the opportunity to talk at peple as much as you can. Do you agree?

3 *Good Behavior*

SPEAKING AND READING

1. Work in groups of three or four and discuss the following.

1. Have you ever been to a foreign country? If so, were there any customs that you found unusual or which made you uncomfortable?
2. Does your country have any customs that tourists find surprising?
3. Do you kiss people to greet them? If so, how many times, and when?
4. Are there any topics of conversation that visitors to your country should avoid?
5. Is punctuality important in your country?

2. Read the following passage. Decide where it comes from:

– A geography textbook
– A guide to Latin American customs and manners.
– A novel about Latin America

Greetings

(1) ____. In many parts of Latin America, greetings are often rather effusive. People sometimes shake hands and sometimes kiss or embrace. In some places, women will be kissed three times on the cheek—twice in greetings and once as a wish for marriage—
5 and should not be offended by this.

Conversation

People from English-speaking countries often believe in being open, frank, and direct. Latin Americans take pride in being tactful and complimentary. Follow suit to avoid giving offense.
10 Try to learn before you go. (2) ____. To make a good impression in business or to strike up an acquaintance, however, it's essential to know something about the other person's world. For instance, learning about soccer, a sport which is almost an obsession in most of Latin America, will give you an instant topic of conversation.

In Public

15 Some public manners and gestures don't travel. You may offend when you least intend to. For example, in conversation Latin Americans naturally tend to stand very close. Don't back away, or you might be considered snobbish and aloof.
Be careful talking with your hands. (3) ____. The cheerful "OK" sign with the thumb and index finger of the right hand in a circle is obscene in most Latin American countries.

20 **Dress**

(4) ____. North Americans are pretty much used to wearing what they want, but dress that is too casual is very offensive in some areas of Latin America. When selecting your travel wardrobe, remember that you rarely err by being on the conservative side.

Appointments

25 (5) ____. If someone has an appointment with you, and a friend drops in, he or she will never say to the friend, "I'm sorry, I can't see you now." Friends always come first, even if they stay three hours! Appointments can happen up to two hours after the agreed time, and no apology is deemed necessary. Frustrating though it may feel, visitors cannot single-handedly change basic cultural traits such as the Latin view of time, nor should
30 they presume that their way is better. Remember, you're the visitor.

3. Are any of the customs mentioned in the passage the same in your country? Do any of them surprise you?

4. Are the following statements true or false?

   1. If a man kisses a woman three times, it means he wants to marry her.
   2. Latin Americans tend to be more indirect than North Americans.
   3. Travelers to Latin America should learn how to play soccer.
   4. Most gestures mean the same in North and South America.
   5. Latin Americans in general dress more formally than North Americans.
   6. It is considered very impolite to be late for an appointment in Latin America.

5. A topic sentence is one that states the main idea of a paragraph. The rest of the paragraph adds details to develop the main idea. The topic sentence is usually the first sentence in the paragraph, but may be in the middle, or even at the end. Five topic sentences have been removed from the passage. Choose from the sentences a–f the one which fits each gap 1–5. There is one extra sentence which you do not need to use.

   a. A visit to any country is richer when you know something about it in advance.
   b. Do not make appointments before ten o'clock.
   c. One of the easiest ways to offend is to dress inappropriately.
   d. Remember that a Latin American's sense of priorities may be different.
   e. To make a good impression, it's important to know how you will be greeted and to react properly.
   f. Gestures mean different things in different countries.

6. Work in pairs and try to guess the meaning of the words in italics below, as they are used in the passage.

   1. *Follow suit* to avoid giving offense (line 8).
   2. *...strike up* an acquaintance (line 10).
   3. Some public manners and gestures *don't travel* (line 15).
   4. *...you rarely* err *by being* on the conservative side (line 23).
   5. *...visitors cannot* single-handedly *change basic cultural traits* (line 29).

VOCABULARY AND SPEAKING

1. Work in pairs. Look at the verbs in the box and answer the questions.

   | beckon blow bow chew clap cuddle frown grin hug kiss kneel laugh nod nudge pat pinch point scratch shrug smile stare stoop stretch wave wink yawn |

   1. Are there any verbs which describe actions that are socially unacceptable to perform in public in your country?
      You shouldn't yawn in public.
   2. Which verbs describe gestures which are warm and friendly?
      cuddle
   3. Which part of the body do you use to perform the actions of the verbs?
      beckon: hand

2. The following conversation takes place in an office. Put the sentences in the right order.

   a. **JANE** You must be Jim Dennis.
   b. **JANE** I'll introduce you to everyone. Let's go and meet your boss. Ah, there she is. Sylvia, this is Jim Dennis, it's his first day. Jim, this is Dr. Sylvia Crewe.
   c. **JANE** Sure, Jim, good to meet you. Welcome to the company! My name's Jane and I'm going to show you around the office.
   d. **JIM** How do you do, doctor.
   e. **JIM** Hello, Jane. Thanks a lot.
   f. **JIM** Yes, that's right, but call me Jim.
   g. **SYLVIA** Call me Sylvia, Jim. Everyone calls me Sylvia. Welcome to the company.
   h. **JIM** Thank you, Sylvia.

   🔲 Listen and check.

3. Work in groups of three. Would a similar dialogue take place in your country?

   Adapt the dialogue so that it is suitable for your country.

   Now act out the dialogue.

4 *Social Customs, Past and Present*

The definite and indefinite article

GRAMMAR

> **The definite and indefinite article**
> **Here are some rules for the use of articles.**
> **You use *a/an*:**
> **– for the first mention of a singular, countable noun.**
> *If **a** friend drops in ...*
> *...**a** sport which is almost **an** obsession...*
> **– with nouns, especially jobs, after *be* and become.**
> *She became **a** successful business traveler.*
> **You use *the*:**
> **– after the first mention of a singular or plural, countable or uncountable noun.**
> *...if **a** friend drops in, she will never say to **the** friend...*
> **– to talk about something unique, when there is only one of something.**
> *...**the** Latin view of time*
> *...**the** thumb and index finger of **the** right hand*
>
> **No article**
> **You don't use any article:**
> **– with plural, abstract, or uncountable nouns when you talk about something in general.**
> *Friends always come first...*
> **– before the names of most countries, towns, and streets.**
> *In many parts of Latin America...*
> **For more information, see the Grammar Review at the back of the book.**

1. Work in pairs. Use the rules in the grammar box to explain the use of the articles (or no article) in these sentences from the passage on page 6.

   1. In many parts of Latin America, greetings are often rather effusive.
   2. A visit to any country is richer when you know something about it in advance.
   3. It's essential to know something about the other person's world.
   4. Gestures mean different things in different countries.

2. Complete the passage with the indefinite or definite article. On some occasions, both may be possible. Can you say why?

   (1) ____ kiss as (2) ____ form of social greeting is, of course, no longer reserved for women. Indeed, men often exchange kisses in countries where it would be considered insulting to kiss (3) ____ woman in public. Except in (4) ____ few countries, it is now regarded as normal for men and women to exchange (5) ____ cheek-to-cheek salutation. There was a time when (6) ____ custom was (7) ____ sign of fairly close friendship; nowadays it has become so pervasive that to shake hands with (8) ____ woman at (9) ____ end of (10) ____ party is regarded as (11) ____ silent equivalent of Groucho Marx's famous remark, "I've had (12) ____ marvelous evening, but this wasn't it."

SOUNDS

Although articles are very important in English, they are rarely stressed in everyday conversation. They are usually pronounced /ə/, /ən/, or /ðə/. Say the following sentences without stressing the articles.

1. I saw an elephant at the grocery store.
2. The back of the bus is the best place to be.
3. A bird in the hand is worth two in the bush.
4. A man and a woman lived in a house in the woods.

   Listen and check your pronunciation. Which words are stressed?

LISTENING

1. You're going to hear Mary Davies and her grandson Pete talking about how social customs in the United States have changed over the last fifty years. First, look at the social customs in the chart below. Think about how they have changed in your country and write notes in the column.

	Your country	Mary Davies	Pete Davies
Behavior of children			
Head of the family			
Age for getting married			
Manners and ways of addressing people			
Living with parents and grandparents			

2. 🔊 Work in groups of three.

Student A: Turn to Communication Activity 8 on page 103.

Student B: Turn to Communication Activity 25 on page 107.

Student C: Turn to Communication Activity 22 on page 106.

3. Work together. What do Mrs. Davies and Pete say about social customs? Complete the chart in as much detail as possible.

🔊 Now listen again and check.

4. Work in pairs. Talk about how customs have changed in your country in the last fifty years. Compare them with customs in the United States.

WRITING

1. Mary Davies is writing to her granddaughter, Ellen, who is doing a project at school about changes in social customs. Ellen has asked her grandmother about social customs when she was young. Put the sections of Mrs. Davies's letter in the right order.

2. Decide if the customs Mrs. Davies describes were similar to those in your country fifty years ago.

3. In groups, discuss the way Americans write informal letters.

1. The address on the letter is Mrs. Davies's. Where has she placed her address?
2. Where is the date?
3. How does the letter begin?
4. How does the letter end?

Do you write informal letters in a similar way? What else tells you that it is an informal letter?

4. Write an informal letter to a penpal about one of the social customs you made notes on in *Listening* activity 2. You can use Mrs. Davies's letter as a model.

A 721 N. 57th Avenue
Portland, OR 97221

B Some people had a boyfriend when they were eighteen or nineteen, but I met my first boyfriend when I was twenty-one. Some people got married at eighteen or nineteen, but most of us waited until we were in our twenties.

C Thanks for your letter. It was good to hear from you and to hear about the friends you have made at your new school. The history project you are working on sounds very interesting and I hope that this information will be helpful.

D If you have any more questions, let me know and I will try to answer them.

Lots of love,

Grandma

E You asked about how I made friends when I was a teenager. Well, when I was your age, I had lots of friends too and I saw them at school or on weekends. They didn't all know each other since I knew people from the tennis club, from school, and from lots of other places. Sometimes, I met people at dances and other social occasions.

F May 26

Dear Ellen,

5 *Passion Play*

Tense review: present tenses

SPEAKING

1. Work in pairs. Make a list of popular hobbies and leisure activities which people in your country enjoy.

Now answer these questions.

Do the activities involve teamwork or individual skill?
Do they involve or interest both men and women?
Do any of the activities involve collecting things?
Do you have a strong passion for them, a mild interest, or no interest at all?
If there are any that you have little or no interest in, do you think people who enjoy them are strange?
How much time do you spend on your hobby or leisure activity?

Our taxi driver has just discovered that one of his passengers supports Cruz Azul. As he hears the name of his team's arch rivals he holds up his Club America season ticket and kisses it as if it were a rosary. The Azteca stadium appears in the distance, a sight as awe-inspiring as Mexico City's Basilica of Guadalupe. Our driver cries: "*El Azteca!—Bellas Artes*—a temple!"

This story illustrates the relationship between Mexico's three great loves: religion, traditional music, and soccer. It's not just a game. Even a moderate sports fan cannot fail to be moved by the spectacle of Mexican soccer and its faithful supporters.

We come as pilgrims in search of the divine sporting experience: a Clasico match at the 120,000-capacity Estadio Azteca, home of Mexico City's twin giants, Club America and Cruz Azul. Today, Club America is playing at home against Las Chivas of Guadalajara. If Las Chivas win today, they can replace Club America at the top of the league! *Ovaciones* is building up the game in dramatic style; the Mexico City sporting newspaper is comparing it to a battle of *mariachis,* Mexico's famous street bands; it is being played under floodlights, the two cities have great dramatic theaters, and the virtuoso performers are the players.

The majority of the crowd at the Azteca are dressed in club colors, with a high percentage of women. Many spectators also don wide *charro sombreros,* the hats typical of *mariachi* musicians. Soccer games, particularly those of the Clasico matches, attract both the rich and the poor of Mexican society. Being seen in a box seat at the Azteca during a Clasico game is as important as attending the opening night of the *Ballet Folklorico* at Bellas Artes.

Passion Play

It is no coincidence that the game is played even on the holy day, Sunday, because *el Futbol* is Mexico's sacred pastime. Mexicans consider the rest of the week as a mere preparation. At noon on Sundays, thousands of Mexicans go to watch soccer games, while millions listen to the game reports on the radio or watch live broadcasts interpreted by the frantic commentary of TV sportscasters.

When the teams file onto the field, the Chivas fans whistle loudly and defiantly at the Club America players. Even before the kickoff, the Club America fans are blowing trumpets, twirling noisemakers, throwing yellow confetti (one of the club colors), waving club flags, and shouting at a fever pitch, producing the most electric atmosphere I've ever experienced at a sporting event.

Club America starts well, but after ten minutes, Las Chivas scores a beautifully simple goal. Then Club America catches up, but the captain is sent out after a deliberate handball. Club America scores again after thirty-seven minutes with a free kick. Las Chivas gets close again just before half time, but Club America scores their third goal. The Club America fans start blowing their trumpets, twirling their noisemakers, and shouting again. Las Chivas scores again, but it's Club America's day at the end of the match.

The Mexicans call the Clasico teams—Cruz Azul, Club America, and Las Chivas—"the best teams in the nation." And they're right.

2. Work in pairs. Discuss these statements about leisure activities. Do you agree with them?

1. Collecting things like stamps or coins is boring.
2. It is better to enjoy a range of activities than to concentrate on just one.
3. Most people prefer to watch sports on television rather than take part themselves.
4. Some sports can only be played by men.
5. Soccer is popular with both men and women.

Now work with another pair and compare your answers.

READING

1. Work in pairs. You're going to read a newspaper article about soccer in Mexico.

Does your country have a national sport? What is it? Is it popular only with men or with women too? Can people become obsessive about a national sport?

2. Read the article and decide which of the following statements best describes why the writer calls it *Passion Play*.

1. Soccer is a game which is played with passion.
2. A *passion play* is a religious drama, and the writer is suggesting that soccer is similar.
3. The fans are passionate about the way their team plays.

3. Read the sentences from the article and answer the questions.

1. *...the name of his team's arch rivals.* —Who are his team's arch rivals?
2. *Even a moderate sports fan cannot fail to be moved by the spectacle...* —Is he moved or not?
3. *...the Mexico City sporting newspaper is comparing it to a battle of mariachis; it is being played under floodlights...* —Who or what does *it* refer to?
4. *...if the rest of the week is a mere preparation.* —A preparation for what?

4. Write down any words or phrases which the writer uses to describe the *passion* of the spectators for soccer.

Even a moderate sports fan cannot fail to be moved by the spectacle.

GRAMMAR

Tense review: present tenses
You use the present simple to talk about:
– a general truth, such as a fact or a state.
*Soccer games **attract** both the rich and poor of Mexican society.*
– something that is regular, such as a routine, custom, or habit.
*At noon on Sundays, thousands of Mexicans **go** to watch soccer games.*
– events in a story or a commentary on a game.
*...after ten minutes, Las Chivas **scores** a beautifully simple goal.*
You use the present continuous to talk about:
– an action which is happening at the moment or an action or state which is temporary.
*Today, Club America **is playing** at home against Las Chivas.*
– the background in a story.
*Even before the kickoff, the fans **are blowing** trumpets, **twirling** noisemakers, **throwing** yellow confetti...*

Look at these sentences from the article. Decide which present tense they use and why.

1. ...one of his passengers supports Cruz Azul.
2. The Azteca stadium appears in the distance.
3. The *Ovaciones* is building up the game...
4. ...the Club Azul fans are blowing trumpets.
5. When the teams file onto the field...
6. The Mexicans call them the best in the nation.

WRITING AND SPEAKING

1. Think of an important sporting event, such as the opening of the Olympic Games, or the final of the World Cup. Imagine you're giving a commentary of the scene to radio listeners. Makes notes on what you can "see."

2. Work in groups of four or five. Give your commentaries to the rest of the group but don't mention the name of the sport. Can the others guess the sporting event you are describing?

6 | *Hobby or Obsession?*

Criticizing behavior and habits; agreeing and disagreeing

VOCABULARY AND SPEAKING

Work in groups of three or four. One student chooses one of the leisure activities in the box. The others have to ask questions to guess the leisure activity you have chosen. You can only answer their questions with *yes* or *no*. Use the following questions to find out about the leisure activity or make up your own.

Do you do it on your own?

Do you do it outside or inside?

Does it need any special equipment?

Do you have to be fit to do it?

Is it usually done by both men and women?

Does it involve collecting something?

Is it a sport?

Is it dangerous?

baseball hunting motor racing surfing tennis riding golf chess track and field boxing knitting dancing mountaineering gambling pottery fishing yoga jogging

SPEAKING AND LISTENING

1. What hobbies do other students in the class have? Find out who has:

– the most interesting hobby
– the most expensive hobby
– the most dangerous hobby

2. 🔲 You're going to hear Dave, Jane, Sarah, and Tim talking about their hobbies. Listen to a section of each of the four interviews and try to guess what their hobbies are.

3. 🔲 Listen to all of each interview. Did you guess the hobbies correctly? Make notes about their hobbies and how long they have been doing them.

4. Work in pairs. Discuss whether Dave, Jane, Sarah, and Tim are describing hobbies or obsessions.

5. Here are some of the things that the speakers' friends and families have said about their hobbies. Put the name of the speaker referred to next to each comment.

1. "If only she'd do something different too—at least on the weekend!"
2. "He's always watching them. If only he were interested in something more normal."
3. "It's definitely an obsession. You know he even watches it on TV when he's seen it live!"
4. "It can't be good for you to do it so often."
5. "It's boring. All they do is throw a ball around. I wish he spent more time with me."
6. "I wish it were more exciting. I just can't see the point of digging up the past."
7. "She looks terrific! I just wish I could be that disciplined."
8. "He's absolutely right. They <u>are</u> the best things on TV."

Compare your answers with your partner.

6. 🔲 Now listen to the tape and check your answers.

FUNCTIONS

Criticizing behavior and habits	
keep + *-ing*	She *keeps going* to the gym.
present continuous + *always*	He's *always watching* football on TV.
present simple + *just*	He *just watches* movies all day.
If only + past simple	*If only* it *were* more exciting.
I wish + past simple	*I wish* he *spent* more time with me.
All they do is + infinitive	*All they do is throw* a ball around.
Agreeing	Disagreeing
I couldn't agree more. Exactly.	*I completely disagree. Do you really think so?*
I agree. Absolutely.	*I'm not sure. It depends.*
So do I. (in answer to *I think...*)	*Do you? I don't.* (in answer to *I think...*)
Neither do I. (in answer to *I don't think...*)	*Don't you? I do.* (in answer to *I don't think...*)

1. Which of the expressions in the functions box for criticizing behavior and habits or agreeing and disagreeing did you hear in *Speaking and Listening* activity 6? Can you think of other sentences the speakers might say using the expressions in the box?

   I wish they would only play football once a week.

2. Think of someone you know well, and make a list of his or her annoying behavior or habits. Tell a partner about this person using some of the expressions in the functions box.

   My father is always leaving the cap off the toothpaste.

3. There are some expressions in the functions box which speakers of English might use to agree or disagree. Can you use their equivalents in your language? If not, what do you say?

4. Work in pairs.

   Student A: Turn to Communication Activity 1 on page 102.
   Student B: Turn to Communication Activity 20 on page 106.

   Do you know anyone who behaves like these people? Tell the class about them.

SOUNDS

Look at these sentences. The speakers are making complaints about other people's behavior. Underline the words you think the speaker will stress to emphasize the complaint.

   1. "They keep fighting each other."
   2. "All they do is kick a ball around."
   3. "He's always watching TV."
   4. "He just spends the whole time playing music."
   5. "I wish it were more exciting."
   6. "If only he spent more time with his family."

   🔊 Listen and check. As you listen, say each sentence out loud.

SPEAKING AND WRITING

1. Work in two groups. You're going to take part in a discussion about the following statement:

   Hobbies are a necessary and important part of your life. People without hobbies are boring.

   Group A: You agree with the statement. Make a list of points to support this view.
   Group B: You disagree with the statement. Make a list of points against this view.

2. Choose two people from each group to present the arguments agreeing or disagreeing with the statement. Prepare to talk for about one minute. Your teacher will organize the discussion.

3. A magazine is publishing a series of reports on hobbies. Write a report on your discussion for the magazine.
   Introduce the subject and say what it's about.
   The discussion was about the statement that hobbies are a necessary part of your life and that people without hobbies are boring.

   Say what the arguments of people who agreed with the statement were and give some examples.
   People who agreed with the statement argued that...

   Say what the arguments against the statement were and give some examples.
   The arguments against were...

   Describe the result of the vote.
   The result of the vote was five people agreed with the statement and two people disagreed.

7 *Making Plans*

Tense review: talking about the future;
making and responding to suggestions

VOCABULARY AND LISTENING

1. Work in pairs. Look at the words in the box and decide what you could use them to talk about. Put them in groups of your own choice.

> aisle *à la carte* box office café cashier circle cloakroom course opening hours department store display escalator exhibit guided tour intermission lobby menu reservation row scenery sculpture service shelf snack stage stalls stroll till tip

Movies: aisle, box office...

Think of other words which can go in these groups.

2. 🔊 Listen to five conversations. Put the number of the conversation by its purpose.

a. asking about opening and closing times ☐
b. making a complaint ☐
c. making a reservation ☐
d. getting information about services ☐
e. buying concert tickets ☐

3. Work in pairs and write down the times mentioned in each conversation.

🔊 Now listen again and check.

GRAMMAR AND FUNCTIONS

Tense review: talking about the future	*will*	*going to*	present continuous	present simple
predicting the future/ future hopes	*	*		
an intention		*		
a decision made at the moment of speaking	*			
a definite arrangement			*	
fixed times, such as timetables				*

Making suggestions and responding to them.

How about going to a play on Friday?   That's a great idea.
*We **could** take Tony to the museum on Saturday.   I'm afraid I'm busy on Saturday.*
*Why **don't** we have lunch in the Union Oyster Bar?   Yes, that would be wonderful.*
***Let's** go to the movies tonight.   I'm sorry I'm having dinner with my parents tonight.*
***Can I** get the tickets?   Yes, please.*

1. Look at these sentences. Decide which future tense is used and why. Use the information in the grammar box to help you.

1. It's going to rain.
2. I'm sure it'll rain.
3. It starts at eight.
4. I'm going to be there to meet you when you arrive.
5. I'm taking the train at ten o'clock.
6. I'll give you a ride if you want.

2. Look at these sentences from the conversations you heard in *Vocabulary and Listening* activity 2. Which tense do the speakers use to talk about something they decide as they speak? Which tense do they use to talk about something which is already planned?

1. "We open at ten Monday through Saturday, and at at noon on Sunday."
2. "OK, Mr. Stein, we'll see you tomorrow. Bye."
3. "Good, I'll try to get down there tonight. You're open until nine, aren't you?'
4. "...and tonight it's going to stay open until four."
5. "So it's going to be just the same tonight?"
6. "How about row D?"   "Sure, that'll be fine."

3. Work in pairs. Talk about your intentions for the weekend. Use *going to* for plans, and *I think I'll...* or *I'll probably...* for anything you're not sure about.

On Saturday I'm going to a tennis match, and on Sunday I think I'll stay home.

LISTENING AND SPEAKING

1. 🔲 Listen to a conversation between Gary and Angela who are going to spend a day with their boss, Tony Baxter, showing him around Boston. Put a check (✓) beside the activities they mention.

a walk along Commonwealth Avenue ☐

lunch at Union Oyster Bar ☐

breakfast in Harvard Square ☐

finish the evening at Quincy Market ☐

shopping at Back Bay ☐

drinks at the Hyatt Regency ☐

a stroll around Beacon Hill ☐

dinner at Joseph's Aquarium ☐

sightseeing in Cambridge ☐

visit the Public Garden ☐

2. Work in pairs. Write down the times they decide on and compare your answers with your partner.

🔲 Now listen again and check.

3. Work in pairs. One of you is Angela and the other Gary. Plan a day's sightseeing in Boston for your boss. Make suggestions about what you'll do and at what time. Think about what other arrangements you need to make and decide who will do them.

How about having lunch at the Union Oyster Bar?
OK, I'll call them and reserve a table. At what time?

WRITING

1. Work in pairs. Angela is going to send Gary a letter confirming the arrangements they discussed on the phone. Decide if the letter is likely to be very formal or fairly informal.

Now read Angela's letter below. There are some expressions which aren't appropriate in the letter. Can you decide what they are?

> September 5
>
> Saltonstall Building 13th floor
> 100 Cambridge Street
> Boston Mass 02178
>
> Dear Sir,
> Regarding our conversation the other day, it was good to hear from you and to figure out the arrangements for Tony's visit. I have attached the schedule for Sunday's visit to Boston.
> With reference to the aforementioned visit, I'm writing to say that I'll collect Tony from the airport on Saturday night and take him to his hotel. I'll see him on Sunday at his hotel at 8 A.M. Can you fax him and let him know what's happening on Saturday and Sunday? I would be grateful for your help in this matter.
> See you then.
> Yours sincerely,
> *Angela*

2. Decide if these are opening or closing remarks for a formal or informal letter. Write F for formal and I for informal in the box.

1. Thank you for your letter of August 20. ☐
2. It was good to speak to you the other day. ☐
3. Regarding our conversation of August 13... ☐
4. Please give my best wishes to... ☐
5. Looking forward to seeing you on Saturday. ☐
6. I look forward to seeing you on Saturday. ☐
7. It was good to hear from you. ☐
8. I look forward to hearing from you. ☐

3. Rewrite Angela's letter above in more appropriate language.

4. Write a formal letter to Tony Baxter. Think about:
addresses, greetings, opening remarks, closing remarks, conclusion.

Make sure you include information about the arrangements for Saturday and Sunday.

Twenty-four Hours in Your Town

**Tense review:
talking about the future**

Cambridge, Massachusetts

Cambridge, Massachusetts, lies over the Charles River across from Boston. A university town since shortly after its 1630 founding, site of the only college in the Americas until nearly the eighteenth century, Cambridge has a worldwide reputation as a respected seat of learning. Nearly half its 95,000 citizens are connected in some way to Harvard, Massachusetts Institute of Technology, or the smaller colleges in the city.

Sights to See

The heartbeat of Cambridge is *Harvard Square*, where life revolves around the many bookstores, coffee shops, boutiques, and newsstands. No one would come to Cambridge without taking a walk through *Harvard Yard*. A stroll through the yard's winding paths, stately trees, grassy quadrangles, and handsome brick buildings is a walk through a long history of higher education.

Six U.S. Presidents have graduated from Harvard. The *Longfellow National Historic Site* is the house where the poet Henry Wadsworth Longfellow lived for 45 years and wrote most of his famous works. In the house you will find many fine Victorian furnishings, among them Longfellow's desk, pen, and inkstand. A few miles east of Harvard Square lies Cambridge's other famous university, the *Massachusetts Institute of Technology* (MIT), which has offered a premier education in engineering and technology since 1865.

Museums

Harvard is also home to a number of museums. The *Busch-Reisinger Museum* is noted for central and northern European

works of art from the Middle Ages to the present, and for its collection of musical instruments. The *Fogg Art Museum* holds European and American art, with a notable Impressionist collection.

Shopping

In the very center of Harvard Square you will see the *Out of Town News and Ticket Agency* kiosk, a Harvard Square landmark for many years, famous for its thousands of national and foreign periodicals. Visitors will find a wealth of shopping in Harvard Square, with everything from boutiques to chain stores. Most notable are the many bookstores surrounding the square.

Yet another Harvard institution is the *Harvard Co-op*, formed in 1882 by several Harvard students as a cost-saving measure. The Co-op holds three floors of clothing, gifts, computers and calculators, games and toys, records, art prints, posters, and books.

Nightlife

Ryle's features nightly jazz, rhythm-and-blues, Latin music, and swing in a casual atmosphere. At the *Mystery Café*, the audience participates in solving a murder over a four-course dinner. Harvard's professional theater company, American Repertory Theater, produces world premieres and classical works, often taking a non-traditional approach. *Catch a Rising Star* showcases rising young comics seven nights a week in a dark and cozy basement club.

Restaurants

East Cambridge is a treasure chest of colorful and ethnic restaurants. A 50s style decor of diner stools, neon, and a black-and-white tiled floor enlivens the *East Coast Grill*. Southern cooking is represented by the *Cajun Yankee* which serves seafood gumbo, Cajun popcorn, and shrimp remoulade. It would be hard to find a friendlier place than the *Casa Portugal,* one of only a handful of Boston Portuguese restaurants, and serving spicy dinners of marinated pork with potatoes or mussels, and squid stew. The family-owned *La Groceria* looks like an Italian *trattoria* and is famed for its hot antipasti and homemade pasta. *Troyka* is a real Russian restaurant, and serves excellent caviar and *blinis*. Its hearty peasant fare includes *borscht*, *piroshki*, meat-potato pie, and Russian dumplings.

VOCABULARY AND READING

1. You're going to read a passage about the city of Cambridge in Massachusetts. Work in pairs. Under which of these headings would you expect to find the words in the box?

– sights to see – restaurants
– museums   – shopping
– nightlife

ethnic diner fare boutique
Victorian Impressionist company
collection kiosk landmark
chain store premiere comic
star audience Latin quadrangle

2. Read the passage. Find out what place in Cambridge you would recommend for someone who:

1. likes live music
2. loves 19th-century French art
3. likes cooking from Louisiana
4. is interested in the history of music
5. wants to buy some cheap presents
6. likes eating out and the theater
7. enjoys historical buildings
8. loves seafood

3. Answer the questions.

1. Where does this passage come from?
   – a guidebook   – a letter
   – a history book   – an atlas
2. Why would someone read this?
   – to guide them around Cambridge.
   – to help them decide what to see there
   – to tell them how to get there
   – to find out about accommodations

FUNCTIONS

Tense review: talking about the future
You can use *will* to:
– **make an offer.** *I'll get the tickets.*
– **make a prediction.** *We'll have a great time together.*
– **make a promise, threat, or warning.** *If you won't be quiet, I'll call the waiter.*
– **make a request. Will** *you ask them to be quiet?*
– **to invite someone to do something. Will/Won't** *you join us?*
– **refuse something.** *No, I **won't** be quiet.*

1. Match the sentences on the left with the replies on the right.

1. I'll buy you another drink.
2. I'll get there as soon as I can.
3. Will you get me something to eat?
4. Won't you sit with us?
5. You'll have a wonderful evening.
6. I'll call the manager if you won't be quiet.

a. Yes, they say it's very good.
b. OK, what would you like?
c. Thank you. That's very nice of you.
d. Thanks. I'll have an orange juice.
e. Don't bother. We're leaving.
f. OK, make sure you're not late.

2. Decide which use of *will* each exchange shows.

SOUNDS

1. 🔲 Listen to the sentences in *Functions* activity 1. Put a check (✓) by the ones which sound polite and friendly.

2. Work in pairs. Say aloud the sentences you checked in 1. Try to sound polite and friendly.

SPEAKING AND WRITING

1. Work in groups of three or four. Choose a town or region that you all know well. Make notes on the following aspects:

– sights to see   – museums   – nightlife   – restaurants
– shopping

Now use your notes to write a short tourist guide to the place you have chosen. Each member of the group could write about one aspect. You can then display your guide for other members of the class to read.

2. Plan a day trip to the place you have chosen. Think about what you will do at different times during the day.

We'll start by going to the old Town Hall.
OK, and then we'll walk along the river.

Present your plan to the rest of the class. Explain where you are going to go and what you are going to do.

Fluency **1** *Mind Your Manners!*

Apologizing and thanking

LISTENING AND SPEAKING

1. Read the dialogue below and decide where it takes place and who the speakers might be.

A Good morning. And how are you today?

B Good morning, miss, and welcome. What can I do for you?

A I'd like to pay this bill, please.

B Sure.

A Here you are.

B Sorry, I'll need your signature. Could you sign here, please?

A Oh, sure. There! Is that OK now?

B Yes, thank you.

A Don't mention it.

B I'm extremely sorry to have kept you waiting.

A So you should be.

B Here's your receipt. Thank you very much, miss. Have a nice day.

A Thanks. Bye!

B Bye. See you later.

2. Work in pairs and check your answers to 1. Is there anything you wouldn't say in your language?

3. 🔲 Listen to the dialogue in 1 and cross out anything you don't hear.

4. Work in pairs and act out the dialogue you heard.

5. What do you say when:

– someone holds open a door for you?
– a neighbor brings in your laundry when it starts to rain?
– a friend lends you a pen?
– you break a neighbor's window while playing baseball?
– a sales clerk gives you what you want to buy?
– you buy a bus ticket?
– you're leaving a dinner party?
– you bump into someone in the street?
– someone serves you a cup of coffee?

Are there any occasions when you say nothing?

6. 🔲 Listen to Sharon talking about her answers to activity 5. Write down the expressions she uses for each situation.

7. Work in pairs. Make notes on Sharon's answers to 5. Try to remember as much detail as possible.

FUNCTIONS

Apologizing	Thanking	Ways of addressing people	
Please forgive me.	*I'm very grateful.*	*Sir*	*(First name)*
I (do) apologize.	*Thank you.*	*Ma'am*	*Mr. (family name)*
Sorry.	*That's very kind of you.*		*Mrs. (family name)*
I'm so sorry.	*Thanks.*		*Miss (family name)*
Excuse me.	*I (do) appreciate that.*		*Ms. (family name)*
I beg your pardon.		*Doctor*	*Dr. (name)*
Pardon me.		*Professor*	*Professor (name)*
		Judge	*Judge (name)*
			Mr. President
			President Clinton

1. Look at the expressions for apologizing or thanking people in the functions box, and answer the questions.

1. Which expressions are very formal?

2. Which ones are direct translations of what you say in your language?

2. Work in pairs and check your answers to *Listening and Speaking* activity 5.

3. How would you address the following people?

- Helen Smith, a director of a company
- Marjorie Helman, a secretary, who is unmarried
- Philip Jones, a manager
- Your teacher, Angela Freeman
- Your colleague and friend, Joe Wallis
- Ken Lavery, your superior at work

4. Work in pairs and talk about your answers to the questions.

1. How would you like people to address you in your class?
2. What are the ways of addressing people in your country?
3. How do you feel if someone addresses you in a way you're not accustomed to?

READING AND WRITING

1. Work in pairs and talk about if and when you:

- touch people
- stand very close to people
- speak loudly
- look someone in the eye
- say *please* and *thank you*
- are very formal
- are very informal

2. Read the passage and note down anything it says about the features in 1.

Americans are what is known as a "non-contact people." Outside of hugs given in greeting and parting, touching—among adults—is generally limited to very intimate relationships. Latin Americans find us cold in this regard. Many Americans are envious of people who can reach out freely and affectionately, but our strong sense of the private space around each person inhibits us. In conversation, Americans usually stand at least an arm's length apart and are made uncomfortable by people who stand closer.

Because it is important to be assertive, Americans speak fairly loudly, at least compared to Asians. Foreigners sometimes mistake the loudness for anger when an American is only trying to make himself understood.

We are taught to look into people's eyes during a conversation. Someone who looks around or down appears shifty to us, although in fact you shouldn't stare continuously at the other person, but glance elsewhere every few seconds.

Visitors usually find Americans, for all their informality, very polite. This reputation seems to rest largely on the great number of "pleases" and "thank yous" we deliver, but also on the general recognition given to strangers. One should be considerate of waiters, garage attendants, and household help as well as of doctors and senators. Americans are shocked to see the peremptory manner in which servants are treated in other countries.

Informality is everywhere in our culture. The forms of our language do not change when we address a superior, as they do in many languages. People dress casually as much as possible. We use slang in nearly all circumstances. We slouch in chairs, lean against walls, and put our feet on our desks. But there are limits. In church you sit up straight. You do not use slang before a judge. If your boss comes into your office and puts his feet on your desk, you are flattered; he regards you as an equal. But you don't put your feet up on his desk. A lot of these distinctions are subtle and foreigners can step on toes by trying to become too casual before understanding the culture very well.

3. Work in pairs. Talk about the similarities and differences between behavior in the United States and in your country.

4. Write a few sentences advising foreign visitors about behavior in your country. You may like to write about ways of addressing people and the points in activity 1.

Progress Check 1–8

VOCABULARY

1. Here are some words from Lessons 1–8. Choose three and answer the questions for each word. Use a dictionary to help you.

blow   collection   display   point   reservation   stretch   service

1. How do you pronounce it?
2. Where does the stress go?
3. How many parts of speech can it be?
4. How many meanings does it have?
5. Are there any prepositions which follow it?

2. Work in pairs. Discuss which of the following pieces of advice about learning vocabulary would be most useful to you.

1. Write down new words under topics or other headings, such as phrasal verbs, words for noises.
2. Write new words in sentences to show how to use them.
3. Look through your vocabulary notes every few days.
4. Test your vocabulary with a friend.
5. Translate all the new words you record.
6. Write down all the other words formed from a word, and their meanings.
7. Only write down words which are useful to you.

GRAMMAR

1. Find the mistakes in these sentences and correct them.

1. When you get up today?
2. What did you last weekend?
3. Where live you?
4. Did she got home late?
5. How long you're learning English?
6. Do you can open the window?

2. Complete these sentences with a suitable tag question, negative question, or reply question.

1. "____ it a beautiful day!"   "Yes, it is."
2. "I'm bored."   "____? I'm enjoying myself."
3. "I don't like the movie."   "____ you? I do."
4. You haven't been here long, ____?
5. "____ she look fantastic!"   "Yes, she does!"
6. You don't like learning grammar, ____?
7. There'll be enough time, ____?
8. "It won't rain, ____?" "No, I don't think so."

3. Complete the passage with the indefinite or definite article, or put a – if no article is needed.

In many countries, you need (1) ____ business card if you want to make (2) ____ good impression. For many (3) ____ people, it makes it easier to understand your name and (4) ____ job you do. Make sure you include your name, (5) ____ name of (6) ____ company you work for, and (7) ____ position you hold. Use your title, such as (8) ____ vice-president or (9) ____ doctor, and don't use (10) ____ abbreviations.

4. Choose the correct verb form.

In the United States, they *play/are playing* a different kind of football. Today, some friends *take/are taking* me to a ballgame between the Redskins and the Cowboys, and I *look /am looking* forward to it. Before the game, everyone *gets/is getting* very excited, and *cheers/is cheering* for their team. But five minutes after kickoff, the game *stops/is stopping* and it *keeps/is keeping* stopping every few minutes while the players and the coaches *have/are having* a discussion. Fortunately, the Redskins *scored/were scoring* a touchdown and the game *got/was getting* more exciting.

5. Write sentences using *will*.

1. Invite someone to stay and have lunch with you.
2. Promise to write to someone.
3. Ask someone to buy some stamps.
4. Refuse to pay the check.
5. Offer to pay the check.

SOUNDS

1. Say these words out loud. Is the underlined sound /ɜː/ or /ɔː/? Put the words into two columns.

<u>her</u>d <u>hear</u>d <u>bor</u>ed <u>boa</u>rd <u>bir</u>d <u>sir</u> <u>sore</u> <u>fur</u>
<u>four</u> <u>pore</u> <u>pour</u> <u>tur</u>n <u>tor</u>n <u>wer</u>e <u>war</u>

Listen and check. As you listen, say the words out loud. Which words sound the same but are spelled differently?

2. Underline the /ə/ sound in these words.

appointment announcement advertisement America
acquaintance business cousin company prisoner
minutes department interval

Listen and check. As you listen, say the words out loud.

3. Predict which words the speaker is likely to stress and underline them.

A prisoner in El Paso, Texas, was allowed out of jail to celebrate his twenty-fifth wedding anniversary. When he arrived home, his wife was absent. He later learned that she was in jail after having stolen his anniversary present from a store.

Listen and check.

4. Write down the words you underlined in 3 on a separate piece of paper. Now turn to Communication Activity 10 on page 104.

SPEAKING AND WRITING

1. Work in groups of three or four. Read this letter from your American friend, and find out:

– what she's going to do – what she needs to know
– what she likes doing

Thanks very much for your letter. I'm really looking forward to seeing you next week. My plane gets in at about four in the afternoon, so I'll get the airport bus to your town. Will you send me directions to your home from the bus station or should we meet somewhere?

By the way, is there anything I can bring from the States which you might like? How about a book, some food, or anything like that? (Nothing too heavy since my suitcase will be full!)

One important thing, can you tell me how I should greet people, like your family and friends? Are people very formal? Is there anything I need to know in order to avoid making any major social gaffes?

Is there any chance of going to a soccer game, or are there any other sports you think I might enjoy? And I hope there'll be plenty to do in the evenings!

See you soon!

Paula

2. In your groups, discuss and respond to your friend's letter. Talk about:

– where to meet   – special social customs
– things to do in the evening   – sports to watch
– presents she could bring   – arrangements for her stay

3. Write a letter giving advice and suggestions about the things you talked about in 2.

⑨ Achievements ...

Tense review: present perfect simple and continuous

VOCABULARY AND SPEAKING

1. Which of the words in the box can you use to describe important events in your life so far?

> acting   agreement   boring   bring up   compromise
> confident   degree   diploma   dream   exciting   fail
> failure   fall in love   family   goal   happy   hate   home
> job   love   major   marry   music   obligation   optimistic
> painting   pass   pessimistic   sad   school   sports   succeed
> success   take an exam   talent   target   travel   uncertain
> university

2. Make two lists. In the first list write your achievements —things you have done in your life which you are proud of. In the second list write your ambitions—things you'd like to do.

3. Now work in pairs, and talk about your achievements and ambitions.

READING

1. The passage comes from *Great Railway Journeys*, in which the novelist Lisa St. Aubin de Terán describes a journey she has always wanted to make in South America. Which of the following words would you expect to see in the passage?

cargo   coconut   destination   drifting   frost   haze
horizon   rhythm   sensual   steamy   transistor   tropical

2. Read the passage and find out if she is at the beginning, middle, or end of her journey.

3. The writer uses a literary style. Find a word or phrase in the passage which means the same as the following (they are in the order in which you'll find them).

on purpose   calmed   call to mind   swollen   fighting

I have set out to travel from the Atlantic Ocean to the foothills of the Bolivian Altiplano, from the once famous coffee town of Santos to Santa Cruz de la Sierra. I have made other great railway journeys by chance, but never by design; this is to be a "proper" journey with a beginning and a prearranged destination. It is early March and I have just left the sharp frosts of a late Italian winter for the steamy heat of the tail end of a tropical rainy season.

Santos is the club that Pele, the King of Football, played for. Beyond the heat haze and the pounding rhythm of transistor radios on the beach, and beyond the sinister lines of gray cargo ships on the horizon, there is a halo: Pele's. His fame is the achieved dream of every Brazilian boy and the pride of his nation.

Every few minutes, people come up and ask me my name and if I like Santos. Between assuring strangers how fond I am of their city, I think about it and decide that I really am. I like the sight of so many people enjoying the sun and the sand and their celebration of themselves.

I have bought a guidebook and map of Brazil which I study. I am lulled by the general feeling of well-being, of drifting with the tide. I have never had any sense of direction, which is, perhaps, why I feel so safe on a train. Trains move implacably along their own tracks, pausing only at predestined places.

I feel at home in Brazil; I can even evoke my paternal grandfather, a moustachioed Señor Mendonca from Belem, to put me further at ease. Bloated as I am with coconut water and roasting under 100°F (38°C), the sensual hum of warring radio stations is lulling me to sleep. I have a train to catch, though. I have been wanting to make this journey for so many years that I am resolved to make it now, no matter what.

4. Complete the sentences 1–4 with a phrase a–f and write the appropriate letter in the box. There are two extra phrases.

1. The other railway journeys she has made were not "proper" ones... ☐
2. She tells people she likes Santos without really thinking about it... ☐
3. She likes traveling by train... ☐
4. She feels at home in Brazil... ☐

a. because she wants them to go away and stop bothering her.
b. since trains will take her effortlessly to where she wants to go.
c. because she wants to be polite.
d. because she used to live in Italy.
e. because she didn't plan them.
f. because she likes the people and she had a Brazilian grandfather.

5. Decide if these statements about the passage are true, false, or if there is no evidence.

1. She has never taken a train before.
2. She has never been to Brazil before.
3. She has just arrived from Italy.
4. She has been staying in Santos for several weeks.
5. She has grown fond of Santos during her stay.
6. She has been writing as she waits for the train.

6. Look at the words in *Reading* activity 1 again and find the words that go with them in the passage.

SPEAKING AND WRITING

1. Work in pairs.

Student A: Turn to Communication Activity 5 on page 103.
Student B: Turn to Communication Activity 15 on page 105.

2. Work in pairs. You're going to find out as much as possible about your partner, but you can only ask questions in writing. Write a question you would like to ask your partner on a piece of paper.
Where were you born?

Now exchange your questions. Write a short answer to your partner's question.
In Quito.

Write another question you would like to ask your partner on the same piece of paper.
Where did you go to school?

Then exchange your questions again. Write a short answer to your partner's next question.
In Caracas.

Continue either until you know everything you want to know about your partner, or until your teacher tells you to stop.

... and Ambitions

Tense review: present perfect simple and continuous

GRAMMAR

> **Tense review: present perfect simple and continuous**
> **You use the present perfect simple:**
> —to talk about an action which happened at some time in the past. We are not interested in when the action took place. You often use *ever* in questions and *never* in negative statements.
> *I **have made** other great railway journeys.*
> —when the action is finished, to say what has been achieved in a period of time, often in reply to *how much/many*.
> *Lisa **has written** several novels.*
> —to talk about a past action which has a result in the present, such as a change. You often use *just*.
> *I **have just left** the sharp frost of a late Italian winter.*
> **You use the present perfect continuous:**
> —to talk about an action which began in the past, continues up to the present, and may or may not continue into the future, and to say how long something has been in progress.
> *She's **been writing** for many years.*
> —to talk about actions and events which have been in progress up to the recent past and show their present results.
> *She's **been working** very hard.* (She's stopped work, but she looks tired.)

1. Work in pairs. Talk about the differences between the two sentences.

1. a. She's known her second husband since 1990.
   b. She's been knowing her second husband since 1990.
2. a. She's been writing her memoirs.
   b. She's written her memoirs.
3. a. She's been living in Venezuela.
   b. She's lived in Venezuela.
4. a. She's been writing since she was sixteen.
   b. She's written since she was sixteen.
5. a. She's been writing her next novel.
   b. She's written her next novel.

2. Work in pairs. Look at the verbs in the sentences in *Reading* activity 5 on page 23. What tense is used and why?

3. Here are the answers to some questions about Lisa St. Aubin de Terán. Work in pairs and use the information you have learned to write the questions.

1. Since 1983.   2. Since 1990.   3. Seven.
4. Seven years.   5. Three, England, Venezuela, and Italy.

1. How long has she been writing novels?

SOUNDS

🔊 Listen to these sentences. Notice how *been* is pronounced /bɪn/. Now say the sentences out loud.

1. Has she been waiting long?
2. He's been sitting here for ten minutes.
3. She's been living in Korea.
4. I've been reading one of her books.
5. You've been working too hard.

LISTENING

1. You are going to hear a radio program in which some people talk about their answers to the following questions. First, think about your answers to the questions.

1. What have you achieved in your life which you are most proud of?
2. Who do you particularly admire, and why?
3. Is there anything you have always wanted to do?
4. Where have you always wanted to visit?
5. Where have you been the happiest in your life?

2. 🔊 Listen to five people talking about their answers to the questions. Each speaker will answer one of the questions. Put the number of the speaker by the question they answer.

3. Work in pairs, and make notes about each speaker's answer. Try to include as much detail as possible.

4. 🔊 Listen again and check your answers to 3.

SPEAKING AND WRITING

1. Work with the same student you worked with in *Speaking and Writing* activity 2 on page 23. Ask and answer the questions in *Listening* activity 1. Make notes about your partner's answers.

2. You are going to write a biography of your partner for the local newspaper called *Achievements and Ambitions.* Use the short answers your partner gave you in *Speaking and Writing* activity 2 on page 23 and the notes you made in *Listening* activity 1 to help you write the article.

3. When you have finished, discuss your article with your partner. Give your partner any other suitable information, and tell him or her about anything which is inaccurate. Now, check the article for correct vocabulary, spelling, and punctuation.

4. Now, write a final draft of your article.

11 | Nurse Coxall's Revenge

Tense review: past tenses

SPEAKING

1. Work in pairs. This lesson is about truth and deception. Which people do you expect to tell the truth?

politicians   teachers   journalists   police officers
sales clerks   car mechanics   lawyers   doctors

2. Do you think it is ever justified not to tell the truth? Can you think of circumstances when it might be acceptable to deceive someone about:

– reasons for being late?   – their appearance?
– reasons for leaving work early?   – an illness?

3. When was the last time someone told you something which turned out to be untrue? What happened?

LISTENING

1. You're going to listen to *Nurse Coxall's Revenge*, by Dawn Muscillo, a story about a deception which takes place in a hospital. First, look at the picture and write down any words you think you'll hear.

2. Work in groups of three or four. Look at the events in part 1 of the story. They are in the wrong order. Try to guess the right order.

Nurse Coxall was in charge of Ward 4. ☐
Dr. Green was interested in psychiatric medicine. ☐
She met the new doctor. ☐
He got out of his car. ☐
She wondered who the new doctor was. ☐
He nearly ran her over. ☐
She offered him some coffee. ☐
He gave her a ride. ☐
She listened to his plans for Ward 4. ☐
He had recently finished his studies. ☐
She walked through the hospital grounds. ☐
He got the new job without an interview. ☐

3. 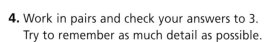   Listen to part 1 of the story. Number the events in the order you hear them.

4. Work in pairs and check your answers to 3. Try to remember as much detail as possible.
 Now listen again and check.

5. Work in pairs. What do you think happens next in the story? Answer the questions, then work with another pair and compare your answers.

1. What was Dr. Green going to do the next day?
2. How do you think Nurse Coxall felt about Dr. Green's plans?
3. How do think she was going to stop him?

 Now listen to part 2 of the story and check your answers.

6. Match each question with one of the answers below.

1. Why was Nurse Coxall angry?
2. Why didn't anybody know what Dr. Green looked like?
3. Why did she want him to come straight to the ward?
4. How do we know it was a lie that Dr. Green was paranoid and confused?
5. Why did she fill the syringe?
6. How do we know this was not the first time she had done this?

a. Because the sedative would make Dr. Green easy to handle.
b. Because she was only pretending to read from a report.
c. Because the ward was full of men who insisted they were doctors.
d. Because he hadn't been to the Personnel Office yet to get his identity badge.
e. Because she didn't want him to suspect that the nurse thought he was a patient.
f. Because she wanted to keep her job.

GRAMMAR

Tense review: past tenses

You use the past simple to talk about a past state or a past action or event that is finished.
*She **looked** around her office.*

You use the past continuous to talk about something that was in progress at a specific time in the past, or when something else happened. The second action is often in the past simple.
*The doctor **was driving** in the hospital grounds when he met Nurse Coxall.*

You use the past perfect to talk about an action in the past which happened before another action in the past. The second action is often in the past simple.
*After she **had spoken** to the nurse, she **wrote** the report on Mr. Green.*

You use the past perfect continuous to focus on an action which was in progress up to or near a time in the past. You often use it with *for* and *since*.
*Nurse Coxall **had been running** her ward **for** many years.*

---

1. Look at the tenses used in these sentences. What is the difference in meaning between *a* and *b* in each pair?

1. a. I left college when I passed my exams.
   b. I had left college when I passed my exams.
2. a. When she became a doctor, she moved near the hospital.
   b. When she became a doctor, she had moved near the hospital.
3. a. She had been reading the patient's notes when the ambulance arrived.
   b. She had read the patient's notes when the ambulance arrived.
4. a. She was walking home when Dr. Green arrived.
   b. She had walked home when Dr. Green arrived.

2. Look at these sentences and choose the best tense.

1. When she took her driving test, she *had/had had* about twenty driving lessons.
2. He *was reading/read* the newspaper when someone knocked at the door.
3. The river *rose/was rising*. It *rained/had been raining* all week.
4. His face *was/had been* red since he *forgot/had forgotten* the sunscreen.

Work with a partner and explain why the tense you have chosen is the best.

3. Answer the questions using the past perfect continuous and the words in parentheses.

1. Why was the patient so angry? (he/wait/an hour)
2. Why was the doctor late? (she/play/golf)
3. Why was the man so stressed? (he/work/too much)
4. Why did the doctor prescribe him some pills? (he/not sleep/very well)

4. Work in pairs and complete these sentences with suitable verbs to give a summary of the story. Use appropriate past tenses.

Nurse Coxall (1) _____ Ward 4 for years. One day she (2) _____ that a new doctor was coming to take over. She (3) _____ the new doctor when she (4) _____ on the grounds of the hospital. He (5) _____ almost (6) _____ over her. Dr. Green (7) _____ Nurse Coxall back to her apartment and she (8) _____ him a cup of coffee. He told her that when he (9) _____ his studies, he (10) _____ for the job at the hospital. He (11) _____ Nurse Coxall that he intended to make many changes, including moving the nurse on Ward 4.

The next day Nurse Coxall (12) _____ in her office when Dr. Green arrived. She (13) _____ the nurse a few minutes before that a new patient was expected and that he (14) _____ he was a doctor. Nurse Coxall (15) _____ a sedative to make Dr. Green easy to handle. Surprisingly, nobody in the hospital seemed to think it was strange that Nurse Coxall's ward (16) _____ full of men who (17) _____ they were doctors.

WRITING

Rewrite the story from Dr. Green's point of view. Use the linking words, *when, as, while, before,* and *after* and suitable tenses.

***When** I finished my studies, I applied for a job in a psychiatric hospital…*

VOCABULARY AND SOUNDS

1. Put these words under the following headings: *people, places, medicine,* and *medical complaints.*

blood pressure   pain   dentist   pill   disease   heart attack   patient   cut   ward   injection   nurse   ointment   wound   temperature   clinic   hospital   pharmacist   physician   surgeon   tablet   operating room

2. Work in pairs. Here are some more words to do with medical matters. In what circumstances would you use them?

ambulance   appointment   bandage   cane   cast   casualty   crutches   disabled   dizzy   emergency   limp   outpatients   prescription   sedative   shiver   wheelchair

3. Underline the stressed syllables in these words.

hospital   pharmacist   injection   patient   attack   consultant   ointment   emergency   disabled   disease   prescription   temperature   ambulance

🔊 Now listen and check. As you listen, say the words out loud.

4. Look at these compound nouns. Underline the stressed word.

hospital ward   outpatients   heart attack   blood pressure   wheelchair

🔊 Now listen and check.

In 1812 a young man called James Barry received his medical degree from Edinburgh University in Great Britain. After graduating, he moved to London where he studied surgery at Guy's Hospital. After that, the popular young doctor joined the army and over the next forty years had a brilliant career as an army medical officer, working in many far-off countries and fighting successfully for improved conditions in hospitals. It was a remarkable career—made even more remarkable by the discovery upon his death that *he* was in fact a *she.* James Barry was a woman.

No one was more surprised at this discovery than her many friends and colleagues. It was true that throughout her life people had remarked upon her small size, slight build, and smooth pale face. One officer had even objected to her appointment as a medical assistant because he could not believe that Barry was old enough to have graduated from medical school. But no one had ever seriously suggested that Barry was anything other than a man.

By all accounts Barry was a pleasant and good-humored person with high cheek bones, reddish hair, a long nose, and large eyes. She was well-liked by her patients and had a reputation for great speed in the operating room—an important quality at a time when operations were performed without anaesthetic. She was also quick-tempered. When she was working in army hospitals and prisons overseas, the terrible conditions often made her very angry. She fought hard against injustice and cruelty, and her temper sometimes got her into trouble with the authorities. After a long career overseas, she returned to London where she died in 1865. While the undertaker's assistant was preparing her body for burial, she discovered that James Barry was a woman.

So why did James Barry deceive people for so long? At that time a woman could not study medicine, work as a doctor, or join the army. Perhaps Barry had always wanted to do these things and pretending to be a man was the only way to make it possible. Perhaps she was going to tell the truth one day, but didn't because she was enjoying her life as a man too much. Whatever the reason, Barry's deception was successful. By the time it was discovered that she had been the first woman in Britain to qualify as a doctor, it was too late for the authorities to do anything about it.

READING

1. You are going to read a story about a deception involving a doctor which took place in the 19th century. The deception was only discovered when the doctor died. Before you read, look at the picture, and try to guess what the deception was.

2. Read the passage and find one sentence which describes what the deception was.

3. Decide if these statements are true or false.

1. James Barry pretended to be a man because there were no women doctors.
2. She worked to improve conditions in hospitals.
3. Many people suspected that she was a woman.
4. She performed operations very slowly and carefully.
5. The army authorities discovered that she was a woman while she was working abroad.

4. Find a word or expression in the passage that has a similar meaning to the words or phrases in italics.

1. James Barry was *liked by a lot of people.*
2. She *tricked* people into thinking she was a man.
3. The undertaker's assistant was very surprised when she *found out* that Barry was a woman.
4. James Barry was skillful at *operating on people.*
5. In the 19th century doctors didn't use *drugs to make people sleep* during operations.
6. To *become* a doctor you have to pass a lot of exams and graduate from medical school.

5. What do the words in italics refer to?

1. No one was more surprised at *this discovery* than her many friends and colleagues…
2. …*an important quality* at a time when operations were performed…
3. While the undertaker's assistant was preparing *her* body for burial…
4. …and pretending to be a man was the only way to make *it* possible.
5. …it was too late for the authorities to do anything about *it.*

6. Work in pairs. Which of the following words would you use to describe the style of the story?

factual   ironic   persuasive   objective   subjective

Now talk about how the story would change if the deception was revealed in the last paragraph. Would this be better?

7. Write some true and false statements about James Barry. When you're ready, show your statements to another student. Can he or she guess which are true and which are false?

FUNCTIONS

Describing a sequence of events in the past

You can use *before* and *after* + *-ing* to describe a sequence of two events which both have the same subject. *After graduating*, he moved to London.

You can use *when*, *as*, and *while* to describe two events which happen at the same time. The second verb is often in the past simple and is used for the event which interrupts the longer action. *When she was working in hospitals overseas, the terrible conditions made her angry.*

1. Look back at the passage and find more examples of describing a sequence of events in the past.

2. Number these events in the order in which they happened.

a. James Barry joined the army. ☐
b. The undertaker's assistant found out that James Barry was a woman. ☐
c. James Barry died. ☐
d. James Barry graduated from medical school. ☐
e. James Barry gained a reputation as a quick and skillful surgeon. ☐
f. James Barry wanted to be a doctor. ☐
g. James Barry pretended to be a man. ☐
h. James Barry returned to London. ☐

3. Write a brief summary of the story of James Barry using the structures in the functions box and the sentences in *Functions* activity 2 to help you.

After graduating from medical school, James Barry moved to London.

SPEAKING

Work in pairs and discuss your answers to these questions.

1. Do you think there was anything wrong with what James Barry did?
2. Are there any jobs today that women are not allowed to do?
3. Are there any jobs that are better done by men?

13 *Wish You Were Here?*

Adjectives

SPEAKING AND WRITING

1. Put the following features of a vacation in the order of their importance to you.

- beautiful countryside
- peace and quiet
- sunshine
- mountains
- sports facilities
- sandy beaches
- good food
- swimming
- old buildings
- good nightlife
- plenty to read

2. Work in groups of three or four and compare your answers to 1. Now write down statements about vacations which you all agree on.

3. Find out which group in your class has:

- the most statements
- the longest statement

READING

1. Read the passage from *The Lost Continent* by the American writer Bill Bryson and choose the best title.

1. What to See in Arizona
2. The Geography of the Grand Canyon
3. The Beauty of the Grand Canyon
4. A Magical Experience

2. Work in pairs. Look back at the passage and find these words and expressions.

gray soup   a set of theater curtains
ants   an old shoelace

What is the writer using these words to describe? Do you think the descriptions are good? What other words could you use to describe these things?

I drove through a snow-whitened landscape toward the Grand Canyon. It was hard to believe that this was the last week of April. Mists and fog swirled about the road. I could see nothing at the sides and ahead of me except the occasional white smear of oncoming headlights. By the time I reached the entrance to Grand Canyon National Park, and paid the $5 admission, snow was dropping heavily again, thick white flakes so big that their undersides carried shadows.

The road through the park followed the southern lip of the canyon for thirty miles. Two or three times I stopped and went to the edge to peer hopefully into the silent murk, knowing that the canyon was out there, just beyond my nose, but I couldn't see anything. The fog was everywhere —threaded among the trees, adrift on the roadsides, rising steamily off the pavement.

Afterward I trudged toward the visitors' center, perhaps 200 yards away, but before I got there I came across a snow-spattered sign announcing a lookout point half a mile away along a trail through the woods, and impulsively I went down it, mostly just to get some air. The path was slippery and took a long time to traverse, but on the way the snow stopped falling and the air felt clean and refreshing. Eventually I came to a platform of rocks, marking the edge of the canyon. There was no fence to keep you back from the edge, so I shuffled cautiously over and looked down, but could see nothing but gray soup. A middle-aged couple came along and as we stood chatting about what a dispiriting experience this was, a miraculous thing happened. The fog parted. It just silently drew back, like a set of theater curtains being opened, and suddenly we saw that we were on the edge of a sheer, giddying drop of at least a thousand feet.

The scale of the Grand Canyon is almost beyond comprehension. It is ten miles across, a mile deep, 180 miles long. You could set the Empire State Building down in it and still be thousands of feet above it. Indeed you could set the whole of Manhattan down inside it and you would still be so high above it that the buses would be like ants and people would be invisible, and not a sound would reach you. The thing that gets you—gets everyone—is the silence. The Grand Canyon just swallows sound. The sense of space and emptiness is overwhelming. Nothing happens out there. Down below you on the canyon floor, far, far away, is the thing that carved it: the Colorado River. It is 300 feet wide, but from the canyon's lip it looks thin and insignificant. It looks like an old shoelace. Everything is dwarfed by this mighty hole.

30

3. Look at these sentences from the passage and answer the questions.

1. *It was hard to believe that this was the last week of April.* – Does this mean he thought time was passing very quickly, or that he didn't expect such bad weather?

2. *Afterward, I trudged toward the visitors' center...* – Is it likely that he walked quickly and lightly or slowly and with difficulty?

3. *The scale of the Grand Canyon is almost beyond comprehension.* – Does this mean he doesn't believe the facts about it or that he thinks it is very big?

4. *The thing that gets you—gets everyone—is the silence.* – Does this mean the silence is impressive or annoying?

4. The writer uses a lot of adjectives to create a "word picture" of his experience. Underline all the adjectives you can find in the passage. Choose four adjectives which you think have been used well and which give you a clear picture of the scene he is describing or how he feels about it. Work with a partner and say why you have chosen these adjectives.

5. Write down any facts the writer tells us about the Grand Canyon.

GRAMMAR

> **Adjectives**
> **When there is more than one adjective, you usually put *opinion* adjectives before *fact* adjectives.**
> *The **beautiful, silent** Grand Canyon.*
> **You can use a noun as an adjective before another noun.**
> ***canyon** floor   **theater** curtains*
> **Nouns used as adjectives do not have a plural form. You use hyphens between the parts of the noun clause.**
> *The Colorado River is 300 feet wide.   It is a **300-foot-wide** river.*
> *The Grand Canyon is 180 miles long.   It is a **180-mile-long** canyon.*

1. Look at the adjectives you underlined in the passage. Are they *fact* or *opinion* adjectives? If they are *fact* adjectives, what kind are they: size, age, shape, etc.?

2. What do you call the following?

1. A journey which takes two days.
2. A walk which lasts twenty minutes.
3. A girl who is ten years old.
4. A road which is ten miles long.
5. A vacation which lasts two weeks.
6. A building which has two stories.

1. A two-day journey.

3. Rewrite these sentences in one sentence.

1. The Colorado is a slow-moving river. It is 300 feet wide and very muddy.
2. The visitors' center has a collection of photographs of the Canyon. They are black and white. They are old and very interesting.
3. Thousands of tourists visit the Grand Canyon every year. They are international. They are excited.
4. The Grand Canyon National Park has a visitors' center. It is new and big.
5. There is a road along the southern lip of the canyon. It is thirty miles long. It is winding.
6. There are some rock formations in the canyon. They are a strange shape. They are huge.

1. The Colorado is a slow-moving, very muddy, 300-foot-wide river.

SPEAKING

1. Work in groups of three or four and discuss your answers to the questions.

1. Which are the most beautiful regions in your country?
2. What is their special appeal?
3. Is there anywhere which is particularly special which few people have heard of?
4. What kind of threat is there to the environment in these regions?
5. What do you think should be done about the threat?

2. Find out how other groups have answered the questions in 1.

14 | *Dream Vacation*

Describing position

LISTENING AND SPEAKING

1. You're going to hear two Americans, Terry and Kathy, talking about vacations. First, think about your answers to the following statements.

– my vacation nightmare is…
– my vacation paradise is…
– my favorite vacation activity is…
– I never travel without…
– when I'm away, I usually miss…

2. 📼 Work in pairs.

Student A: Listen and take notes on Terry's answers to the questions.
Student B: Listen and take notes on Kathy's answers to the questions.

Now work together and tell your partner what you have found out.

3. Complete the sentences below with suitable words or phrases. Use the information in 2 to help you.

1. Terry doesn't enjoy staying in big cities because ____.
2. Kathy really liked the house in _ Hawaii because ____.
3. Terry first learned to dive when ____.
4. Terry takes his walkman because ____.
5. Kathy always takes her hat because ____.
6. Kathy would like to have entertainment for her children because ____.

📼 Listen again and check your answers.

4. Look at these extracts from the listening passage. Answer the questions and try to guess the meaning of the phrases in italics.

1. *"All the people on the trains made me feel like I was in a can of sardines."* – Why does Terry say he felt like he was in a can of sardines?
2. *"The shopkeepers really make you feel special."* – Did Terry enjoy the attention he was given in shops?
3. *"I'm kind of addicted to my hour a day."* – What is Kathy's "hour a day"? Is she proud or embarrassed about this habit?
4. *"I love to catch up on my reading when I'm on vacation."* – Does Kathy read a lot when she is not on vacation?

VOCABULARY

1. Here are some nouns to describe places. Write down the nouns which go together to make compound nouns.

bank   beach   cathedral   center   city   country   fishing   hall   market   mountain   river   square   state   town   university   village

river bank

2. Which words in the box below can you use to talk about the landscape in your country?

> unspoiled plain peak waterfall valley stream wood forest hill
> meadow river field village path quiet jungle desert fence oasis
> industrial mountainous low-lying flat tropical vegetation overcrowded
> picturesque agricultural fertile rugged canyon island range temperate
> estuary coastline cliff beach

FUNCTIONS

> Describing position
> **Here are some useful expressions for describing position.**
> *To the north/south...   70 miles from...*
> *In central (country/region)   In the North/South/East/West...*
> *Half-way between...   About 200 yards/miles from...*
> *On each/either side...*
> *The road leads to...   The stream goes/winds/flows past...*
> *At the top/bottom of the hill.*
> *The house is set among the trees.   It's surrounded by fields.   All around...*
> *As far as the eye can see...   In the foreground/background/distance...*
> *A little/long way off...*

1. Work in pairs. Take turns describing the photos on these pages. Use the words in the vocabulary boxes and the expressions in the functions box.

2. Work in pairs. Take turns describing two of the following views.

– the view from your classroom
– a view you particularly like
– the view from your house
– a view you particularly dislike

SOUNDS

1. 📼 Listen to the following phrases and decide what sound links the words which are joined.

1. on the edge of the oasis
2. at the end of the estuary
3. on two or three islands
4. empty areas in the East
5. on the open sea
6. as far as the eye can see
7. high above the entrance
8. down to a river

2. Can you figure out a rule for the sounds which link the words in 1 in connected speech?

WRITING

1. You've been asked to write a magazine article about an attractive region in your country. Make notes on:

– where it is
– how large it is
– what the landscape is like
– what the buildings are like
– any historical information
– any other special features

First focus on facts.

The island of Bali, east of Java, in Indonesia

2. Write sentences using the notes you made in 1.

The Indonesian island of Bali is just east of Java.

3. Think about why the region is attractive or interesting. Rewrite the sentences you wrote in 2 by adding *opinion* adjectives and adjectival phrases.

The beautiful Indonesian island of Bali is found just east of Java.

15 | *Spooky Stories*

Participial (-ing) clauses

One night, quite late, I was still awake in the room I shared with my husband. I was lying on my right side and could hear a child crying. Getting up, I went to see if our son was all right. He was sleeping soundly, breathing deeply and gently. So I climbed the stairs to the attic where our daughters were. They too were sleeping very quietly. I stayed a while but nothing changed and I could not hear any sound other than the sea and a slight breeze. I went back to our room and got back into bed.

Laying my head on the pillow, I could hear the crying again. And so, without consciously thinking about it, I sat up, arms around my knees and said clearly but softly, "Stop crying, darling. Everything's OK. Mother's here." And the crying stopped.

I used to walk to the bus stop with the elderly gentleman living near us. He became ill and I did not see him until one bright, sunny morning a few months later. As I walked down the path, I glanced to the left and I saw the elderly gentleman walking slowly up past the fence, around the front yard.

He turned and looked straight at me, and I was struck by how pale he appeared to be. Not until later did I realize I could not hear the sound of his footsteps, although he appeared to be walking in his usual manner, except for being slower.

I happened to glance away, and when I looked back there was no one there. There was nowhere he could have disappeared to, and he had not collapsed on the sidewalk.

In the evening I discovered that he had died about half an hour before I had seen him that morning.

My brother and I were staying with friends. On the second night I just couldn't get to sleep and didn't want to disturb him with a light. Eventually I lay down and placed my hand under the pillow. As I did so, I felt someone grasp my hand, squeezing it in a comforting manner. My eyes were open and I could see the room, but I was paralyzed with fear.

I took a deep breath and told myself to relax, then moved my legs. My hand was still being held. I then slowly withdrew my hand and rolled onto my back. I felt no other "presence" in the room.

Arriving late at the colonel's house, I was shown to my room immediately and offered a bath before changing for dinner. Tired and travel-stained, I accepted gratefully. On my way down the passage I saw someone enter the bathroom. Thinking this was another guest, I said hello and returned to my bedroom to wait my turn, leaving the door ajar. A few minutes later I went back, found the bathroom empty, and took a bath.

As I came down the stairs, I saw my host waiting for me. I noticed that the table was laid for two people only, and to satisfy my curiosity, I made some remark about the other guest going into the bathroom just before me, to which the colonel replied: "There's no other guest. Just you and me!"

Not wishing to contradict him, I said nothing and we took our seats. Then I became aware of the same figure suddenly appearing directly behind the colonel's chair.

"But there's the gentleman I saw upstairs!" I said.

The colonel turned his head. "Where? Who?" he asked.

"There!" I said. "Standing behind your chair, now!"

The colonel turned his head to look and said with some amusement: "I can never see him. It's our monk, you know! I find it so disappointing. He often appears upstairs and on the staircase, but never for me, I'm sad to say."

Adapted from *True Ghost Stories of Our Time*

VOCABULARY AND READING

1. Put the words in the box under these headings: *sight, sound, smell, taste, touch.*

> bitter scented sweet-smelling deafening
> fragrant gaze glance glimpse grab grasp
> loud pat noisy notice observe sweet
> peer press punch salty silent slap
> smelly snatch sour spicy squeeze
> stinking stroke stare

2. Look at the words you wrote under each heading in 1. Find a word to describe the following:

Sight
a. look at quickly   *glance*
b. look at fixedly
c. look at carefully

Sound
a. very loud   b. very quiet

A smell to describe:
a. petals   b. strong cheese
c. sewer   d. perfume

A taste to describe:
a. sugar   b. bacon
c. curry   d. vinegar

Touch
a. to take roughly
b. to touch kindly with the hand
c. to hold tightly then loosely
d. to hit with your fist
e. to hit with an open hand

3. Read the four stories and decide which of the senses each one features. Think of a suitable title for each story.

4. Look back at the stories and find a word which means the same as:

– *top rooms in the house   light wind* (story 1)
– *quite old   very aware   fallen down* (story 2)
– *wake someone up   unable to move   took away* (story 3)
– *open   interest* (story 4)

5. Work in pairs. Which story did you enjoy most, or find most strange? Can you explain why?

GRAMMAR

> Participial *-ing* clauses
> **Participial clauses are often used in stories to describe background information. They focus on the action by leaving out nouns, pronouns, auxiliary verbs, and conjunctions. This often creates a more dramatic effect. You can use a participial clause:**
> **– when two actions happen at the same time. You use it for one of the actions.**
> *Laying my head on the pillow, I could hear the crying again.*
> **– as a "reduced" relative clause.**
> *I used to walk to the bus stop with the elderly gentleman **living** near us. (= who lived near us)*
> **– when one action happens immediately after another action. You use it for the first action.**
> *Getting up, I went to see if our son was all right.*
> **– when an action happens in the middle of a longer action. You use it for the longer action.**
> *Thinking this was another guest, I returned to my room.*
> **– to say why something happens.**
> *Not **wanting** to contradict him, I said nothing.*

1. Rewrite these extracts from the stories as participial clauses.

1. I went back to our room and got back into bed.
2. I lay down and placed my hand under the pillow.
3. I took a deep breath and told myself to relax.
4. As I walked down the path, I glanced to the left...
5. Because I found the bathroom empty, I took a bath.
6. As I came down the stairs, I saw my host...
7. The colonel turned his head to look and said...

1. Going back to our room, I got back into bed.

2. Look at the sentences in *Grammar* activity 1. Use the information in the grammar box to decide which type of participial clause each one of your answers is.

SPEAKING

1. Work in groups of three or four and discuss your answers to the questions.

1. Are there stories of ghosts or spirits in your country?
2. Where do the best-known ghost stories come from?
3. Do you believe in ghosts? Do you like ghost stories?
4. The stories in this lesson are supposed to be true. Do you believe they really happened?
5. Can you think of an explanation for what happened?

2. Find out what the rest of the class thinks.

16 *Strange Sensations*

Verbs of sensation

SOUNDS AND VOCABULARY

1. 🔊 Listen to someone reading the first story on page 34 in a dramatic way. Note how the speaker uses pauses, word stress, intonation, and pitch of voice (loud or soft).

2. Work in pairs. Choose one of the other stories and decide which effects in 1 you would use and where, to make the story sound dramatic.

Now read the story out loud in a dramatic way.

3. These words all describe sounds. Say who or what makes these sounds.

> hum creak groan sigh whistle clatter
> buzz cry bark whisper hiss sniff sob
> roar gasp crash bang rustle thud clang
> rumble rattle beep screech cough
> hiccup snore

4. 🔊 Listen and check (✓) the sounds in 3 which you hear.

GRAMMAR

> **Verbs of sensation**
> *See, hear, feel, watch, listen to,* and *notice* are verbs of sensation. You can use an object + *-ing* when you only see or hear part of an action and the action continues over a period of time.
> *I heard **a child crying**.*
> *I felt **someone squeezing** my hand.*
> **You can use an object + infinitive without *to* when you see or hear the whole action and the action is now finished.**
> *I felt **someone grasp** my hand.*
> *I saw **someone enter** the bathroom.*

1. Work in pairs and say what you heard happen or happening in *Sounds and Vocabulary* activity 4. Use the infinitive if you heard the whole sound.

I heard a bee buzzing.

2. Complete the sentences with a verb from below in its infinitive or *-ing* form.

sing bark walk nod wave

I had a strange dream last night. I dreamed I was in bed when suddenly I heard a dog ____, then scratching at the front door. I went to the door and opened it, but there was nothing there. Then I heard someone ____ in the distance. It went on for a minute or so. I stood there and suddenly I saw a man ____ slowly toward me, singing and dancing along the path. Behind him was a dog. I asked him who he was. He called out that he used to live in the house. I knew the previous owner was dead, so I asked him if he was a ghost. I saw him ____ his head and say "yes." Then I saw him ____ once and then he was gone.

3. Think back to the ghost stories you read on page 34.

Write sentences using verbs of sensation and object + *-ing* or infinitive.

In the first story, the woman heard a child crying.

LISTENING

1. Work in pairs. You're going to hear Linda telling some friends a story about something strange which happened to her. Here are some words and phrases from part 1 of her story.
Discuss what you think the strange event was.

vacation Utah inn spooky dark isolated sharing tower housekeeper singing Bing Crosby Christmas

2. 🔊 Listen to part 1 and decide which of the following statements are true.

1. Linda shared a bedroom with Cynthia.
2. They had a television in their room.
3. They kept hearing someone singing.
4. Cynthia heard someone playing the piano.
5. Linda's sister believed Cynthia's story.
6. Bing Crosby had once stayed at the inn.
7. Cynthia didn't recognize his voice.
8. She heard the music on the anniversary of Crosby's visit.

Did you guess correctly in 1?

3. Work in pairs and check your answers to 2.
🔊 Now listen again and check.

4. 🔊 Listen to part 2 and complete these sentences.

1. One night after they had been asleep for some time, Cynthia and Linda _____.
2. There was a strong smell of smoke in _____.
3. They thought it was a _____.
4. When they told Linda's sister, she said they were _____.
5. The same thing happened _____.
6. The old housekeeper told them that the bedroom that they were sleeping in had belonged to _____.
7. She had been killed _____.
8. They smelled the smoke on the anniversary of _____.

5. Work in pairs and check your answers.
🔊 Now listen again and check.

6. What do you think Linda means by the following expressions? Say them in a simpler way.

1. "It reminded me of the kind of place that could have been the setting for a horror movie."
2. "She was really cool."
3. "She said Cynthia was completely out to lunch."
4. "She was really mad."
5. "He was just pulling our legs."
6. "They thought we were making it up."
7. "They just sat there cracking up."
8. "She looked kind of spooked."

1. She felt uncomfortable there.

7. Which of these words would you use to describe her friends' reactions to Linda's story?

amused incredulous frightened mocking unbelieving sarcastic sympathetic astonished

What is your reaction to the story?

SPEAKING AND WRITING

1. A national newspaper is running a series called *Ghost Stories from Around the World.*

Work in groups of two or three. You're going to write a ghost story together. First decide where your story will take place. Choose from one of these places or think of a place of your own.

– a dark wood   – an old house   – a school   – a cemetery

Now decide who the characters are. Did the story happen to you or someone you know?
Next, decide what happened. Did the person *see, feel, hear,* or *smell* something strange? What did the person do?
Finally, decide what happened at the end of the story. Did the person escape from the ghost or not?

2. In your groups, write the story. Use linking words to join each event.

You can use *meanwhile* for something that was happening at the same time.
*I tried to fix my car. **Meanwhile**, it was getting dark.*

You can use *eventually* for the last in a long sequence of events.
***Eventually**, he found a door that led to the room.*

You can use *finally* for the last event of all.
***Finally**, he locked the front door and drove away.*

When you have finished, display your story for the rest of the class to read. Which group wrote the most frightening story? Were any of the stories amusing?

Fluency ❷ Family and Friends

Giving opinions; expressing emotions

LISTENING AND SPEAKING

1. Look at the illustration of a family tree on page 39. Draw your family tree.

Now work in pairs, and show your family trees to each other. Who has drawn the larger family tree?

2. Work in pairs and talk about the members of your family. Ask and say:

– how old they are   – where they live   – where they were born
– what they do or did

3. Read the questions below and think about your answers to them.
- [ ] Who is the head of the household?
- [ ] Do children ask their parents' approval of the person they wish to marry?
- [ ] Where do the grandparents live?
- [ ] What is a typical family in your country?
- [ ] Who would you turn to if you had an emotional problem?
- [ ] Do grandparents help to look after their grandchildren?
- [ ] How often is there a reunion of all the members of a family?
- [ ] Does the whole family discuss important decisions?
- [ ] Do you look after relatives who cannot look after themselves?
- [ ] When do children leave the parents' home?
- [ ] If you had a financial problem, would you expect your family to help?
- [ ] When do parents stop their financial support of their children?

4. 📼 Listen to Roseanne answering some of the questions. Number the questions in the order she answers them.

5. Which of these statements do you think Roseanne would agree with?
1. Children should ask their parents' permission to get married.
2. Parents should pay for their children until they leave university.
3. The housework should be shared among everyone in the family.
4. Older members of the family who are ill should be taken care of in special homes.
5. The whole family should discuss important decisions.
6. Grandparents shouldn't be expected to look after the grandchildren.
7. The family should always try to help anyone with financial difficulties.

6. Work in pairs and check your answers to 5. Make notes on Roseanne's opinions. Try to remember as much detail as possible.

📼 Now listen again and check.

FUNCTIONS

> **Giving opinions**
> *The point is … Frankly, I think…*
> *In my opinion, … If you ask me, …*
> *It seems to me that … As I see it, …*
> *Wouldn't you say that…*
>
> **Agreeing**
> *Sure./Right. I couldn't agree more.*
> *It sure is. Of course. I agree.*
> *Yes, I think so too.*
> *That's just what I was thinking.*
>
> **Disagreeing**
> *It depends. Maybe. I'm not so sure.*
> *Well, you have a point there, but…*
> *Don't make me laugh! No way!*
> *You've got to be kidding!*
>
> **Saying how you feel**
> *It makes me happy/sad/furious/angry.*
> *I couldn't care less.*
> *It doesn't worry me at all.*
> *I get really mad when …*
> *I'm not interested in (doing) …*

1. Look at the expressions in the functions box. Which ones express strong opinions, agreement, and disagreement? Which ones have direct translations in your language?

2. Say how you feel about the following:

- people who smoke
- people who smile all the time
- people who ask you to lend them money
- people who speak loudly
- people who drive too fast
- people who stand too close
- people who litter
- people who look you in the eye

3. Work in pairs. Are there any circumstances in which you are not expected to give an opinion or say how you feel in your culture?

4. Read this dialogue and try to guess what the missing words are. Use the expressions in the functions box.

A I (1) ... it's ridiculous for sons and daughters to ask their parents who they can marry.

B Well, I'm (2) ... Wouldn't you say that their parents could help them make a suitable choice?

A Maybe, but (3) ... I think that if you're old enough to get married, you're old enough to choose for yourself.

B Well, you have (4) ... there but it (5) ... to see people who marry so young and then realize they've made the wrong choice.

A (6) ... ! It doesn't matter if you make a mistake once or twice, does it?

B Well, yes, if there are children involved.

📻 Now listen and check.

5. Work in pairs and act out the dialogue.

6. Work in pairs. Look at the other statements in *Listening and Speaking* activity 5 and act out dialogues giving your opinions and saying how you feel.

READING AND WRITING

1. Here are some extracts from an interview with Kelly, who is eighteen years old, about dating customs in the United States. Read them and write the questions the interviewer asked.

> "I guess it starts when you're about thirteen or fourteen and you get invited to birthday parties or dances. And if you meet someone you like, then maybe you'll go to a movie together or something like that."
>
> "No, there's no one who comes with you, to keep an eye on you, if that's what you mean. No, your parents are supposed to trust you to behave, if you know what I mean."
>
> "Usually my mom and dad will let me stay out until ten o'clock. And my dad gets mad if I get back any later."
>
> "Well, my date usually comes around and picks me up from home, in his car if he's got one, and we go from there. Actually, I usually make sure I only date guys with cars!"
>
> "The guys I date are usually the same age as me, or maybe a year or two older. They don't usually date girls who are older than they are, though."
>
> "I guess it's still usual for the boy to invite the girl. But a lot of the time girls ask guys now. That's OK, too."
>
> "I don't expect the guy to pay for me all the time. I mean, once or twice is fine, but if we go to the movies, I buy my own ticket, and if we go to a restaurant, I pay for my own meal. I wouldn't pay for him, though."
>
> "No, my parents don't expect to tell me who I can date, although my dad often gives an opinion about my dates."
>
> "Most of my friends and I go out with guys from all sorts of different backgrounds, social, ethnic, or religious, yes, sure."

2. Work in pairs. Is there anything which is similar to dating customs in your country? Is there anything which surprises or shocks you?

3. Find another student and ask him or her the questions you wrote in 1. As you listen to his or her answers, make notes.

4. Write a short account of dating customs in the country of the student you spoke to in 3.

Progress Check 9–16

VOCABULARY

1. *Connotation* refers to the feeling or image an adjective creates rather than its meaning. There are many adjectives which usually have either positive or negative connotations.

Positive   *practical, hard-working, romantic*
Negative   *mean, nosy, careless*

In different contexts the same adjectives can have the opposite connotation.

He was very dull and serious. He didn't laugh a lot.
I am serious about my work and passed my exams.
She was proud of her children.
She was a little proud and unfriendly.
His piano playing was very sensitive.
She was very sensitive and kept bursting into tears.

Now decide if the adjectives in these sentences have a positive or a negative connotation.

1. She was wearing a very curious hat.
2. He was very ambitious and was prepared to do anything to succeed.
3. He was very talkative and interesting.
4. She has a naïve charm.
5. He's very extravagant when he throws a party and we all enjoy ourselves.
6. It was a simple idea and everyone liked it.

2. Write sentences using the same adjectives as the sentences above, but with the opposite connotation.

3. You can often make an adjective from nouns or verbs by using the following suffixes:

-able -al -ant -ar -ual -atic -ific -ative -erial
-ish -ive -ful -y

comfort – comfortable

Now use the suffixes to make adjectives from the following words. You may have to change the noun or verb by taking off the last one or two letters.

talk innovate fruit child smell create thought
manage boss pain haze tropic fragrance
notice

GRAMMAR

1. Choose the best tense.

1. I*'ve* never *learned/been learning* Spanish.
2. She *has* just *left/been leaving* for work.
3. For the last year he *has written/been writing* his autobiography.
4. I *have* always *wanted/been wanting* a Mercedes.
5. They *have* just *gone/been going* shopping.
6. He*'s lived/been living* in Japan for a long time and he's going to stay.

2. Look at these sentences and explain the difference between them. Which sentences mean the same?

1. a. I had left the office when I heard the explosion.
   b. I left the office when I heard the explosion.
2. a. She changed her mind when she saw him.
   b. She changed her mind when she had seen him.
3. a. I felt better when I heard the news.
   b. I felt better when I had heard the news.
4. a. She ran away when he arrived.
   b. She had run away when he arrived.
5. a. When he became a pilot, he earned a lot of money.
   b. When he became a pilot, he had earned a lot of money.
6. a. She bought a car when she moved to Seattle.
   b. She bought a car when she had moved to Seattle.

3. Answer the questions using the words in parentheses and the past perfect continuous.

1. How long had you been at the bus stop? (I/wait/for twenty minutes)
2. How many years had he had the same job? (He/work/there/since 1967)
3. Why did you look so tired? (I/study/vocabulary/all evening)
4. Why hadn't you spoken to your parents? (I/work/too much)
5. Why was the river so high? (It/rain/for two weeks)
6. What had you been doing before the accident? (I/drive/from Washington to Philadelphia)

4. Which pairs of sentences have the same subject? Rewrite them as one sentence using *after + -ing*.

1. I had lunch. Then my boss called me.
2. She got married. Then she had a baby.
3. They bought a car. Then he lost his job.
4. They left on vacation. Then she got sick.
5. We went to the movies. Then we had dinner.
6. He got to the hotel. Then he called home.

5. Decide if these are usually *opinion* or *fact* adjectives.

tropical sensual dizzy plump bald agricultural west smelly frosty

6. Rewrite these sentences with participial clauses.

1. I lay down on the bed. I went to sleep.
2. She told everyone to be quiet and listened.
3. I felt relaxed at the party. I talked to most of the people.
4. I sat in the garden. I could hear birds singing.
5. The man who was standing by me was wearing a hat.
6. I saw the accident. I called an ambulance.

7. Complete the sentences with the verb in parentheses in its infinitive or *-ing* form.

1. She saw him (work) in the store.
2. He heard something (fall) to the ground.
3. I noticed her (look) quickly at him.
4. I felt her (touch) my hand for a moment.
5. They watched the children (play) all day.
6. I saw him (crash) the car.

SOUNDS

1. Underline the /ɔɪ/ sound and circle the /əʊ/ sound. Put the words in two columns.

nose noise toe toy bow boy sew soil boil choice chose loin loan cone coin

 Now listen and say the words out loud. How many different spellings are there for each sound? What letters follow the letter(s) you have underlined or circled?

2.  Listen and underline the words which the speaker stresses.

I used to walk to the bus stop with the elderly gentleman living near us. He became ill and I didn't see him until one bright, sunny morning a few months later. As I walked down the path, I glanced to the left and I saw the elderly gentleman walking slowly up past the hedge, around the front yard.

3. Underline the words you think the speaker will stress.

He turned and looked straight at me, and I was struck by how pale he appeared to be. Not until later did I realize I could not hear the sound of his footsteps, although he appeared to be walking in his usual manner, except for being slower.

 Listen and check. As you listen, say the passage out loud.

LISTENING AND SPEAKING

1.  Work in pairs. You're going to hear a story about a chauffeur in a hospital. Listen and make notes about what happened.

2. Work together and check that you remember the story. Make sure you get the sequence of events correct. Expand your notes with as much detail as possible.

The husband had died before his wife.

3. Work with another partner.

Student A: Start telling the story and try to include as much detail as possible. Answer Student B's questions. If you cannot answer a question, Student B will continue telling the story and you must ask questions.
Student B: Listen to Student A telling the story. Ask questions about any details he or she leaves out. If he or she cannot answer your questions, continue telling the story.

Keep asking and answering questions. The person telling the story at the end is the winner.

17 | *First Day at School*

Talking about memories: *remember + noun/-ing*

SPEAKING

1. This lesson is about school and your impressions.
Can you remember:

– how old you were when you first went to school?
– the names of the friends you made?
– the name of your first teacher?
– how you felt about going to school?
– if you were ever punished?

2. Work in groups of two or three and take turns telling
each other about the things you remembered in 1.

3. It is often said that your schooldays are the best days
of your life. Decide in your groups if you agree. Tell
the class whether you agree or disagree and why.

READING

1. The passage is taken from the novel *To Kill a
Mockingbird* by Harper Lee. Scout lives with her
father, Atticus, who is a lawyer, and her older brother,
Jem. Her mother is dead. The passage describes her
first day at school. Work in pairs. The following words
are in the order in which they appear in the passage.
Check that you know what they mean.

haul   palm   auburn   crimson   board   haze
cunning   wriggle   ragged   hogs   immune   fail
stock-market   literate   distaste

Can you use the words to guess what the answers to
these questions might be?

Where does the teacher hit Scout with the ruler?
What animals did the children feed?
What did the children in Scout's class look like?
How did the children do in school?
How did the teacher feel about Scout?

2. Read the passage and check your answers to 1.
Did you guess correctly?

Before the first morning was over, Miss Caroline Fisher, our
teacher, hauled me up to the front of the room and patted the
palm of my hand with a ruler, then made me stand in the corner
until noon.

Miss Caroline was no more than twenty-one. She had
bright auburn hair, pink cheeks, and wore crimson fingernail
polish. She also wore high-heeled pumps and a red-and-white
striped dress. She looked and smelled like a peppermint drop. She
boarded across the street one door down from us in Miss Maudie
Atkinson's upstairs front room, and when Miss Maudie
introduced us to her, Jem was in a haze for days.

Miss Caroline began the day by reading us a story about
cats. The cats had long conversations with one another, they
wore cunning little clothes and lived in a warm house beneath a
kitchen stove. By the time Mrs. Cat called the drugstore for an
order of chocolate malted mice the class was wriggling like a
bucketful of catawba worms. Miss Caroline seemed unaware
that the ragged, denim-shirted and floursack-skirted first grade,
most of whom chopped cotton and fed hogs from the time they
were able to walk, were immune to imaginative literature. Miss
Caroline came to the end of the story and said, "*Oh*, my, wasn't
that nice?"

Then she went to the blackboard and printed the alphabet
in enormous square capitals, turned to the class and asked,
"Does anybody know what these are?"

Everybody did; most of the first grade had failed it last
year. I suppose she chose me because she knew my name; as I
read the alphabet a faint line appeared between her eyebrows,
and after making me read most of *My First Reader* and the stock-
market quotations from *The Mobile Register* aloud, she
discovered that I was literate and looked at me with more than
faint distaste. Miss Caroline told me to tell my father not to teach
me any more, it would interfere with my reading.

"Teach me?" I said in surprise. "He hasn't taught me
anything, Miss Caroline. Atticus ain't got no time to teach me
anything," I added, when Miss Caroline smiled and shook her
head. "Why, he's so tired at night he just sits in the livingroom
and reads."

"If he didn't teach you, who did?" Miss Caroline asked
good-naturedly. "Somebody did. You weren't born reading *The
Mobile Register*."

"Jem says I was."

Miss Caroline apparently thought I was lying. "Let's not
let our imaginations run away with us, dear," she said. "Now
you tell your father not to teach you any more. It's best to begin
reading with a fresh mind. You tell him I'll take over from here
and try to undo the damage—"

"Ma'am?"

"Your father does not know how to teach. You can have
a seat now."

5. Work in pairs. Talk about Scout's experience of her first day at school. Was it a positive one? Was it similar to yours?

GRAMMAR

> **Talking about memories: *remember* + noun/-ing**
>
> You can use *remember* + noun or *-ing* to talk about a memory.
> *She remembers **Miss Caroline's clothes**.*
> *She remembers **standing** in the corner until noon.*
> **When the subject of the memory is different from the subject of the sentence, you put a noun or a pronoun subject between *remember* and the *-ing* form.**
> *She **remembers her teacher printing the alphabet**.*
> *She **remembers Miss Caroline smiling**.*
> **For other uses of *remember*, see the Grammar Review at the back of the book.**

3. Look at these sentences from the passage and answer the questions.

1. *She looked and smelled like a peppermint drop.*
   What does a peppermint drop look like?
2. *Jem was in a haze for days.*
   Why do you think Jem was in a haze?
3. *The class was wriggling like a bucketful of catawba worms.*
   Do you think the class enjoyed the story?
4. *The ragged, denim-shirted, floursack-skirted first grade....*
   Are these students likely to be rich or poor?
5. *...were immune to imaginative literature.*
   What does the writer mean?
6. *"Does anybody know what these are?" Everybody did.*
   Why did everybody know the alphabet?
7. *She looked at me with more than faint distaste.*
   Was Miss Caroline happy that Scout could read?
8. *"Jem says I was."*
   What does the writer mean?

4. Which of these statements about the passage are true?

Scout remembers ...
1. being patted with a ruler on the head.
2. standing in the corner until noon.
3. Miss Caroline's clothes.
4. her teacher printing Scout's name on the blackboard.
5. the story about dogs that Miss Caroline read.
6. watching the other students wriggle.
7. the numbers that her teacher printed on the blackboard.
8. reading the alphabet, a book, and a newspaper out loud.
9. telling Miss Caroline that Atticus hadn't taught her to read.
10. Miss Caroline shouting.

1. Look at the sentences in *Reading* activity 4. Do they show examples of *remember* + *-ing*, *remember* + noun, or *remember* + noun + *-ing*?

2. Correct the false statements in *Reading* activity 4.

She remembers being hit on the hand with a ruler.

3. Write down five things you remember doing as a child. Talk about them to a partner.

I remember arriving at the school gates with my mother.

VOCABULARY AND SPEAKING

1. Here are some words to do with school. Put them under these headings: *people, places, equipment*.

> lunch room   teacher   janitor   blackboard
> classroom   playground   gym   chalk   pen
> notebook   roll   principal   desk   bench   track
> auditorium   staff

2. Work in pairs. Are there any words in the box which bring back particular memories of school for you? Tell your partner about them.

Memories of School

Used to and *would* + infinitive,
be/get used to + noun/-*ing*

LISTENING

1. Work in pairs. You're going to hear Ben Philips, an American, talking about his experience of teaching in a school in the Sudan. First, write down some questions which you'd like to find out the answers to.

Why did he go to Africa?

2. Look at the chart below. Try to guess what Ben Philips will say about each point.

School subjects	
Students	
Classroom	
Equipment	
Length of classes	
Exams	
Amusing or embarrassing incidents	

3. Work in pairs:

Student A: Turn to Communication Activity 6 on page 103.
Student B: Turn to Communication Activity 16 on page 105.

4. Work together and complete the chart. Were your predictions in 2 right?

5. Complete these sentences with suitable phrases.

1. Ben used to work in _____.
2. He used to teach _____.
3. Every day he would _____.
4. At first he wasn't used to _____.
5. After a while, he got used to _____.
6. There didn't use to be _____ in the classroom.

📼 Now listen again and check.

6. Work in pairs. What can you guess about Ben's life when he left Africa?

GRAMMAR

> *Used to and would* + infinitive
> Remember that you use *used to* and *would* + infinitive to talk about past habits and routines which are now finished. You often use them to contrast past routine with present state.
> You can also use *used to* to talk about past states, but not *would*.
> *Be/get used to* + noun/-*ing*
> You use *be used to* + noun/-*ing* to mean *be accustomed to.*
> You can use *get used to* to mean *become used to.*

1. Look at the sentences in *Listening* activity 5 and find examples for each of the rules in the grammar box.

2. In which of these sentences can you rewrite the underlined verbs using *used to* or *would*?

When I <u>was</u> a child I went to a school which <u>was</u> about fifty miles away from home, so I <u>stayed</u> there the whole semester, and only <u>returned</u> home for vacations. At first I <u>missed</u> my parents, but I got used to it. In fact, during the long summer vacations, I <u>got</u> bored and <u>wanted</u> to see my friends. My parents <u>were</u> pleased that I enjoyed school, but I think they <u>regretted</u> encouraging me to be so independent at such a young age.

3. Write sentences describing things which you have to *get used to* doing:

– when you learn a foreign language
– when you live in a foreign country
– when you finish school
– when you buy a house

When you learn a foreign language, you have to get used to learning lots of vocabulary.

SOUNDS

1. Which words contain the /j/ sound in American English?

New York you used tune clue
few duke drew blue

🔊 Listen and check. As you listen, say the words out loud.

2. Which words in 1 contain the /j/ sound in British English?

🔊 Listen and check. As you listen, say the words out loud.

WRITING

1. Here's an old report card about a student's progress in different subjects. It was written in a very positive way. An old school friend has interpreted the report in a much more realistic way. Read it and match the interpretations below with five of the subjects.

a. She never used to open her mouth.
b. She didn't use to be able to count from one to ten.
c. She used to like making bombs.
d. She used to send the boys love letters.
e. The teachers didn't use to know where she was most of the time.

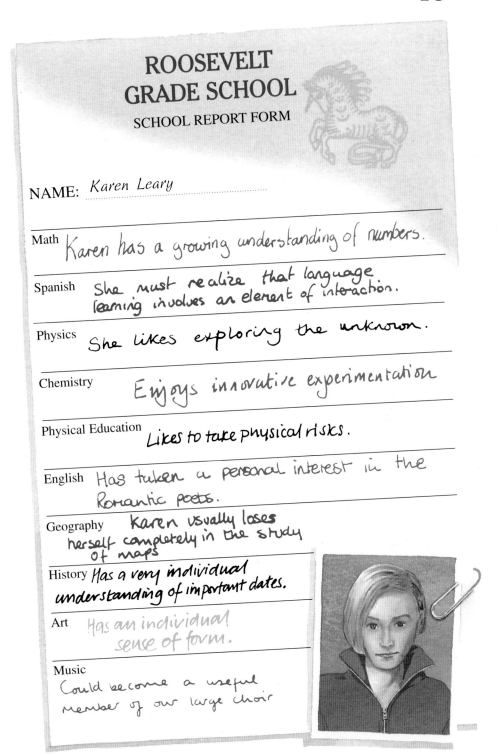

ROOSEVELT GRADE SCHOOL
SCHOOL REPORT FORM

NAME: *Karen Leary*

Math *Karen has a growing understanding of numbers.*

Spanish *She must realize that language learning involves an element of interaction.*

Physics *She likes exploring the unknown.*

Chemistry *Enjoys innovative experimentation*

Physical Education *Likes to take physical risks.*

English *Has taken a personal interest in the Romantic poets.*

Geography *Karen usually loses herself completely in the study of maps*

History *Has a very individual understanding of important dates.*

Art *Has an individual sense of form.*

Music *Could become a useful member of our large choir*

2. Write realistic interpretations about the other five subjects.

3. Think about how good you were in different subjects in a report card. Write a positive report about yourself.

Now show it to another student. Can he or she interpret it in a more realistic way?

19 | *Law and Order*

Modal verbs: *must, have to, have got to, can't, must not*

VOCABULARY AND SOUNDS

1. Look at the sentences below. Match the definitions of crimes to words from the box.

> blackmail   kidnapping   arson   trespass   hijacking
> manslaughter   murder   smuggling   drug dealing
> forgery   fraud   mugging   spying   shoplifting   libel
> bribery   burglary   speeding

1. When someone kills someone else deliberately.
2. When someone offers you money to do something.
3. When someone steals something from your home.
4. When someone captures you and demands money for your release.
5. When someone attacks you in the street and takes your money.
6. When someone writes something false and offensive about someone.

Find out what the other words in the box mean.

2. Underline the stressed syllable in these words.

illegal   blackmail   forbidden   compulsory
manslaughter   forgery   libel   obligatory

Put the words in two columns according to the stressed syllable.

🔲 Now listen and check.

3. Work in pairs. Decide on punishments for some of the crimes in the vocabulary box in 1.

prison sentence   fine   caution   life sentence
damages   community service   revoked license

READING

1. Read *Law and Order* and decide which laws the cartoons illustrate. Now work in pairs and discuss which law you find most amusing or strange.

Law and Order

- In Lancashire, England, it is against the law to hang male and female underwear on the same line.
- **In Saskatchewan, Canada, you must not drink water in a beer house.**
- A transportation law in Texas, U.S.A.: When two trains approach each other at a crossing, they should both stop, and neither shall start up until the other has gone.
- **In Waterloo, Nebraska, U.S.A., it is illegal for a barber to eat onions between 7 A.M. and 7 P.M.**
- The town council of Widnes, England, introduced a fine of £5 for those who made a habit of falling asleep in the reading rooms of libraries.
- **Dueling in Paraguay is legal as long as both participants are registered blood donors.**
- In New York City there is still a law which makes it illegal for women to smoke in public.
- **The citizens of Kentucky, U.S.A., are required by law to take a bath once a year.**
- In 1659 it became illegal to celebrate Christmas in Massachusetts.
- **In New York State you are not allowed to shoot at a rabbit from a moving trolley car. You have to get off the car, or wait for it to come to a complete stop, then fire away.**
- In Malaysia it is against the law to dance on the backs of turtles.
- **In Madagascar it is illegal for pregnant women to wear hats or eat eels.**
- In Alaska, it is illegal to look at a moose from the window of an airplane or any other flying vehicle.
- **It is illegal to hunt camels in the state of Arizona.**
- In Indiana, U.S.A., it is against the law to travel on a bus within four hours of eating garlic.
- **During the reign of Elizabeth I, the wearing of hats was made compulsory in England.**
- In 1937, in Hungary, spring cleaning became compulsory. All lofts and cellars had to be cleaned.

2. Answer the questions. Try to do this in one minute.

1. Where can't barbers eat onions during the day?
2. Where and when did you have to wear a hat?
3. Where and when did you have to clean out your lofts and cellars?
4. What must two trains do at a crossing in Texas?
5. What can't you do if you've just eaten some garlic?
6. What can't you do from an airplane window?

3. Work in pairs. Here are some possible reasons why some of the laws were introduced. Match the reason and the law.

1. Because it makes their breath smell.
2. Maybe they're an endangered species.
3. It doesn't give the animal a sporting chance.
4. Because it distracted people from the true meaning of their religion.
5. Maybe because it was considered unsuitable behavior for a woman.
6. In case people snored.

Can you think of reasons why the other laws were introduced?

GRAMMAR

Modal verbs: *must, have to, have got to, can't, must not, can't*

You usually use *must* when the obligation comes from the speaker.
You often use it for strong advice or safety instructions.
*You **must** call me as soon as you arrive.   You **must** drive carefully.*

You usually use *have to* when the obligation comes from someone else.
You often use it for rules.
*I **have to** pay taxes.*
*You **have to** drive on the right in the United States.*

But you use *have to* for things which happen regularly, especially with an adverb or adverbial phrases of frequency.
*We **have to** buy a new car **every year**.*
You can often use *have got* to instead of *have to*, especially for a specific instance.
*I've **got to** fill out my tax form this week.*
You use *can't* and *must not* to talk about what you're not allowed to do or what it is not possible to do. *Must not* is formal, and is not often used in conversation.
*You **can't** hunt camels in Arizona.*
*Women **must not** smoke in public in New York.*

You can only use *must, must not* and *have got to* to talk about the present and future. This is how you talk about obligation and prohibition in the past.

Present	must	have to	have got to	must not
Past	had to	had to	had to	couldn't or wasn't/weren't allowed to

---

1. Look back at the passage and find sentences using the present or the past form of a modal verb. Are they examples of obligation or prohibition?

2. Rewrite these rules using the present or the past form of a modal verb.

1. In Malaysia, it is against the law to dance on the backs of turtles.
2. During the reign of Elizabeth I, the wearing of hats was made compulsory.
3. In 1659 it became illegal to celebrate Christmas in Massachusetts.
4. It is illegal to hunt camels in Arizona.
5. In 1937, in Hungary, the spring cleaning of all lofts and cellars became compulsory.

3. Choose six other laws in *Law and Order* and rewrite them using the present or the past form of a modal verb.

SPEAKING AND WRITING

1. Work in groups of two or three. Are there any laws you would like to introduce in your country? Think about:

– use of mobile phones   – smoking in public places   – use of cars
– pollution   – health care   – housing   – pets   – language learning
– compulsory education

2. Write some new laws for your country. They can be as amusing or strange as you like.

20 | *Guilty or Not Guilty*

**Modal verbs: *don't need to/don't have to,
didn't need to/didn't have to, should/shouldn't***

VOCABULARY AND LISTENING

1. Work in groups of two or three. Look at the words in the box and use them to complete the gaps in the questions.

> innocent   guilty   prison   offense
> weapon   arrest   suspect   crime
> legal   charged with   confess
> custody   trial   executed   jury
> judge   bail   attorney

1. Are you innocent until you're proven ____, or the other way around?
2. If you're convicted of drug dealing, are you always sent to ____ or is there sometimes a fine?
3. Is it an offense to carry a ____, such as a gun or a knife?
4. If the police arrest you, are you allowed to call an ____?
5. If the police ____ you for a crime, is it legal to remain silent when they question you?
6. If you're ____ a crime, are you always kept in custody while you wait for a trial?
7. If you ____ to a crime, do you always get a lighter sentence?
8. Are there any crimes for which you can be ____?
9. Is there always trial by ____ for serious crimes?
10. Who decides on a sentence? Is it the ____ or the jury?

Now answer the questions in 1 for your country.

2. Check that you know what the other words in the box mean.

3. 🔊 Listen to a radio show about law and order in the United States. What are the speaker's answers to the questions in 1?

4. Work in pairs. Complete these sentences about law and order in the United States.

1. In the United States, you are innocent until _____.
2. It isn't an offense to carry a _____.
3. When you are arrested, they read you your _____.
4. You can legally call a _____.
5. If you don't want to talk, you can remain _____.
6. There is always trial by jury for _____.
7. The jury decides whether you're _____ or _____.
8. The judge decides how long your _____ will be.

🔊 Now listen again and check.

GRAMMAR

> *Don't need to, didn't need to, should/shouldn't*
>
> **You can use *don't need to* + infinitive to say what isn't necessary or what you don't have to do.**
> *You **don't need to** call a lawyer, but it's a good idea.*
>
> **You use *didn't need to* + infinitive to say that something was unnecessary. We don't know if the person did it or not.**
> *He **didn't need to** take a gun (= It wasn't necessary; we don't know if he did it or not.)*
>
> **You can use *should/shouldn't* to say what is right or wrong.**
> *It **should be** the judge who decides on the sentence. It **shouldn't be** the jury.*
>
> **You use *should have/shouldn't have* to say that someone did something wrong in the past.**
> *He **should have stayed** in bed, but he didn't.*
> *He **shouldn't have gotten up**, but he did.*

1. Write sentences saying what you *don't need to/don't have to* do or *should/shouldn't* in your country.

– carry an ID card at all times
– have a work permit
– be twenty-one before you can marry
– be twenty-one before you can drive
– call a police officer sir or ma'am
– have a license to own a gun

2. Make sentences using *should have* and *shouldn't have* and the words in parentheses.

1. I'm sure he was guilty. (He/go/to prison)
2. The fine was very high. (It/be/so high)
3. He didn't have a permit. (He/have/the gun)
4. There was a lot of traffic. (He/drive/more slowly)
5. She didn't have her ID. (They/serve/her alcohol)
6. He didn't have a green card. (They/employ/him)

3. Complete the sentences using an appropriate form of *should* or *need to* and an appropriate verb.

1. If you didn't have any money, you _____ a cab!
2. You _____ a cab. I have a car.
3. They _____ anyone about their tax evasion. Now they're in real trouble.
4. His boss just found the lost report, so he _____.
5. He confessed to the crime, but they let him go anyway! They _____.
6. You _____ some eggs. We can't make the cake without them.

READING AND WRITING

1. Read the newspaper article and the letter in reply to it. Who do you agree with—the judge or the writer of the letter?

2. Work in pairs and talk about what Jack Lewis *didn't need to* do, *should have*, or *shouldn't have* done.

He shouldn't have shot him.
He didn't need to use his gun.

3. Write a letter to a newspaper giving your opinion about the judgment. If you need some arguments for and against it, turn to Communication Activity 11 on page 104. Use the linking words and expressions to help you write the letter.

Explain why you're writing.
I am writing to you because...
Give your opinion. *In my opinion,...*
Give the opposite opinion.
It may be true that... However,...
Many people believe that...
Give your opinion again, more strongly.
But as far as I am concerned,...
But in practice,...

A judge ordered an 82-year-old man to pay $6000 in damages to a burglar who was trying to break into his house. Jack Lewis was asleep in his house in Lewiston, Idaho when he heard noises. He picked up his shotgun and went downstairs where he found Michael Phillips in the hall with a bag full of electrical equipment. Phillips claimed that he was unarmed, so he put the goods down and raised his hands when he saw the shotgun. Lewis said Phillips had turned to run out of the open front door, so he shot him. Phillips suffered minor wounds to the legs. In the trial, the judge said that despite the fact that Lewis was defending his own property, it was not acceptable for people to take the law into their own hands. Lewis was charged with assault with a deadly weapon.

I am writing in disbelief at the judgment passed on Jack Lewis yesterday. In my opinion, it is totally absurd to make him pay for his act of self-defence. In theory he committed an offense by firing at an unarmed intruder, and he should be prosecuted for this. But in practice the law should be more flexible. As far as I'm concerned, for a criminal to receive compensation for an injury sustained while carrying out a crime is outrageous.

Brian Forbes.

Brian Forbes
Boise, Idaho

READING

1. You're going to read a passage about people traveling west in the United States in the 19th century. Which of these words would you expect to see in the passage?

television farmland wagon
dentist oxen trek plain
prescription trail guide
pioneer tennis moccasin
winch chain ingenuity
disabled prairie bread dough

2. Read the passage and choose the best title.

1. How The West Was Won
2. Survival On the Oregon Trail
3. A Hard Journey
4. Tips for Travelers

3. Find a word in the passage which means the same as:

1. accidents
2. loaded and heavy
3. difficult and tiring
4. unwelcoming
5. cross
6. friendly
7. drag something in
8. make something feel better
9. keep something for a long time
10. skill and intelligence
11. turn milk into butter
12. speed

4. Read the passage again and find out how many tips are mentioned.

In the 1840s people were beginning to feel crowded in the eastern part of the United States. Many people decided to go west to the Oregon Territory, what is now the states of Oregon, Washington, Idaho, and parts of Montana and Wyoming. Stories told about Oregon made it sound like a magical place, where flowers bloomed all year and there was plenty of good farmland. So people set out from Independence, Missouri, in covered wagons with teams of six or eight oxen to pull them more than 2,000 miles along the Oregon Trail. A big wagon, laden with supplies, could travel only ten or fifteen miles a day, so it might take four to six months to complete the journey, depending on weather conditions and mishaps. The trek usually started in May, so that the travelers could arrive before winter.

It was a long, arduous, and dusty journey across an unknown and inhospitable land. Many wagon trains hired trail guides who had done the journey before them to help them safely traverse the mountains, plains, and rivers. These guides taught the travelers many survival tips, some of which they learned from the amicable Native Americans with whom they traded along the way.

There were many rivers to cross on the long journey, some far too deep to walk or ride across. So the travelers painted the bottom and sides of their wagons with tar to keep the water out, and then floated them across the river like boats. When they came to the mountains, they had to haul the wagons up to the mountain tops with winches and chains. The oxen had to be treated with great care—if they died, were injured, or even if their feet became sore, it could considerably slow up the journey. The pioneers learned a trick from the Indians to relieve the oxen's sore feet: they put moccasins, or shoes made of deer skin, over the oxen's feet until they healed.

Since they didn't have any method of refrigeration along the route, the pioneers had to learn how to dry the meat of the buffalo that they shot in order to preserve it. They tied strings from the front to the back of the wagon and hung strips of meat over the strings. The meat would dry while they kept traveling westward. The ingenuity of the pioneers helped them to solve many small but troublesome problems. For instance, they would put eggs in the flour barrel, making sure they didn't touch each other, so that the eggs didn't break along the bumpy wagon trail.

When the travelers were on the wide open plains with no trees in sight, they had to find something to burn in order to make fires. They discovered that dried buffalo droppings, called buffalo chips, made a hot fire with little smoke and no smell.

Because they didn't have ovens, the pioneers couldn't make bread. Instead, they ate bread dough which they fried in a pan. Everybody wanted butter because it made the fried bread taste better. They had milk from the cows they brought with them, but the constant pace of the journey didn't leave much time to churn it into butter. However, they found that if they tied a milk can to the side of the wagon, the milk would bounce around so much as the wagon bumped along the trail that when they opened the can, they found that the butter made itself.

Many of these and hundreds of other survival tips were common knowledge to the Native Americans whose land the pioneers had to cross during their travels. Still others were the result of trial and error—and nobody knows how many lives were lost before the best methods were discovered. It is strange to reflect that less than 100 years after these travelers made their way across the vast expanse of the West, it became possible to fly from Missouri to Oregon in just a few hours!

5. Look at these sentences from the passage. What do the words in italics refer to?

1. ...some of *which* they learned from the amicable Native Americans...
2. ...then they floated *them* across the river...
3. ...or even if *their* feet became sore...
4. ...in order to preserve *it*...
5. ...making sure *they* didn't touch each other....
6. ...*whose* land the pioneers had to cross...

GRAMMAR

> ### Clauses of purpose
> You use *to/in order to* to describe the purpose of an action when the subject of the main clause and the purpose clause are the same.
> *They painted the bottom and sides of their wagons with tar* **to** *keep the water out.*
>
> **In order to** makes a clause of purpose sound formal.
> *They hired trail guides who had done the journey before* **in order to** *help them.*
>
> **In negative sentences, you have to say *in order not to*.**
> *In order not to break the eggs, they put them in the flour barrel.*
>
> You use *so (that)*:
> –when the subjects of the main clause and the purpose clause are different.
> *The trek usually started in May,* **so that** *the travelers could arrive before the winter set in.*
> –when the purpose is negative.
> *They would put eggs in the flour barrel,* **so that** *they* **didn't** *break along the bumpy wagon trail.*
> –with *can* and *could.*
> *The trek usually started in May,* **so that** *the travelers* **could** *arrive before the winter set in..*

1. Complete these sentences using *to, so (that),* or *in order to.*

1. The pioneers decided to go west...
2. People traveling on the Oregon Trail started their journey in May...
3. They put moccasins on the oxen's feet...
4. They used buffalo droppings...
5. Everybody wanted butter...
6. They tied strings from the front to the back of the wagon...
7. They tied milk cans to the sides of their wagons...
8. The pioneers traveled with winches and chains...

2. Work in pairs. Discuss the answers to these questions using *to, so (that),* or *in order to.*

1. Why do people go on diets?
2. Why do people learn English?
3. Why do people go on vacation?
4. Why do you need to eat good food?

Compare your answers with another pair.

SPEAKING AND WRITING

1. Work in groups of four or five. Imagine it is 1840 and you are going on a six-month-long journey in a covered wagon along the primitive, dangerous Oregon Trail. You and your group have six oxen and one covered wagon. Look at the following list of supplies. Imagine that you can only take seven of the twelve things. Talk about what you need each thing for, which ones you would choose, and why.

one milk cow   two laying hens   one rooster   a length of rope   10 lb. of flour   2 lb. of sugar   a hammer   a violin   a religious book   a barrel of water   an ax   a knife

Tell the rest of the class what you have decided. As a class, choose five more important and useful things you will need for the journey. Talk about what you will need each thing for. Use the structures in the grammar box.

2. Write a short account of the things that you chose to take with you and your reasons for choosing them. Use the structures in the grammar box.

22 | *Inventions*

Noun/adjective + *to* + infinitive

VOCABULARY

1. Work in pairs. Look at these words for tools and household equipment. Which do you think are the most and least useful? Are there any that you never use?

> hammer fork spade mop
> broom screwdriver wrench
> chisel scissors corkscrew can
> opener strainer grater
> breadboard peeler carving knife
> tweezers ladle ironing board
> lawnmower saw drill toaster
> coffee grinder nail saucepan
> trash can watering can sieve
> brush chopping board

Work with another pair and compare your ideas.

2. Work in pairs. Take turns to choose a tool or piece of household equipment. Tell your partner what you use it to do. Your partner must guess what it is.

You use it to bang nails into wood. Is it a hammer?

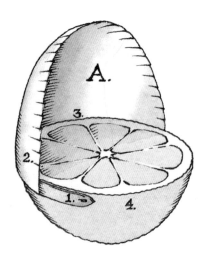

SPEAKING AND LISTENING

1. Work in pairs. You're going to hear someone talking about the inventions in the illustrations. Look at the illustrations below and discuss what you think their purpose is.

I think you use it to...   I think it's for...

Work with another pair and compare your answers.

2. 🔊 Listen and number the inventions in the order you hear them described.

3. Work in pairs and make notes on the following aspects of each invention.

name of invention   purpose   advantages   possible disadvantages

4. Complete the sentences with a few words about each invention.

1. At night, it's difficult for the parents to ____ and to ____ fall asleep.
2. When your hands are full, it's impossible to ____.
3. When you're boiling something, it's sometimes difficult to ____.
4. It's way too big and dangerous to ____.
5. After a meal, we're often surprised to ____.
6. But it would be unusual for you to ____.
7. When eating grapefruit, it's essential for you to ____.
8. But it might be easier for you to ____.

🔊 Listen again and check.

5. Which do you think is the best invention? Can you think of any more advantages and disadvantages of them?

6. Which of these inventions do you think were really invented?

Turn to Communication Activity 23 on page 106 to find out.

GRAMMAR

> Noun/adjective + *to* + infinitive
>
> **You can put *to* + infinitive after certain nouns and pronouns, usually to describe purpose.**
> *It's a thing **to pat** the baby.   Where are the keys **to lock** this door?*
>
> **You can put *to* + infinitive after some adjectives, such as *pleased, disappointed, surprised, difficult, easy.***
> *It's **impossible to raise** your hat when your hands are full.*
>
> **You can put *of* (someone) + *to* + infinitive after certain adjectives, such as *nice, kind, silly, careless, good, wrong, clever, stupid, generous.***
> *It's **stupid of the inventor to use** electricity.*
>
> **You can put *for* + object + *to* + infinitive after certain adjectives, such as *easy, common, important, essential, (un)usual, (un)necessary, normal, rare.***
> *It's **rare for men to wear** a hat these days.*
>
> **You can put *for* + -*ing* to describe the purpose of something.**
> *It's a thing **for patting** a baby.*
> *It's a device **for shaving.***

1. Use *to* + infinitive to describe the purpose of the following tools and pieces of equipment.

1. a key ring   3. a fan   5. a toothbrush
2. a knife   4. a kettle   6. a fax machine

2. Make sentences beginning with the words in brackets and *of* (someone) or *for* + object + *to* + infinitive.

1. You spilled the milk. (It was careless)
2. After a few days, bread goes stale. (It's normal)
3. He used all the hot water. (It was wrong)
4. You turned the lights on. (It wasn't necessary)
5. He did all the housework. (It was unusual)
6. She left the oven on. (It was stupid)

1. It was careless of you to spill the milk.

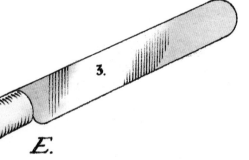

SOUNDS

In connected speech, the last /t/ or /d/ sound in some words disappears before the first consonant of the next word. Listen and repeat these phrases.

first class   difficult time
cardboard   different table
household task   bread toaster
hand drill   felt tip

WRITING

1. Work in groups of three or four. You are going to persuade the company you work for to manufacture *either* one of the inventions in the illustrations, *or* an invention of your own choice. First, choose an invention. Make sure that you choose something which will make a great contribution to improving people's lives.

2. Prepare a description of the invention. Use the notes in *Speaking and Listening* activity 3 to help you. Think of a name for your invention.

3. Design a poster for your invention to display in the classroom. Make sure that it says clearly the name of the invention, what it does and what its advantages are.

23 | *Food, Glorious Food!*

Conditionals (1): zero, first, and second conditionals; *if* and *when*

VOCABULARY AND SPEAKING

1. Look at the words in the box and put them under these headings: *breakfast, lunch, dinner, preparation,* and *cooking.* Some may go in more than one category.

apple	eggplant	bake	boil
butter	cake	carrot	chop
coffee	cut	dice	fry	grate
grill	grind	milk	oil	onion
peel	pepper	potato	pour
roast	spread	steam	stew
tomato	trout	water	

2. Work in pairs. Look at the words in the box for food and drink and answer these questions.

– how do you prepare them?
– how do you usually cook them?

READING AND LISTENING

1. Read and answer the questionnaire. Now turn to Communication Activity 3 on page 102 to find your score.

2. Work in groups of two or three and talk about your answers to the questionnaire. Do you all have similar answers or different attitudes and tastes?

3. Listen to Josie and Phil having a conversation in a restaurant. Decide which one of them lives to eat.

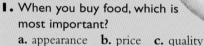

Do You Eat to Live or Live to Eat?

1. When you buy food, which is most important?
   a. appearance **b.** price **c.** quality

2. If you buy apples, which kind do you choose?
   a. red **b.** green **c.** the cheapest

3. When you have a meal, what do you enjoy it most for?
   a. the food **b.** the company **c.** the relaxation **d.** the television

4. If you were stranded on a desert island, what food would you miss most?
   a. chocolate **b.** steak **c.** bread

5. If a waiter suggests water, which do you ask for?
   a. bottled **b.** tap

6. When you look at the menu in a restaurant, what do you usually choose?
   a. a dish you know **b.** a dish you don't know

7. If you're having dinner in a restaurant, will you always have a dessert?
   a. yes **b.** no

8. If someone offered the following unusual food, which would you try?
   a. cheese-flavored ice cream **b.** strawberry-flavored potato chips **c.** neither

9. If someone suggested a quick meal, what would you choose?
   a. fast food **b.** a sandwich **c.** a picnic **d.** something more substantial

10. What would you be happiest to leave out of your present diet?
   a. meat **b.** fruit and vegetables **c.** desserts **d.** wine

11. If you could put a flavor on stamps, what would you choose?
   a. chili **b.** cheese **c.** banana **d.** another **e.** none

12. If someone said "Never eat anything you can't pronounce" what would you say?
   a. I couldn't agree more! **b.** Nonsense!

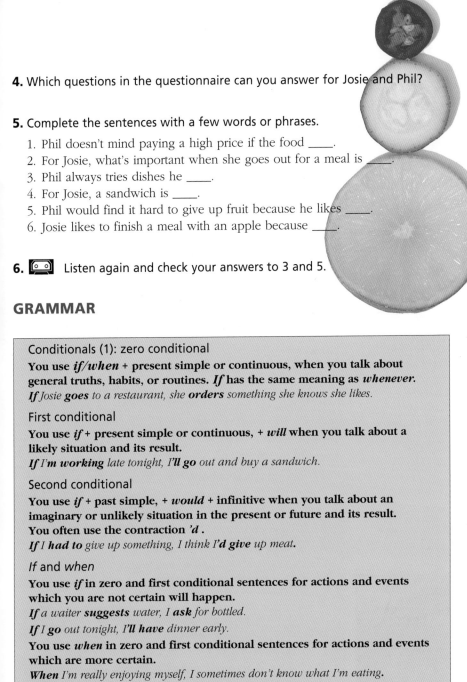

4. Which questions in the questionnaire can you answer for Josie and Phil?

5. Complete the sentences with a few words or phrases.

1. Phil doesn't mind paying a high price if the food ____.
2. For Josie, what's important when she goes out for a meal is ____.
3. Phil always tries dishes he ____.
4. For Josie, a sandwich is ____.
5. Phil would find it hard to give up fruit because he likes ____.
6. Josie likes to finish a meal with an apple because ____.

6. 🔲 Listen again and check your answers to 3 and 5.

GRAMMAR

> ### Conditionals (1): zero conditional
> You use *if/when* + present simple or continuous, when you talk about general truths, habits, or routines. *If* has the same meaning as *whenever*.
> *If Josie **goes** to a restaurant, she **orders** something she knows she likes.*
>
> ### First conditional
> You use *if* + present simple or continuous, + *will* when you talk about a likely situation and its result.
> *If I**'m working** late tonight, I**'ll go** out and buy a sandwich.*
>
> ### Second conditional
> You use *if* + past simple, + *would* + infinitive when you talk about an imaginary or unlikely situation in the present or future and its result. You often use the contraction *'d* .
> *If I **had to** give up something, I think I**'d give** up meat.*
>
> ### If and when
> You use *if* in zero and first conditional sentences for actions and events which you are not certain will happen.
> *If a waiter **suggests** water, I **ask** for bottled.*
> *If I **go** out tonight, I**'ll have** dinner early.*
> You use *when* in zero and first conditional sentences for actions and events which are more certain.
> *When I'm really enjoying myself, I sometimes don't know what I'm eating.*
> *When I go out tonight, I'll have dinner in a restaurant.*

1. Look at these sentences and explain the difference between them.

1. a. If you give me $1, I'll spend it all.
   b. If you gave me $25,000, I'd spend it all.

2. a. I'll give it to you if you get here at 9 A.M.
   b. I'll give it to you when you get here at 9 A.M.

2. Complete the sentences using a suitable conditional form. There may be more than one possibility.

1. If you ____ to the new restaurant, I'm sure you ____ yourself.
2. If I ____ too much to eat, I ____ sleepy.
3. If I ____ you, I ____ the chef's specialty.
4. If I ____ a lot of money, I ____ out more often.
5. If you ____ the vegetables, they ____ more quickly.

3. Complete the sentences with *if* or *when*.

1. She's coming with us tonight. ____ you see her, you can ask her.
2. ____ we're late, start without us.
3. I'm going to the restaurant now. ____ I get there, I'll call her.
4. ____ it's a nice day tomorrow, we'll have a barbecue.
5. They may not be at home, but ____ they are, I'll invite them over.

SOUNDS

1. Underline the words you think the speaker will stress in *Grammar* activity 3.

2. 🔲 Listen and check your answers to 1. As you listen, say the sentences out loud.

SPEAKING

Work in pairs. Talk about food and drink in your country. Discuss the following:

– most typical dish   – typical drinks
– typical produce   – typical snacks
– eating out   – family meals

The most typical dish for us in Korea is rice.

Meals on Wheels

Conditionals (2): *unless, even if, as long as, provided (that), or/otherwise*

READING AND SPEAKING

1. Work in groups of three. You are going to read a passage called *Meals on Wheels*. Before you read the passage, try to predict what it might be about. Try to think of at least five ideas.

2. Read the passage and write a sentence saying what it is about. Were any of your ideas correct? (For the moment, ignore the blanks in the text.)

3. Find a word in the text that means the same as the words and phrases below:
   1. not cooked
   2. a kind of seat you put on a horse
   3. soft or easy to cut and eat
   4. a break in a journey for rest or food
   5. something which is wrapped
   6. to tie something to something else
   7. to make a hole in something

It is perfectly possible to use the engine in your car to cook food. It's not a new idea. After all, Genghis Khan is believed to have put raw meat under the saddle of his horse to make it tender as he rode. This is said to be the origin of *steak tartare*. (1) _____ the food should be ready when you arrive or at some convenient pit stop. It allows you to eat good, freshly-cooked, hot food anywhere on the way even if you find yourself in a remote place. Anyone can try car-engine cooking (2) _____. Driving conditions can vary the cooking process considerably. Most of the recipes are based on cooking times generated by empty freeways in America and its 55-mile-an-hour speed limit. But if you ignore the speed limit (3) _____, this will affect the process. It's probably not a good idea to use your engine for cooking in Midtown Manhattan (4) _____. The classic cooking method is *en papillote*, or wrapped in foil. There's usually room to do six small foil-wrapped packages at a time (5) _____. Here are a few tips for car engine cooking:

1. Do not expect to boil anything; if your engine is boiling, you'll have to stop anyway. But you can still bake, roast, poach, and stew, even if you have a cool-running diesel engine.

2. Don't choose dishes which need careful timing.

3. On long journeys, provided that you choose dishes which cook slowly, your cooking will be very successful. For short journeys, only fish, diced vegetables, and sliced meat will be ready in time.

4. Always wrap everything in three layers of foil. Otherwise it will smell or get dirty. If you use baking paper, it burns. As long as you wrap everything carefully, the food will be all right.

5. Make sure you don't pierce the package when you put it in place or there will be a serious loss of sauce, which only smells good at first.

6. Try using the foil trays in which you buy frozen dinners.

7. Wrap sweet peppers, tomatoes, potatoes (which can take some time), bits of eggplant, apples, and hamburgers in small round packages. Long, thin packages are better for pieces of meat, mackerel, trout, and sausages.

8. Strap sausages, lamb chops, and fillets of fish to the exhaust pipe to brown them on one side.

9. Take care not to let the cooking paackages get in the way of the accelerator cable or any other moving part of the engine.

10. Make sure you pierce any cans you intend to heat with two holes. Unless you do this, they will explode.

11. Never use the car engine fan as a food processor for slicing carrots.

Adapted from *Meals on Wheels* by Robin Young, *The Times*

4. What do you think?

1. Why did Genghis Khan put raw meat under his saddle?
2. Why will ignoring the speed limit affect the cooking process?
3. Why isn't it a good idea to use your engine for cooking in Midtown Manhattan?
4. Why will you still be able to cook with a cool-running diesel engine?
5. Why shouldn't you choose dishes which need careful timing?
6. Why should you take care not to let cooking packages get in the way of the accelerator cable?
7. Would it have occurred to you to use the car engine fan to slice carrots?

5. Work in pairs. Look back at the passage and decide where these conditional clauses go in the gaps.

a. even if you have an average car
b. if the driving conditions are suitable
c. As long as you plan your journey and your cooking carefully
d. or if you come up against heavy traffic jams
e. unless you like raw food

6. Look back at the passage and put a check (✓) by the tips which say what you *should* do and a cross (✗) by the ones which say what you *shouldn't* do.

7. Work in pairs and answer the questions.

1. What do you think of the idea of car engine cooking?
2. Would you like to try it?
3. If so, where would you try it?
4. What would you cook?
5. How would you cook it?
6. How long would it take?

Now work with another pair and compare your answers.

GRAMMAR

Conditionals (2): *unless, even if, as long as, provided (that), or/otherwise*
You can use *unless, even if, as long as, provided (that)* with zero and first conditionals to talk about likely situations and their results.
You can use *unless* to mean *if... not.*
Unless you pierce the cans, they will explode.
(= If you don't pierce the cans, they will explode.)
You use *even if* to express a contrast or to give some surprising information.
You can cook food ***even if*** *you have a cool-running diesel engine.*
You use *as long as* or *provided (that)* to mean *on condition that.*
The food will be ready ***as long as (provided that)*** *you plan your journey carefully.*
You can also use the expressions with second conditional sentences, when you talk about an unlikely situation and its result.
You can follow an instruction with *or (else)* or *otherwise* + a clause describing the result if you don't follow the instruction. Notice the difference in usage:
Always wrap everything in three layers of foil, ***or (else)*** *it will smell or get dirty.*
Always wrap everything in three layers of foil. ***Otherwise,*** *it will smell or get dirty.*
(= If you don't wrap everything in three layers of foil, it will smell or get dirty.)

1. Look back at *Meals on Wheels* and find some examples of conditional sentences. Say which type of conditional (zero, first, or second) they are and why they are used. You can use the grammar box to help you.

2. Complete these sentences with *if, even if,* or *as long as.*

1. I wouldn't use my car engine for cooking _____ I was starving.
2. I'd try car engine cooking _____ the food stayed clean.
3. _____ there were no restaurants on a long journey, I think I'd try it.
4. _____ there was no risk of the food falling off, I'd try cooking some steak.
5. _____ it was easier to take a picnic, I'd still want to try it out.

3. Choose four or five tips for car engine cooking, and rewrite them using *if, unless, even if, as long as,* and *provided that.*

As long as you choose dishes which cook slowly, you can use your engine to cook food.

4. Rewrite the sentences in 3 using *or (else)/otherwise* + a clause describing the result.

WRITING

Choose one of the following topics and write a list of ten tips for it.

– having a picnic
– having a barbecue
– eating a meal out in your country
– an unusual method of cooking

Give your tips.   *Always take a picnic blanket...*
Explain your reasons.   *...since the ground may be damp.*
Describe the result if you don't follow the instructions.
Otherwise, you might catch a cold.

Fluency **3** *Home Visit*

Expressing ability; making and responding to compliments; asking a favor

SPEAKING AND LISTENING

1. Draw a plan of your house.

Now work in pairs. Talk about what the rooms are and what they're used for.

2. Which of the following items of furniture and features of a house or apartment would you expect to see in a typical home in your country?

fireplace bathtub balcony attic telephone yard
bidet laundry room television dishwasher
barbecue swimming pool shower basement
garage sofa deck refrigerator carpet patio
central heating

Which items do you have in your home?

3. 📼 Listen to Joan talking about a typical home in the United States, and check (✓) the furniture and features she mentions.

4. Read the questions below and think about your answers to them.

1. What would you prefer, a new or an old house?
2. Would you be prepared to buy an old house with character and renovate it?
3. How many rooms does a typical home have?
4. What is more common for people of your age group, rented accommodation, property you own, or accommodation with your parents?
5. Do you often entertain guests at home? If so, in which rooms do you usually entertain them?
6. Are there any rooms which visitors do not go into?
7. Are there any particular customs on entering or leaving a home?

5. 📼 Listen to Joan talking about her answers to the questions in 4 and make notes.

6. Work in pairs and check the notes you made in 5. Try to remember as much detail as possible.

📼 Now listen again and check.

7. Work in pairs and talk about your answers to the questions in 4.

FUNCTIONS

Making compliments	Responding to compliments
Your home is beautiful!	*(Why,) thank you.*
What an amazing view!	*That's very kind of you.*
This is a very nice chair.	*Yes, it is.*
You speak English really well.	

Asking for help

I don't have a chair. Could I possibly have some more?
I don't seem to have a cup. Could you pass the salt, please?
Could you tell me where the bathroom is?
I wonder if you could pour me some water.
Would you mind sitting here?
I hope you don't mind my asking, but could I have a smaller portion?
Sorry to trouble you, but I'd rather not have any meat.

Agreeing	Refusing
By all means!	*I'm awfully sorry, but ...*
Go right ahead.	*I'd like to say yes, but ...*
Sure!	*I can't really because...*
Why, yes of course.	*No way, José.*
I'd be glad to.	

1. When do you usually make compliments in your language? How do you usually respond to them? Which expressions for making and responding to compliments in the functions box have direct translations in your language?

2. Work in pairs.

Student A: Turn to Communication Activity 2 on page 102.

Student B: Turn to Communication Activity 24 on page 107.

3. Look at the expressions for asking for help. Which are the most and least direct? Which are the most polite? Which is not a polite way of refusing to help.

4. Look at this dialogue. Is there anything which surprises you?

TED Hi! Come in. How are you? What an amazing haircut!

BILLY Oh, it's nothing, really. I'm fine, thanks, how are you? I hope I'm not too early.

TED Not at all. Come on in and join us. Would you like a drink?

BILLY Yes, please. I'm sorry to trouble you but could I have a Coke?

TED Sure. Ice?

BILLY That'll be fine. I hope you don't mind my asking, but do you have any lemon?

TED Uh-huh. Here you go.

BILLY Wow, this really is a beautiful place! What a great view!

TED Why, thank you. Here's your drink. Would you be so kind as to sit down? Make yourself at home.

BILLY Thank you. This is great. I hope you don't mind my asking, but is it OK to put it here on this table?

TED No way, José. Go right ahead.

🔊 Now listen and cross out anything you don't hear.

5. Work in pairs and act out the dialogue.

6. Work in pairs.

Student A: Turn to Communication Activity 14 on page 105.
Student B: Turn to Communication Activity 26 on page 107.

READING AND WRITING

1. Read the advice on visiting customs in the United States. Put a check (✓) by the advice which is also true for your country.

☐ We usually offer visitors something to drink whenever they come by. During the day, it may be a cup of coffee or a Coke, and in the evening, maybe a glass of wine or a cocktail.

☐ If someone invites us for lunch or dinner, we usually invite them back after a few weeks.

☐ We like to have visitors so they can admire our home. We spend a lot of money making sure it looks good.

☐ When you're offered food or drink, it's OK to accept it immediately. If you say you don't want any more, your host will believe you and certainly won't insist.

☐ It isn't very usual to come by without an invitation, certainly not in the evening, in case the person we're visiting already has guests.

☐ You don't wander around the house unless you're invited to do so by your host. It's common to introduce yourself to other people at an informal party. You don't wait for the hosts to do it as they may be very busy.

☐ If you've accepted an invitation, you'd better show up or call. They could be very upset if you don't come.

☐ If you arrive much later than twenty minutes after the time you were invited for, people will start to worry. But don't arrive early—your host may still be in the bathtub!

☐ You shouldn't start to eat or drink as soon as you're served. Wait until everyone has got something in front of them.

☐ When you take your first sip of your drink, say something like "Cheers," "To your health," or "Break a leg!" But don't drink the glass in one swallow, though, even if you're thirsty!

2. Work in pairs and talk about your answers to 1.

3. Write some advice on customs for visiting for foreign visitors to your country. Include advice on:

– things to say   – things to do   – things to eat   – things to drink

Progress Check **17–24**

VOCABULARY

1. After the following verbs you can use the *-ing* form or *to* + infinitive but the meaning changes: *remember, forget, try, stop, regret.*

I remember him saying he felt sick.
(= He said he felt sick and I remember this.)
I remembered to call him.
(= I remembered, then I called.)
You've forgotten asking for my help.
(= You asked for my help, then you forgot.)
I forgot to tell you what I'd done.
(= I didn't tell you because I forgot.)
He had even tried working on weekends.
(= as an experiment.)
He had tried to study for about eight hours a day.
(= He made an effort to do so.)
I stopped feeling so generous.
(= I was feeling generous, then I stopped.)
He stopped to get some gas.
(= He stopped his car in order to get a some gas.)
I now regret being so stingy.
(= I regret something I have already done.)
I regret to tell you that I can't come.
(= I'm sorry to have to tell you that I can't come.)

For more information, turn to the Grammar Review at the back of the book.

Now complete these sentences with the verb in brackets in the correct form.

1. I remember ____ her at a party a year ago. (meet)
2. During the trip we stopped ____ something to eat. (have)
3. She regretted not ____ an earlier flight. (take)
4. Please try ____ very carefully. (drive)
5. Don't forget ____ me some money. (give)
6. Remember ____ a newspaper when you go shopping. (buy)

2. You often use a prefix to give a word an opposite or a negative meaning. Here are some common prefixes:

dis- il- im- in- ir- over- re- un- under-

Use your dictionary to find out which prefixes the following words take. Some words may take more than one prefix.

able   agree   approve   charge   convenient   edible
fair   legible   literate   load   patient   place
probable   read   replaceable   reversible   use   work

GRAMMAR

1. Write down five things you remember doing last year.

2. Put a check (✓) by the sentences where you can use *used to* or *would* and a cross (✗) where you can only use *used to.*

1. When I was young, I *used to/would* be very shy.
2. We *used to/would* spend our holidays in Maine.
3. There *used to/would* be a store on the corner.
4. In the summer, they *used to/would* go out every day.
5. Years ago he *used to/would* have a mustache.
6. I *used to/would* be afraid of the dark.

3. Complete the sentences with *must* or a form of *have to.* Sometimes both are possible.

1. You ____ take your passport when you go abroad.
2. She's not at home. I'll ____ call her again tomorrow.
3. I'm tired. I ____ leave before I fall asleep.
4. She ____ go home because she felt sick.
5. I ____ take a bus this morning because my car broke down.
6. He doesn't enjoy ____ cook every day.

4. Choose the best verb.

1. We *must not/don't need to* get up early since it's Sunday.
2. She *doesn't have to/can't* pay for the repairs because it's still under warranty.
3. We *must not/don't have to* annoy him as he gets very angry.
4. You *must not/don't need to* call a taxi. I'll drive you home.
5. I *didn't have to call/shouldn't have called* her because she came by to see me.
6. You *don't need to/must not* drive so fast. We've got plenty of time.
7. You *must not/don't have to* drive on the left in the United States.
8. I didn't go shopping yesterday. I *didn't have to/ shouldn't have to* because I still had plenty of food.

5. Answer the questions with *in order to, to,* or *so that.*

1. Why do some people spend their vacations in sunny places?
2. Why does the government make us pay taxes?
3. Why do some people wear hats?
4. Why do some people keep guard dogs?
5. Why do you carry an umbrella?
6. Why should you exercise?

6. Rewrite these sentences using the words in parentheses and *of* or *for.*

1. You called me. (It was nice)
2. She brought some flowers. (It wasn't necessary)
3. Speak clearly. (It's important)
4. He refused a second helping. (It was unusual)
5. She left her bag in the taxi. (It was careless)
6. She bought me lunch. (It was generous)

7. Complete the sentences with *if, when, even if,* or *as long as.* There may be more than one possibility.

1. I wouldn't go ____ you paid me.
2. ____ you help clean up, I'll help you with your homework.
3. I'm going to work now. ____ I get there, I'll speak to my boss.
4. She may not be there, but ____ she is, I'll tell her.
5. ____ it was well-cooked, I wouldn't eat meat.
6. ____ it's not illegal, I'll try anything.

SOUNDS

1. Say these words out loud. Is the underlined sound /aʊ/, /oː/ or /ɔː/? Put them into three columns.

sh<u>ore</u>   sh<u>ow</u>   sh<u>ow</u>er   t<u>ore</u>   t<u>oe</u>   t<u>ow</u>er
fl<u>oor</u>   fl<u>ow</u>   fl<u>ow</u>er   s<u>ore</u>   s<u>ew</u>   s<u>our</u>

Listen and check. As you listen, say the words out loud.

2. Say these words out loud. In which two words is *ough* pronounced the same?

through   though   bough   rough   cough   enough

Now listen and check.

3. Underline the words you think the speaker will stress in this dialogue.

A How are you?
B Fine. How are you?
A OK. Did you have a good weekend?
B Yes, I did. Did you?
A Very nice. What did you do?
B I played tennis. What did you do?
A I went to the movies. I saw the latest Woody Allen movie. Have you seen it?
B Yes, I have. Did you like it?
A Yes, I did. Did you?
B Yes, I did.

Listen and check. Then work in pairs and act out the dialogue.

LISTENING AND WRITING

1. Listen to three news stories and take notes.

2. Work in groups of three, and compare notes. Check that you have noted down as much detail as possible.

3. In your groups, write out the news stories in full. Try to reconstruct them as accurately as you can.

4. Listen again and check your stories in 3. Did you remember everything?

25 | *High-tech Dreams or Nightmares?*

The passive

VOCABULARY AND READING

1. Look at the words for items of technology in the box. Which ones would you find at work, which at home, and which at both work and home?

> computer   video recorder   microwave   CD player
> food processor   camcorder   camera   photocopier
> washing machine   telephone   refrigerator   stereo
> security system

2. Work in groups of three or four. Discuss whether you are happy with or afraid of technology. Which items in the box do you most or least like using? What can go wrong with technology?

3. Read the passage about a computerized home. Is the writer's home a high-tech dream or a high-tech nightmare?

4. Read the passage again and find six things that went wrong in the writer's home.
Now work in pairs and check your answers.

5. Which of these statements are true?
  1. On December 3, the computer damaged all the electrical appliances.
  2. The software company tested the system from a distance.
  3. Vibrations on the window set off the security alarm and called the police.
  4. The universal remote usually changes the TV channels.
  5. On December 12, the computer caught a virus from inside the home system.
  6. Usually, you could raise or lower the garage doors automatically.
  7. On December 21, the programmers upgraded the system.

Nov 28: Moved in at last. Finally, we live in the best house in the neighborhood. Everything is networked. The cable TV is connected to our phone, which is connected to my personal computer, which is connected to the power lines, all the appliances, and the security system. Everything runs off a universal remote.

Nov 30: Hot Stuff! Programmed my video recorder from the office, turned up the thermostat, and turned on the lights with the car phone. Everything nice and cozy when I got home.

Dec 3: Yesterday the kitchen CRASHED. As I opened the refrigerator door, the light bulb blew. Immediately, all the electrical appliances were shut down by the computer. So the software company ran some remote telediagnostic tests via my house processor. Turns out the problem was that the network had never seen a refrigerator bulb failure while the door was open. The burned out bulb was interpreted as a power surge and THE ENTIRE KITCHEN WAS SHUT DOWN.

Dec 7: The police are not happy. Our house keeps calling them for help. We discover that whenever we play the television or stereo above 25 decibels, it creates vibrations which are amplified when they hit the window. The police computer concludes that someone is trying to break in.

Another glitch: the universal remote won't let me change the channels on my television. That means I actually have to get up off the couch and change the channels by hand! The software and the utility people say this flaw will be fixed in the next upgrade— SmartHouse 2.1.

Dec 12: This is a nightmare! There's a virus in the house. My personal computer caught it while browsing on the public access network. I come home and the living room is a sauna, the bedroom windows are covered with ice, the refrigerator has been defrosted, the basement has been flooded by the washing machine, the garage door is going up and down, and the television is stuck on the home shopping channel.

Dec 18: They think they've disinfected the house, but the place is a shambles. Pipes have burst and we're not completely sure we've got the part of the virus that attacks the toilets.

Dec 19: Apparently our house isn't insured for viruses.

We call our lawyer. He laughs. He's excited!

Dec 21: I get a call from a SmartHouse sales rep. As a special holiday offer, we get the opportunity to become a site for the company's new SmartHouse 2.1 upgrade, free of charge! He says I'll be able to meet the programmers personally. "Sure," I tell him.

6. Work in pairs and talk about your answers to the questions.

1. Is the writer enthusiastic or indifferent about his home at first?
2. Why does the system keep calling the police?
3. Why do you think the lawyer is excited?
4. How does the writer feel about meeting the programmers?

GRAMMAR

> **The passive**
> **You use the passive:**
> **– when you do not know *who* or *what* does something.**
> *The cable TV **is connected** to our phone.*
> **– when you are not interested in *who* or *what* does something.**
> *All the electrical appliances **were shut** down.*
> **– when you want to take away the focus on the personal responsibility.**
> *This flaw **will be fixed** in the next upgrade.*
> **You use *by* to say *who* or *what* is responsible for an action.**
> *The basement **has been flooded by** the washing machine.*
> **You use *with* to talk about the instrument which is used to perform the action.**
> *The lights **were switched** on by the writer **with** his car phone.*
> **You also use *with* to talk about materials or ingredients.**
> *The bedroom windows **are covered with** ice.*
> **The passive is often used in sales brochures and product information to give an "official" tone.**

1. Look at these pairs of active and passive sentences.
In each pair, which do you think is the better sentence?
Explain why.

1. a. My computer is checked for viruses every six months.
   b. A company checks my computer for viruses every six months.
2. a. As the refrigerator door was opened, the light bulb blew.
   b. As I opened the refrigerator door, the light bulb blew.
3. a. Many children are being shown how to use computers in schools.
   b. Teachers are showing many children how to use computers in schools.
4. a. You can change channels by using the remote control.
   b. Channels can be changed by using the remote control.
5. a. We will install a security system free of charge.
   b. A security system will be installed free of charge.

2. Complete these sentences with *by* or *with*.

1. All the appliances are controlled ____ the universal remote.
2. The floor was flooded ____ water ____ the washing machine.
3. Nothing was detected ____ the security sensors.
4. He was told ____ the claims adjuster that the house wasn't insured.
5. The system was attacked ____ a virus.
6. The computer was tested ____ special software ____ the software company.

WRITING

Think of a piece of electrical equipment, for example a computer or a video recorder, and write down three things that could go wrong with it. Imagine that you bought one by mail order and now you are writing to the manufacturers to explain what went wrong and to demand a replacement or your money back.

Begin your letter by saying what you bought and when you bought it.

Next, explain what the problems were and when they happened.

Finally, tell them that you would like a replacement or your money back.

Use these expressions to help you.

Dear Sir or Madam,
I am writing to inform you that...
First, the box was damaged when the computer was delivered...
I would be grateful if you would...
Yours sincerely,

26 | *In Touch*

Passive infinitive; passive gerund

VOCABULARY AND LISTENING

1. Match the definitions below with these means of communication.

> CD-ROM e-mail fax
> the Internet satellite TV cable TV

a. a system which allows messages to be sent and received by a group of computer users

b. a means of storing information on a computer disk

c. a system of TV broadcasting using a satellite in space

d. a means of sending or receiving printed material in electronic form along a phone line

e. a network allowing computer users around the world to communicate with each other

f. a system of TV broadcasting by cable, giving more channels

Which of these means of communication do you use?

2. 🔲 Listen to Anna describing the words in the box to Rich.

3. Work in pairs. Which of the following uses for the new technology might Anna mention?

– shopping
– taking a correspondence course
– making travel arrangements
– booking concert tickets
– having access to research
– playing games
– having access to the latest news
– visiting museums and galleries
– communicating with people around the world

4. Look at the chart and decide who is likely to have these opinions, Anna or Rich. Put a check (✓) in the appropriate column.

	Rich	Anna
CD-ROMs are much better than books because more information can be stored on them.		
Being connected to an e-mail system is very useful.		
Most people like being contacted by e-mail.		
To be contacted by e-mail is not very sociable.		
The Internet should be controlled by the government.		
Some people are now afraid of being censored by the government.		
There's no point in being connected to TV stations around the world if you don't speak the language.		

5. 🔲 Listen and check your answers to 4.

6. Complete the sentences summarizing what Anna says. Use the information in activity 5 to help you.

1. It's good to be connected to e-mail because it is _____.
2. A fax is a good way of sending _____.
3. Watching foreign TV stations helps you to _____.
4. Being connected to cable and satellite TV isn't _____.

🔲 Listen again and check your answers.

7. What do you think the speaker means by the following sentences? Say them in a simpler way.

1. "When it comes to art there's no substitute for the real thing."
2. "A friend convinced me that LPs and tapes were out."
3. "It sounds really impersonal to me."

8. Work in pairs. Discuss your own reactions to the opinions in 4.

GRAMMAR

> Passive infinitive, passive gerund
> **You can use the passive infinitive as the subject of a sentence for emphasis.**
> *To be contacted by e-mail is not very sociable.*
> **You can use the passive infinitive without *to* after modal verbs.**
> *The Internet should be controlled by the government.*
> **You can use the passive gerund:**
> **– as the subject of a sentence.**
> *Being connected to an e-mail system is very useful.*
> **– as the object of a sentence.**
> *Most people like being contacted by e-mail.*
> **– with a preposition.**
> *People are afraid of being censored by the government.*

1. Rewrite the sentences using the words in parentheses and a suitable passive.

1. I won't come to the party without (invite).
2. She's concerned about (send) unwanted mail.
3. (Lose) in the snow is very frightening.
4. You should (pay) for the work you do.
5. He cannot (give) more time to finish the test.
6. The medicine must (take) twice a day.

1. I won't come to the party without being invited.

2. Rewrite these sentences in the passive.

1. He doesn't like people calling him after 10 P.M.
2. She's nervous about people charging too much.
3. He's interested in someone connecting him to cable TV.
4. She's looking forward to people inviting her over to visit.
5. She wants to communicate with friends without other people overhearing.
6. He needs someone to tell him what to do.

1. He doesn't like being called after 10 P.M.

SOUNDS

1. Say these compound nouns out loud. Underline the stressed word.

computer screen   travel arrangements
concert tickets   satellite dish   television channel

Listen and say the words out loud.

2. Say these compound nouns out loud. Underline the stressed word.

mobile phone   late-night phone call
electronic mail   cable TV

Listen and say the words out loud.

SPEAKING AND WRITING

1. Work in groups. You're going to take part in a discussion about the statement: *More technology means less communication.*

Group A: You agree with the statement. Make a list of Rich's opinions and add some of your own.
Group B: You disagree with the statement. Make a list of Anna's opinions and add some of your own.

2. Start the discussion. Your teacher will explain what to do.

3. Write a summary of your discussion using the statement as a title.

Introduce the subject and explain what it's about.
There has been much discussion recently about the communications revolution. More people are using e-mail, cable TV, and the Internet...

Present the arguments in favor.
On the one hand, using the new technology means faster communication...
The advantages are...
In addition,...
Moreover...

Present the arguments against.
However, many people think technology makes it more difficult to communicate.
The disadvantages are...

Present your conclusion.
In conclusion, I think that...

27 | *The Amish*

Relative clauses

Now, America is as modern a place as you will find in all the world, I imagine, but when you travel a few miles into Pennsylvania from Philadelphia and enter a place called Lancaster County, you could believe you had traveled back in time to the last century and even beyond. This is where the Amish established themselves and held fast to their customs and beliefs. They are farming people who are immediately recognizable by their unusual dress—severe black suits for the men, long skirts and bob caps for the women (heads must be covered at all times, even the children's). The men wear broad-brimmed black hats for best, and straw ones for working. They will not use electricity or motor-propelled vehicles of any kind; they work the land with horses and light their homes with kerosene lamps and candles.

Lancaster County is very rural. And down every narrow lane you can see half a dozen of those distinctive, black, horse-drawn buggies, totally enclosed and usually driven by an old, white-bearded man. The Amish are people whose ancestors came from Switzerland in the sixteenth century. The community living in Lancaster County came from Germany, and still speaks a Rhine dialect. Indeed, the children do not begin to learn English until they start their education, and even then they go to one-room Amish schools. And from a very young age they are all given jobs to do in the home or on the farm, which gives them even less time to mix with non-Amish children. After baptism, you cannot marry outside the faith. Owning motorized transport is banned.

Sunday worship is held in one of their homes, and the location is known only to the Amish, week by week. The services start at 11 A.M. and last for three hours.

On my last day I was invited by the Meyer family to go for a buggy ride and then join them for dinner. I sat beside Mr. Jack Meyer, a large, bearded man, who was dressed in the traditional manner.

He told me the standard Amish day starts at 4:30 A.M. and the milking goes on until breakfast at seven. Half an hour later the children are sent off to school, which starts at eight, and then the men start work until lunch is served by the women at eleven. Around three in the afternoon the final milking of the day begins. That is followed by supper, and by seven-thirty most farmers are in bed.

Dinner with the Meyers was a remarkable experience. They do take in paying guests, but you are not supposed to use alcohol prior to your arrival, and you cannot smoke on their property. Most important, you are specifically requested not to bring a camera with you. But for my benefit, they allowed us to film them at their table.

Lancaster Amish are famous for their food, and justifiably so. Jugs of water washed down the feast, but midway we were offered tea made from herbs which grow wild.

There was clearly a lot of love and laughter in the Meyer household, and the children were exceedingly well behaved. They all returned obediently to the dining room when the final ritual of the evening was to begin. They formed a group with their mother and father and sang a hymn in a manner I had not heard before, all harmonizing beautifully.

All in all, a vivid and memorable occasion.

SPEAKING AND READING

1. Make a list of important things in your life. Number them in order of their importance with 5 being the most important and 1 being the least important.

family, good health, money...

Now work in pairs and compare your list.

2. Read the passage, which is about a woman who is visiting the Amish people of Pennsylvania. Make notes about these aspects of their lifestyle.

– clothing   – work   – transport   – education   – meals   – customs and beliefs

Compare your notes with a partner.

3. Work in groups of three or four. Discuss your answers to these questions.

1. Was the writer sympathetic to the Amish way of life?
2. What aspects of the Amish life was she impressed by?
3. What things did she find strange?
4. What do you think about the lifestyle of the Amish?
5. What are some good and bad points about the Amish lifestyle, in your opinion?

Work with another group and compare your answers.

GRAMMAR

> **Relative clauses**
> You use a restrictive relative clause (without commas) to give essential information about the subject or object of the sentence. You use:
> – *who* or *that* for people, and *which* or *that* for things.
> – *whose* to talk about possession.
> – *where* for places.
> – *when* for times. You can usually leave out *when*.
> You use a nonrestrictive relative clause (with commas) to give more information about the subject or object of the sentence. It is more common in formal English, especially writing. You use:
> – *who* for people.
> – *which* for things. You cannot use *that*.
> You can use *which* to refer back to a whole clause.

1. Look at the passage and find sentences with *who, whose, which, where,* and *when.* Use the information in the grammar box to decide if they are restrictive or nonrestrictive relative clauses. Are there any sentences with *which* referring to the whole clause?

2. Use the information in the passage to complete these sentences about the Amish with restrictive relative clauses.

1. The Amish are people ____.
2. Lancaster County is the place ____.
3. Eight o'clock is the time ____.
4. Food is one of the things ____.
5. Smoking and drinking are things ____.

3. Rewrite these sentences adding the extra information in parentheses, using a nonrestrictive relative clause.

1. The Amish live in Lancaster County. (Their ancestors came from Switzerland.)
2. Men and women wear black hats or caps. (Their heads must be covered all the time.)
3. The buggies are usually driven by old, white-bearded men. (The buggies are horse-drawn.)
4. The children are given work to do. (They are not allowed to mix with the non-Amish.)
5. Worship is held at someone's home. (They meet there every Sunday at 11 A.M.)

SPEAKING AND VOCABULARY

1. Work in pairs. Talk about how your lifestyle would change if you had to live without:

– electricity   – heating
– motor vehicles   – plumbing

If there was no electricity, there wouldn't be any television and I couldn't live without that.

Is there any other aspect of your modern lifestyle which you couldn't live without?

2. In pairs, take turn defining words.

Student A: Choose a word in the box and ask Student B to define it.
Student B: Define the word Student A chooses. You can use the passage to help you.

When you've finished, it's Student B's turn.

> custom   horse   lamp   candle   buggy   ancestor
> dialect   baptism   home   farmer   guest   alcohol
> jug   herb   hymn

28 | *Lifestyles*

Relative and participial clauses

VOCABULARY AND LISTENING

1. Work in groups of three. Use the information you learned about the Amish way of life to answer the lifestyle questionnaire below. Give a score of 1–5 with 5 being the most important and 1 being the least important.

Lifestyle Questionnaire

1. How important are these things in your life?	The Amish	California	Your country
Possessions			
Leisure interests			
Physical fitness			
Mental and spiritual development			
Work			
Attitude toward visitors			
2. Give the pace of your life a score from 1–5 with 5 being fast and 1 being slow.			

2. You are going to listen to Don Wright talking about the lifestyle in California. In your groups, try to predict the answers to the questionnaire for California. Write the score in the appropriate column.

3. 🔲 Listen and check if your predictions in 2 were correct.

4. Check (✔) the words in the box that you heard.

anti-conformist materialistic limousine laid-back tense jogging fortune vineyard racist mild diverse stress calm elegant wealthy cosmopolitan

5. Complete these statements with a few words or phrases from the interview.
1. The man the interviewer spoke to is a ____.
2. The county she visited was ____.
3. The house Don lives in is ____.
4. The family living next door have ____.
5. Any house, located on the beach is ____.
6. The beach, located close to the town, is used ____.

6. 🔲 Listen again and check your answers to 4 and 5. Can you add any extra information?

7. Now complete the questionnaire for your own country.

SOUNDS

🔲 Listen to these sentences. Mark where the speaker pauses.
1. The Californians are people who are famous for their relaxed lifestyle.
2. They are generally very friendly people, whose pace of life is fast.
3. It has an economy which is one of the richest in the world.
4. The climate, which is mild, is very pleasant.
5. It has wonderful beaches, which make it attractive to tourists.

Can you figure out a rule for pauses in restrictive and nonrestrictive relative clauses?

GRAMMAR

Relative and participial clauses

In a restrictive relative clause you can leave out the relative pronoun if the clause is defining an object.

The man (who) the interviewer spoke to was Don Wright.
The county (which) she visited was Marin County.

If you leave out *where*, you have to add a preposition.

*The house **where** Don lives is near the beach.*
*The house Don lives **in** is near the beach.*

Participial clauses

You can use a participial clause instead of a relative clause if the noun or pronoun is the subject of the clause. You use:

– a present participle to replace the relative pronoun + a present or past tense in a restrictive relative clause.

*The family **that** lives next door is very friendly.*
*(= The family **living** next door is very friendly.)*

– a past participle to replace the relative pronoun + *be* in passive sentences in a restrictive relative clause.

*Any house **(which is)** located on the beach is in danger from storms.*

It is also possible, but less common, to do this with a nonrestrictive relative clause.

*The people, **who** were working hard...*
(= the people, working hard...)
*The beach, **(which is)** located close to the town, is used by everybody.*

1. Read the passage below. Underline any relative pronouns which can be left out.

Last year we visited my cousin who lives in Southern California, which was very exciting. We stayed with him in his huge house in Pasadena, which is north of Los Angeles. The people who we met were very friendly and made us feel at home. There is no real downtown area in Los Angeles, which we found strange. We drove everywhere on the freeways, which are excellent, in a car which we borrowed from my cousin, who has several. The place which we liked best was Santa Barbara, which is about sixty miles away.

2. Rewrite these sentences using participial clauses.

1. The houses which were built in the thirties are the largest.
2. There are freeways which lead to most cities in the state.
3. The mountain range, which is called the Sierra Nevada, has good ski resorts.
4. The beaches, which are cleaned every day, are very popular.
5. Disneyland, which attracts millions of people a year, is the number-one tourist attraction.
6. There are guided tours of the studios for anyone who is interested in television and the movies.

1. The houses built in the thirties are the largest.

WRITING

1. Think about the two different lifestyles of the Amish people and people in California. Choose one of them and make notes about aspects of the lifestyle that you like or dislike.
Work with a partner who has chosen the same lifestyle, if you wish.

2. Imagine you have spent a day either as part of an Amish family or in a Californian home. Write your diary for the day. Begin by saying what time you got up and what you had for breakfast.

I woke up at six o'clock and went for a run on the beach, then I had a light breakfast of toast and coffee.

Next, describe what you did during the day.

First of all, we went to the mall.

Use your notes from 1 to describe anything you enjoyed or didn't enjoy about your day.

29 Lucky Escapes

Third conditional

VOCABULARY AND SPEAKING

1. This lesson is about occasions when people have been lucky. Look at the adjectives in the box and put a + by the positive feelings and a – by the negative feelings.

ecstatic +   disappointed –

ecstatic disappointed devastated grateful fed-up frustrated frantic happy confused excited inspired enthusiastic thrilled furious anxious tired nervous upset worried depressed

Which adjectives can you use to describe mild feelings, and which ones extreme feelings?

2. Think of situations you have experienced when you could use some of the adjectives to describe how you felt.

Now work in pairs and talk about these situations.

LISTENING

1. 🔲 You're going to hear Janet, Paul, and Lisa talking about three situations in which they had a lucky escape. Listen and put the name of the speaker by the situation below which he or she is talking about.

– a plane crash   – a traffic accident   – a fight

2. Choose the best answer.

Janet says that:
a. If she hadn't been delayed in Curaçao, she would have been on the plane that crashed.
b. If her plane hadn't crashed, she would have been in Caracas on time.
c. If she had arrived in Caracas on time, the plane wouldn't have crashed.

Paul says that:
a. If he had known the kid had a knife, he wouldn't have tried to stop the fight.
b. If the kid had attacked him with a knife, his injuries would have been more serious.
c. If the police hadn't arrived, the kid wouldn't have attacked him.

Lisa says that:
a. She would have been killed if the truck had been driving faster.
b. She would have worn her seat belt if she had known that there would be an accident.
c. She might have been killed if she hadn't been wearing her seat belt.

3. Which speaker did the following things? Put the name of the speaker in the box.

1. Who intends to complain? ☐
2. Who became very anxious? ☐
3. Who was furious at the end? ☐
4. Who thinks he or she was extremely lucky? ☐
5. Who managed to stay calm at the start? ☐

🔊 Now listen again and check.

GRAMMAR

> **Third conditional**
> **You use the third conditional to talk about an imaginary or unlikely situation in the past and to describe its result. You separate the two clauses with a comma.**
> *If she **hadn't been delayed**, she **would have been** on the plane that crashed.*
> **You can also use *may have*, *might have*, or *could have* if the result is not certain.**
> *If he **had pulled** out his knife, I **could have been** in real trouble.*

1. Complete this sentence saying how you form the third conditional.

You form the third conditional by using *if* + _____ for the condition and _____ for the result.

2. Complete these sentences using suitable words or phrases.

1. If Janet hadn't _____, she would have _____.
2. If she had _____.
3. If Paul hadn't _____.
4. If he had _____.
5. If Lisa had _____.
6. If she hadn't _____.

READING AND WRITING

1. Read this story about a lucky escape. Decide what the lucky escape was.

1. Jennifer nearly had an accident.
2. Alan's plane was diverted from JFK airport.
3. The taxi driver stopped for gas.

My daughter, Jennifer, had decided to meet her husband at JFK airport when he was flying in from Toronto. As I was working in the kitchen, I had a sudden vision. A freezing fog had come down and my daughter was involved in an accident on the freeway to JFK.

My daughter arrived and I tried to persuade her not to go, without telling her why. The sun was still shining brightly after lunch when she left for JFK. About two and half hours later a thick, freezing fog came down. I tried to call the airport but there was no answer.

The next four hours were the longest of my life—then the telephone rang. A man spoke and told me what had happened. "The young lady was getting off the freeway to go to the airport and braked behind the truck in front of her. Her brakes failed. Somehow she managed to pull up, stopping with the hood of the car just under the tail of the truck. I promise you she's OK," he added quickly. "I have the car here at my garage, and she was told by the airport that her husband's plane has been diverted to Newark. She's on her way there now in a cab."

Soon, the telephone rang again. It was Jennifer's husband, Alan. "My plane's been diverted to La Guardia (another airport near New York)," he said. "I've been trying to get through to JFK to tell Jennifer to wait for me at the information desk 'cause I'll be arriving on the airport shuttle."

I explained that she was on her way to Newark. I put the phone down, closed my eyes and tried to imagine Jennifer on the freeway, thinking desperately, "Please, wherever you are, call me." Five minutes later the phone rang. I heard Jennifer's voice say, "What's the matter? I felt like I had to call you."

Later, I learned that on the way to Newark, the cab driver said he had to stop at a service station for gas and as he pulled up, Jennifer said, "I have to call my mother right now." They returned safely to JFK and Jennifer made her way to the information desk, arriving at the same time as Alan.

Adapted from the Fortean Times

2. Work in pairs and say what would have happened *if*:

1. Jennifer had not gone to meet her husband.
2. The writer had not had a vision.
3. Jennifer had not managed to stop the car.
4. Alan had not called.
5. Jennifer had not called.
6. The cab driver had not stopped for gas.

3. Write a summary of the woman's story in about 100 words. You may like to use the sentences in 2 to help you, although you will have to adapt them slightly. Begin like this:

A woman described how her daughter, Jennifer, was going to meet...

30 | *Bad Luck!*

Expressing wishes and regrets

READING AND WRITING

1. You are going to read some stories about people who had some bad luck. The first story is about a young man taking his driving test. Guess what kind of bad luck he might have had.

2. Read the story. Did you guess correctly in 1?

A young man was taking his driving test and was looking forward to passing it and buying himself a new car. He began very attentively and successfully until the examiner slightly raised his clipboard. The driver had heard about this sort of test of reactions, and interpreting this as the sign for an emergency stop, he slammed his foot on the brake.

To his horror, his passenger had forgotten to fasten his seatbelt, and taken completely by surprise, hurtled forward and hit his head against the windshield, then fell back, bleeding and unconscious. The distraught man immediately drove him to a hospital then went home in a miserable mood.

The very next day he received official notice that he had failed his test for driving recklessly. Attached to the form was a note from the examiner himself. On it he explained that...

3. Try to guess what the missing line is. Now turn to Communication Activity 12 on page 104.

4. Work in pairs. You're going to read a story about a couple having a meal in a restaurant. Put the parts of the story in the right order.

a. Feeling good about themselves, the couple asked for their check. But after looking at it, they called the manager demanding to have the massive total explained.

b. They smiled back politely and the old lady made her way to their table. "I'm sorry to trouble you," she began. "But you look so like my daughter. She was killed last year and I do miss her terribly. I wonder if you'd do me an enormous favor?"

c. "That includes the charge for the lady's meal," the manager explained. "She said her daughter would pay."

d. "Certainly," the couple replied. How could they possibly refuse? A few minutes, later the old lady gathered her belongings and stood up to leave, and the two diners cheerily waved and said goodbye as "mom" left the restaurant.

e. The couple nodded compassionately. "It would give me such a thrill if, just as I am leaving, you would say, 'Goodbye Mom,' and wave me off," the old lady said.

f. Our sister's friend and her new husband were enjoying a meal at a good restaurant. As they were eating, they noticed sitting next to them an elderly lady, alone and gazing in their direction.

5. Work in pairs. You're going to recreate a story about a woman who goes on a shopping trip.

Student A: Turn to Communication Activity 7 on page 103.

Student B: Turn to Communication Activity 17 on page 105.

6. Write a sentence saying what would have happened in the three stories if someone had done something different.

FUNCTIONS

Expressing wishes and regrets
You can express:
– regret about a present state with *wish* + past simple or continuous.
I wish I knew what I was going to do.
– regret about the past with *wish* + past perfect.
I wish I hadn't acted so badly.
– a wish with *could*.
I wish I could travel more.
You can use *if only* if the feeling is stronger.
If only I had called the store to check that the call was genuine!
You use *should have* or *shouldn't have* to express regret or criticism about actions in the past.
I should have called the store to check that the call was genuine.

1. Explain the difference between these two sentences.

a. I wish I knew what was going to happen.
b. I wish I had known what was going to happen.

2. Work in pairs. Talk about what each person in the stories wished or regretted about what happened.

3. Write sentences saying what the people in the stories *should* or *shouldn't have* done.

4. Work in pairs. Talk about three wishes and regrets you have for the present and three for the past.

SOUNDS

1. Say these words out loud. Is the underlined sound /s/ or /ʃ/? Put the words into two columns.

<u>s</u>hould <u>s</u>end <u>s</u>un Engli<u>s</u>h depre<u>ss</u>ed
an<u>xi</u>ous frustra<u>ti</u>on depre<u>ss</u>ion affec<u>ti</u>onate
gue<u>ss</u> <u>s</u>chool

Listen and check. As you listen, say the words out loud.

2. Look at these sentences. Underline the words you think the speaker will stress.

1. If only I could speak to her.
2. I wish you'd be quiet.
3. If only you'd listened to me.
4. I wish I'd kept quiet.
5. If only I understood Chinese.
6. I wish he wouldn't do that.

Now listen and check.

VOCABULARY AND SPEAKING

1. Work in pairs. Which words in the box are similar in meaning?

peculiar sad amusing farfetched boring uneventful
exciting gloomy profound pathetic fascinating
charming delightful stimulating bizarre eccentric
touching hilarious

2. Which words could you use to describe the stories you read in this lesson? Which of the words would you use to describe the following stories?

1. A story about a woman who looks after injured animals.
2. A story about a couple who take a vacation in which everything goes wrong.
3. A story about a person who discovers a cure for cancer.
4. A story about a child with a serious illness who finds ways to help other children who are in trouble.

3. Did you like the stories in this lesson? Which story did you like best? Tell a partner and give your reasons.

31 All-time Greats

Phrasal verbs

SPEAKING

1. Work in groups of three. Look at the list of types of music below. Add as many more kinds as you can.

classical   jazz   opera   rock   folk   reggae   blues

2. Now choose one of the types of music on your list. Think about what instruments are used to play it, what country it comes from, and any famous musicians who play it.

3. Work with another group and guess what type of music they have chosen. They must try to guess the type of music you have chosen. Take turns asking questions. You can only answer *yes* or *no*. You cannot guess the type of music until you have received a *yes* answer.

Can you dance to it?   No.
Is it played by an orchestra?   Yes.
Is it classical music?   Yes.

4. Go around the class and find someone who shares your taste in music. Are there many people who share your taste or are you on your own?

VOCABULARY AND READING

1. Look at the words in the box. Find:

– four words for *types of music.*
– two adjectives to *describe* music.
– three words for *musicians.*
– three words for a *form of recording.*
– one word for a *song.*
– one word for a *great success.*

> lyrics   bossa nova   melody   samba   cool   mellow
> chord   tenor   guitarist   LP   album   feature   number
> hit   chart   guitar   single   disc   composer   jazz
> saxophonist   rock

Find out what the remaining words mean.

2. Work in pairs. Write down five more words for musical instruments and five words for the musicians who play them.

piano – pianist

Compare your list with another pair.

3. Read the passage, which comes from a magazine, and decide what it is about.

– Stan Getz   – Astrud and Joao Gilberto   – Tom Jobim
– The *bossa nova* – *The Girl from Ipanema*

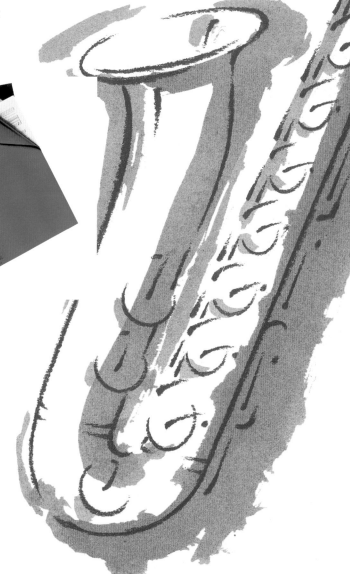

Tall, and tan and young and lovely,
The girl from Ipanema goes walking,
And when she passes
Each one she passes goes Ah!

These are the lyrics Antonio "Tom" Jobim wrote down on the back of a cocktail napkin as he looked at a beautiful sixteen-year-old girl on a beach in Rio de Janeiro in 1964. And with these opening lines he not only brought about a musical revolution but also came up with one of the best-known songs in the world. The 1960s craze for the *bossa nova* caught on and made Tom Jobim's name, and today many years later his melodies remain highly popular with singers and jazz musicians alike, and none more so than *The Girl from Ipanema*.

The musical revolution of *bossa nova*, "new flair," came about in the early sixties. It was a mixture of jazz and samba and, in those days, came second in importance only to rock 'n' roll. With its cool, mellow chords, it captured the upbeat mood of a generation of Brazilians whose country was beginning to emerge as a great industrial power. Brasilia, its futuristic capital—built from scratch on an arid stretch of land in the country's interior—was nearing completion and the world was looking at the Latin American giant as a great example of modernity. Brazil became known to the rest of the world as "the country of the future."

"Jobim took the traditional street samba and combined it with our North American cool school," the jazz tenor saxophonist Stan Getz said. "And that's what came out—the *bossa nova*." In 1962, after a tour of Brazil, Getz and the guitarist Charlie Byrd made an LP called *Jazz Samba*. The album featured two Jobim songs: *Samba de una nota so*, "One Note Samba," and *Desafinado*, "Slightly Out Of Tune." Both numbers became hits and *Jazz Samba* was on the best-seller chart in the United States for over a year.

In 1964 Getz got together with the Brazilian singers Joao and Astrud Gilberto. On the *Garota de Ipanema*, "The Girl from Ipanema," track, Joao sang in Portuguese and Astrud joined in in English, with Getz on saxophone and Jobim on guitar. When the song came out as a single they did away with Joao Gilberto's vocal and the only voice heard on the disc was his wife Astrud's. The song went on to be an international hit, selling more than a million copies, staying at Number 5 on the U.S. charts for two weeks and winning a Grammy.

Soon such Jobim songs as *Corcovado*, "Quiet Nights, Quiet Stars," achieved similar fame, and were sung by such celebrities as Ella Fitzgerald, Dionne Warwick, Nat King Cole, and Frank Sinatra. But when people think of *bossa nova*, it's still *The Girl from Ipanema*, which nearly everyone remembers and loves.

How did Tom Jobim feel about being the composer of one of the world's greatest songs? He admitted it had helped make him Brazil's foremost composer for thirty years. But toward the end of his life (he died in 1994), when audiences at concerts asked for the song he often turned them down. "A guy writes 400 songs in his life and they only remember him for one. There's no justice."

4. Decide if these statements are true or false.

1. Stan Getz was the creator of *bossa nova*.
2. *Bossa nova* was relaxing but optimistic music.
3. Tom Jobim had two successful songs in 1962.
4. The international version of *The Girl from Ipanema* was sung in Portuguese.
5. Tom Jobim's other songs were more successful.
6. He never liked playing it.
7. He didn't want to be known just for one song.

5. Look at the phrases from the passage. Answer the questions and try to guess the meaning of the phrases in italics.

1. *...with singers and jazz musicians alike.* – Why are they alike?
2. *...came second in importance only to rock 'n' roll.* – Which was first?
3. *...and none more so than* The Girl from Ipanema. – Are Jobim's other songs more or less popular than *The Girl from Ipanema?*
4. *...made Tom Jobim's name...* – Made his name what?
5. *...built from scratch...* – What was there before they started building?

6. Find phrasal verbs in the passage which are similar in meaning to the following words and phrases:

put on paper   watched   caused to happen
composed   became popular   evolved
played with   participated   was released
got rid of   continued its progress
call to mind   requested   refused

SPEAKING

Work in pairs and discuss your answers to the questions.

1. Can you think of a song from your country which is known around the world?
2. Are there any musicians in the past or the present who are internationally famous?
3. What is the most popular style of music in your country?
4. Has rock ever been the most popular style of music in your country?

32 | *What's Your Favorite?*

Phrasal verbs

GRAMMAR

> **Phrasal verbs**
>
> 1. **Phrasal verbs are verbs with a particle which have a different meaning from the verb when it is on its own. Sometimes the meaning is obvious because it is a combination of the meanings of verb and particle.**
>   *Tom Jobim **wrote down** the lyrics on the back of a cocktail napkin.*
>   *He **looked at** a beautiful girl on a beach.*
>
>   **Sometimes the meaning is not obvious because it has a different meaning from the meaning of the verb and particle.**
>   *He **brought about** a musical revolution.*
>
> 2. **There are four types of phrasal verbs.**
>   **Type 1   These do not take an object.**   *The craze for bossa nova **caught on**.*
>   **Type 2   These take an object. The noun object goes before or after the particle.**   *He **wrote down** the lyrics. or He **wrote** the lyrics **down**.*
>   **The pronoun object goes before the particle.**   *He wrote **them** down.*
>   **Type 3   These also take an object. The noun and the pronoun object go after the particle.**
>   *He looked at **a beautiful girl** on a beach.*   *He looked at **her**.*
>   **Type 4   These have two particles and take an object. The noun and the pronoun object go after the particle.**
>   *He came up with **one of the best known songs**. He came up with **it**.*
>
> 3. **It is common to use phrasal verbs, especially in spoken English. But it's usually possible to replace them with another verb or verbal phrase.**
>   *When audiences **asked for** the song, he often **turned them down**.*
>   *When audiences **requested** the song, he often **refused**.*

1. Look back at the passage on page 75 and decide if the meaning of the phrasal verbs in the passage is obvious from the meaning of the verb + particle, or not. Decide what types the phrasal verbs in the passage are.

2. Look at the phrasal verbs which have a similar meaning to the words and phrases in *Vocabulary and Reading* activity 6 on page 75. Which do you think is better, the phrasal verb or the alternative?

SOUNDS

Underline the words you think the speaker will stress in these sentences.

1. Turn it up.
2. I'll look into it.
3. Please stand up.
4. He put it on.
5. I'll let it out.
6. Please carry on.
7. Don't tear it up.
8. Won't you sit down?

🔊 Listen and check. As you listen, say the words out loud.

VOCABULARY AND LISTENING

1. You're going to hear Steve and Jessica talking about their favorite pieces of music and favorite books. Which are they likely to use the following words to talk about?

> symphony   violins   volume
> biography   novel   literary   plot
> fiction   diary   paperback
> soprano   beat   lead singer   key
> lyrics   concerto   band   movie

2. Write a definition of six words from the box.

A symphony is a piece of music for a full orchestra.

3. In pairs, take turns defining words.

Student A: Tell Student B one of the words you have defined.
Student B: Give a definition of Student A's word.

Decide which is the better definition. When you've finished, it's Student B's turn.

WRITING AND SPEAKING

1. Look at some attitude words and their uses.

To express an opinion   *I suppose, I guess*
as far as I'm concerned, I think, personally
To emphasize   *really, definitely, clearly, obviously,*
in fact, actually
To express surprise   *amazingly, curiously, strangely*
To express a generality   *in general, overall*

Now complete this review of a favorite book with a suitable attitude word or phrase.

(1) ____, my favorite book is *The House of the Spirits* by Isabelle Allende. (2) ____ it's her best book, although (3) ____, I only read it for the first time a couple of months ago; I'd already read most of her other novels. (4) ____, I've read a lot of novels by South American writers, but what I (5) ____ like about this book is the atmosphere, which is (6) ____ incredible, and the plot, which is wonderful. (7) ____, after reading the book I felt that I would like to live in the world that she describes. (8) ____, it's the most magical book I've read.

4. 📻 Listen to Steve and Jessica talking about their favorite pieces of music and their favorite books. Work in pairs.

Student A: Turn to Communication Activity 21 on page 106.
Student B: Turn to Communication Activity 18 on page 105.

5. Work together and complete the chart with as much detail as possible.

	Favorite music	**Favorite book**
Steve		
Jessica		

6. 📻 Listen again to Steve and Jessica, and check your answers to 5.

2. Work in groups of three or four. Talk about your favorite books and pieces of music. Can you explain why you like them?

3. Use the words and expressions in activity 1 to write a review of your favorite pieces of music or your favorite books. You can use the text in activity 1 to help you.

Say what it is.
My favorite pieces of music/books are...
Say who wrote/played it.
...by (writer/composer), with (musicians)
Say when you read/heard it.
The first time I read/heard it...
Say why you like it in general.
The reason I like it is...
Say what you particularly like.
In particular, I like...

Fluency **4** *Business Matters*

Talking about ability

LISTENING AND SPEAKING

1. Read these statements about business practices and decide if they are true or false for your country.

Most people stay with the same company all their working lives. ☐

You expect friends and relatives to help you get a good job. ☐

It's very common to spend the evening with colleagues from work. ☐

It's important to greet all of your work colleagues when you arrive in the morning. ☐

There's no place for social conversation during a business meeting. ☐

Business people don't give gifts because they may be seen as bribes. ☐

If you leave your office door open, it means you're ready to receive visitors. ☐

Business hours are from 9 A.M. to 5 P.M. ☐

The most important people are in the center of an open-plan office. ☐

Most people retire at the age of fifty-five. ☐

2. Work in pairs and discuss your answers to 1.

3. 📼 Work in pairs. You're going to hear Leo talking about American business practices. Listen and put a check (✓) by the statements which are true for the United States.

4. Work in pairs.

Student A: Turn to Communication Activity 27 on page 107.
Student B: Turn to Communication Activity 28 on page 107.

5. Work together and complete the chart for the United States.

	The United States	Your Country
Business hours		
Giving gifts		
Social life at work		
Greeting colleagues		
Office layout		
Retirement age		

6. Complete the chart for your country.

7. Look at the dialogue and decide where the sentences (a–d) go.

A Being a publisher must be very interesting.
B (1) ...
A Oh, so tell me, what special qualities do you think you need to be a good publisher?
B (2) ...
A And I imagine you have to work well in a team.
B Yes, that's certainly true. And you have to be calm and patient as well.
A (3) ...
B Well, it takes a long time to learn how to deal with problems at work. And above all, you have to be able to concentrate for long periods of time.
A (4) ...

a. I'm terrible at that. I just can't concentrate at all.
b. I'm no good at staying calm, especially when I'm dealing with problems!
c. Well, yes, it can be, although it involves a lot of hard work.
d. Well, the first thing is you need to get along well with people.

📼 Now listen and check your answers.

8. Work in pairs and act out the dialogue.

FUNCTIONS

> **Talking about ability**
>
> *I'm good at ...   I'm no good at + -ing   I can ...   I (just) can't ...*
> *I'm not very good at ...   I'm incapable of + -ing   I know how to ...*
> *I'm bad/terrible at + -ing*
>
> **Talking about qualities and skills**
>
> | | | | | |
> |---|---|---|---|---|
> | | *have to* | | *must* | *know how to ...* |
> | *To be a/an ... you* | *must* | *be + adjective* | *You need to* | *be able to ...* |
> | | *need to* | | *have to* | *be good at ...* |

1. Look at the expressions for talking about ability. Decide which ones you can use to say what you can do and what you can't do.

2. Work in pairs. Say if you're good at:
   – swimming   – typing
   – playing a musical instrument – speaking English
   – working hard   – relaxing

3. Is it usual in your culture to say what you are good at? Do you describe your abilities objectively, or do you overstate or understate them?

4. Work in pairs. Say what qualities and skills you need for the following jobs:

   accountant   secretary   receptionist   manager   salesclerk   computer programmer   teacher

5. Think about your job or ideal job and decide what qualities you need for it.

   Now work in pairs. Use the dialogue in *Listening and Speaking* activity 7 to talk about your job or ideal job, and respond to your partner's comments about his or her job.

READING AND WRITING

1. Read the passage about Doing Business in the United States and match the following headings with the paragraphs.

   – Qualities and Skills of a Manager   – Straightforwardness
   – Office Relationships   – Relations with Strangers
   – Time Keeping

2. Work in pairs. Is the business culture described similar to or different from that in your country?

3. Write a brief passage about business practices in your country. Use the paragraph headings in 1 to help you.

Amiability is not necessary to rise to the top, and there are a number of chief executive officers with famous bad tempers. It's not the boss's job to worry about the well-being of his or her employees; it's the company he or she worries about. American executives must be capable of enough small talk to get through the social part of their work, but they may not be highly cultured individuals.

Most offices are informal, with lots of joking around and back slapping. Although everybody knows perfectly well who the boss is, they are less deferential to him or her than one might expect in other cultures. First names are usually used, which sometimes gives foreign visitors a distorted view of the boss–employee relationship.

Most peoples of the world don't negotiate with strangers. Therefore, the first order of business is to get to know their callers, no matter how long it takes. Then they can decide if these are people they want to work with. All this is a mystery to an American. Why sit around talking and drinking coffee when you could be making deals? We just don't think it's necessary to know someone very well to do business with them.

During the work day, Americans are very precise about time. If you're ten minutes late for an appointment, you should apologize. When you see your American host looking at his or her watch, finish the meeting quickly. If you arrive without an appointment, you could discover that your important contacts have no time to see you.

Business people from Asia may be shocked by the bluntness with which an American reports negative news. "Sorry, but we got a better price from someone else." In another culture, your feelings would be considered more important than the truth, whereas we consider that we're doing you a favor by being direct.

Progress Check 25–32

VOCABULARY

1. There are many phrasal verbs which are based on the following verbs:

break bring come do get go let look make put run see set take turn

Make twenty phrasal verbs with the verbs above and the following particles.

about at away with by down down to for forward to in into of off on out out of over around to through up up for up to up with with without

2. Rewrite these sentences replacing the words in italics with a suitable phrasal verb and particle in 1.

1. They couldn't *tolerate* their noisy neighbors any longer so they called the police.
2. She has always *greatly respected* her teacher.
3. We must *deal with* the arrangements for our vacation.
4. She *met unexpectedly* an old friend yesterday.
5. He *refused* the invitation to the party.
6. I've *postponed* the meeting until next week.
7. We should *begin our journey* before seven o'clock.
8. The airline company put us in first class to *compensate us for* the overnight delay.
9. The police are *investigating* the crime.

3. There are many other expressions based on the verbs in 1.

break	the news, your heart, a record
bring	charges against someone, to light, out the best in someone
come	to an end, to a decision, to your senses
do	the housework, homework, your best, business with
get	rid of, even
go	far, to great lengths, broke
let	someone down, it slide
look	someone in the eye, down your nose at something
make	a mistake, arrangements, a suggestion, an excuse
put	your foot down, your mind to something
run	a business, for office
see	the light, the forest for the trees
set	your heart on something, fire to, a good example
take	care of, for granted, advantage of, pride in
turn	over a new leaf

Which verbs go with these phrases? What do the expressions mean?

on the bright side   without saying   into contact with   your sights on two and two together   off to a good start   your breath away   a leg a fuss over someone

GRAMMAR

1. Complete these sentences with *by* or *with*.

1. The principle of radio broadcasting was invented ____ Marconi.
2. The computer is covered ____ a plastic wrapper.
3. We get our television channels ____ cable.
4. The system was sold to us ____ a computer specialist.
5. It was checked ____ the engineer ____ a circuit tester.
6. She was provided ____ lodging ____ her company.

2. Rewrite these sentences in the passive.

1. He likes people calling him by his first name.
2. She doesn't want people to exploit her.
3. She's hoping her boss will give her a raise.
4. I want someone to tell me if anything happens.
5. They were looking forward to their neighbors inviting them to dinner.
6. He wants people to elect him as chairman of the committee.

80

3. Put commas in these sentences if necessary.

1. The city which is growing at the fastest rate is Mexico City. The population which has been estimated at 16 million will grow to over 31 million by the year 2000. This is five times more than all the people who live in Switzerland at present.
2. Mount Isa, Queensland, which is in Australia spreads over 16,000 square miles which makes it the largest town in the world. It covers an area twenty-six times greater than that of London which means that it is about the same size as Switzerland.
3. The city which has the greatest amount of traffic is Los Angeles. At one interchange almost 500,000 vehicles were counted in twenty-four hours which is an average of 20,000 cars and trucks an hour.

4. Rewrite these sentences using participial clauses.

1. The capital which lies farthest to the north is Reykjavik.
2. Twenty-one huts which were discovered in France in 1960 are believed to date from 400,000 B.C., which makes them the oldest buildings in the world.
3. Light which travels from the sun takes eight minutes and twenty seconds to reach the earth.
4. The language which is spoken by the greatest number of people is Chinese.

5. Write down five or six important events which have happened in your life.

I moved to Nagasaki.

Now write sentences saying what *would have* or *might have* happened if these events hadn't happened.

If I hadn't moved to Nagasaki, I wouldn't have met Taeko.

SOUNDS

1. Say these words out loud. Is the underlined sound /θ/ or /ð/? Put them in two columns.

think   thin   this   that   theater   the   thank   tooth   bath   thread   three   thick   they   then   with

Listen and check. As you listen, say the words out loud.

2. Underline the silent consonant in these words.

comb   dumb   lamb   doubt   subtle   debt   could   calm   half   herb   honest   hour   knee   know   knife   psychiatry   receipt   pneumatic   chrome   chord   island   foreign   sign   whistle   bristle   fasten   soften

Listen and check. As you listen, say the words out loud.

3. Listen to someone saying these sentences in four different ways. As you listen, repeat the sentences in the same way.

1. I arrive at nine o'clock. – *factual*
2. Let's meet tomorrow. – *mysterious*
3. He finally called me! – *excited*
4. See you next week. – *vague*

4. Look at the sentences below. Decide in which of the four ways in 3 the speaker says these sentences.

1. This is a photo of Mount Rushmore.
2. I'll mention it when I see him.
3. Maybe I'll go later.
4. I missed my bus.
5. I haven't got any film for my camera.
6. I get home sometime tomorrow night.

Now say the sentences in the same ways.

WRITING AND SPEAKING

Work in pairs. You're going to play a game called *If Things Had Been Different*.

How To Play

1. Look back over the texts in Lessons 23–30, and think about some of the events and situations described. Write as many sentences as possible saying what might or would have happened if they had not happened.
   If the Amish had stayed in Europe, their way of life might not have survived.
2. Work with another pair. Each pair should say one of their sentences in turn.
3. You score one point for each correct sentence.
4. You cannot repeat a sentence which is similar to or the same as one which the other pair has already said.
5. Continue until one pair has no more sentences.
6. The pair which has the largest number of points is the winner.

33 Spending Money

Countable and uncountable nouns

```
loaf of bread
pair of shoes
hat
tube of toothpaste
silk scarf
handkerchief
fresh coffee
newspaper
cushion
necklace
3 silk flowers
```

SPEAKING

This lesson is about spending money. Look at this shopping list. Which of these things have you bought recently? Which do you buy more than once a month?

Discuss your answers with a partner.

READING

1. The passage is taken from the novel *Tender is the Night* by the American writer, F. Scott Fitzgerald, which was first published in 1934. Nicole is doing some shopping. Listed below are some of the items she buys. Do you think Nicole is rich or poor? Is she a young person or an old person?

dress   hat   colored beads   cushion
artificial flowers   love bird   bathing suit
leather jacket

Which items would you like to buy?

2. Read the passage. Were you right about Nicole?

> With Nicole's help Rosemary bought two dresses and two hats and four pairs of shoes with her money. Nicole bought from a great list that ran two pages, and bought the things in the windows besides. Everything she liked that she couldn't possibly use herself, she bought as a present for a friend. She bought colored beads, cushions, artificial flowers, honey, a guest bed, bags, scarves, love birds, miniatures for a doll's house, and three yards of some new cloth the color of prawns. She bought a dozen bathing suits, a rubber alligator, a traveling chess set of gold and ivory, big linen handkerchiefs for Abe, two chamois leather jackets of kingfisher blue and burning bush from Hermès. Nicole was the product of much hard work. For her sake trains began their run at Chicago and crossed the continent to California; in factories men mixed toothpaste in vats and girls canned tomatoes quickly in August or worked hard at the local store on Christmas Eve; Indians worked on Brazilian coffee plantations—these were some of the people who contributed to Nicole's wealth and, as the whole system swayed and thundered onward, it gave a rosy color to such processes of hers as wholesale buying.

3. Work in pairs and discuss your answers to the questions.

1. What impression of Nicole does the author want to give in his description of her shopping list?
2. What type of person do you think Nicole is? Would you say that she is selfish or generous, serious or frivolous? Find words and phrases in the passage to support your opinion.
3. Do you think Nicole has worked hard to earn her wealth?
4. Who has worked hard to make Nicole wealthy?

4. Decide which of the following summaries of the passage is the most accurate.

   a. The first part of the passage is a list of what Nicole buys, and the second is a list of the people who have been exploited and who have contributed to her wealth.

   b. The passage describes Nicole and Rosemary on a shopping trip in which they spend a great deal of money on some expensive and frivolous things.

   c. The passage describes how Nicole and Rosemary exploited the capitalist system and became rich.

5. Read the passage again and decide if Nicole is the sort of person you would like to know.

GRAMMAR

> Countable and uncountable nouns
> **Many nouns can be both countable and uncountable depending on the way they are used. Uncountable nouns can often be countable if you use them to describe different types.**
> *Would you like some* **wine**?   *Burgundy and claret are* **wines** *from France.*
> **Words for materials are usually uncountable but we can often use the same word as a countable noun to describe something made of that material.**
> *made of cloth   several wash cloths*
> **Some countable nouns are seen more as a mass than a collection of separate elements.**
> *bean(s), spice(s)*
> **Sometimes a word is uncountable in English and countable in other foreign languages. For example, *information* is uncountable in English but countable in other languages.**
> **Uncountable: *advice, baggage, information, money, news, travel, work***
> **Countable: *a place to live, a piece of advice, a case/bag, a piece of information, a sum of money, an item of news, a journey, a job***

1. Here are some words from the passage about Nicole's shopping trip. Which are countable and which are uncountable?

dress hat shoe money bead honey bag cloth gold ivory
linen rubber

2. Choose the correct word.

I'm going on a *travel/trip* to Chicago tomorrow because I'm looking for a new *work/job*. I saw a(n) *advertisement/publicity* for a job in a company there which does scientific *research/experiment*. I'm only taking my briefcase and one *bag/baggage* because I'm only going to stay for two nights. I hope the weather is OK, because the snow often causes *retards/delays* at this time of year. I should buy *a paper/some paper* to find what *information/piece of information* there is about the weather. I booked a(n) *place to stay/accommodations* at a hotel close to the center. I hope I get *scenery/a view* of the Sears Tower, because they say it's *too/very* beautiful. I've heard Chicago's pretty expensive, so I'll have to be careful not to *pay/spend* too much money. The last time I was traveling, I did a lot of *buying/shopping* and spent way too *much/many* money.

SPEAKING AND SOUNDS

1. Here are some humorous sayings about money. Match the two parts of these sentences.

  1. I've got all the money I need...
  2. Money can't buy you love...
  3. Money isn't everything,...
  4. Money can't buy you friends,...
  5. Money doesn't go as far as it used to,...

  a. ...but it certainly goes faster.
  b. ...but it certainly puts you in a wonderful bargaining position.
  c. ...but you can get a better class of enemy.
  d. ...but it's certainly handy if you don't have a credit card.
  e. ...if I die by four o'clock.

2. Work in pairs and compare your answers to 1. Which saying did you like best? Which was the funniest?

3. When people say funny things or tell jokes, timing and intonation are very important. The amusing part usually comes at the end after a slight pause.

Listen to the two versions of each saying. Which do you think is better, the first version or the second? Now say the sayings out loud in a lively way.

34 *Born to Shop*

Ways of expressing quantity

VOCABULARY AND SPEAKING

1. Match the definitions below with one or more words from the box.

> bank   cash   check   credit card   currency   deposit
> exchange rate   fee   grant   income tax   interest   loan
> mortgage   overdrawn   receipt   rent   salary   sales tax
> Social Security   statement   unemployment benefits
> wages   withdrawal

1. A document you get when you buy something.
2. Money which is lent to you in order to buy a house or condominium.
3. A document your bank sends you telling you what you have in your account.
4. Money you earn from a larger amount of money or that you pay on money you borrow.
5. A description of your bank account when you have a negative balance.
6. Money which is lent or given to you. (2 words)
7. The actions of taking out and putting money into a bank account. (2 words)
8. A method of paying for things you buy. (3 words)
9. Money the government takes from you. (2 words)
10. Two words to do with money from a foreign country.
11. Money you receive for work you do. (3 words)
12. Three words or expressions to describe money which the government may pay you.

2. Think about your answers to numbers 6–12. What's the difference between the words?

3. Work in pairs. Discuss the answers to these questions.
1. Which of the words in the box have an equivalent in your language?
2. Do people borrow money to buy houses in your country?
3. What money do you have to pay to the government?
4. What does the government pay you?

GRAMMAR

> **Ways of expressing quantity**
> **You can use the following expressions of quantity:**
> **– with countable nouns.**
> *a(n), few, a few, many, both (of), several, neither (of),*
> *a couple (of)checks*   **a few** *dollars*   **several** *people*
> **– with uncountable nouns.**
> *very little, not much, a little, less, much, a great deal of*
> *very little money*   *less tax*
> **– with both countable and uncountable nouns.**
> *some, any, no, none, hardly any, half, all, a lot of, lots of,*
> *(not) enough, more, most*
> **some** *money*   **hardly any** *cash*
> ***Some* is common in affirmative clauses, and *any* is common in questions and negatives. But you use *some* in questions if you expect, or want to encourage, the answer *yes*.**
> *Would you like to borrow **some** more money?*
> **You can use *any* when you mean *it doesn't matter which*.**
> *You can get a loan from **any** major bank.*

1. Complete the sentences with suitable expressions of quantity from the list below.

a few   some   some more   hardly any   a lot   any

A Can you lend me _____ money? I forgot to go to the bank.

B Well, I've only got _____ dollars on me.

A Oh, darn. I need _____. Don't worry. I'll go to the bank when I go shopping.

B If you're going shopping, can you get me a gallon of milk?

A What kind of milk?

B _____ kind is OK. No, actually, get one percent. Oh, and we need _____ cans of tomatoes. I'm making spaghetti tonight. We've got _____ pasta. Could you get _____ pasta too?

B Sure.

🔲 Now listen and check your answers.

2. Work in pairs. Imagine that you are planning to invite some friends to a barbecue. You have already got the items listed below. Make a list of the things that you will need to buy.

– a small piece of cheese   – two tomatoes
– five bottles of water   – half a bottle of milk
– one sausage   – one bread roll

Now prepare a conversation about the things you need to buy using the dialogue in 1 to help you. Act out your dialogue for the class.

LISTENING AND SPEAKING

1. You are going to hear two people talking about shopping. First, look at this questionnaire, which is about shopping habits. What do you think the title *Were You Born to Shop?* means?

Were You Born to Shop?	Jorge	Nanthapa
How often do you go shopping?		
What do you spend most money on?		
How often do you buy clothes?		
How often do you buy things for the home?		
Which items that you buy are necessities?		
How often do you buy presents for other people?		
Which do you prefer to use, cash, credit cards, or checks?		
Do you ever borrow money from friends or from a bank?		
Do you try to save any money?		

2. Work in pairs.
Student A: Turn to Communication Activity 4 on page 103.
Student B: Turn to Communication Activity 9 on page 104.

3. Work together and complete the chart.

4. Listen again and complete these sentences with suitable words or phrases.

1. Nanthapa buys food every day at the market because _____.
2. Jorge thinks clothes are a necessity if _____.
3. Nanthapa buys presents if _____.
4. Jorge would never ask a friend _____.
5. Nanthapa thinks saving money is _____.
6. Jorge usually spends money _____.

SPEAKING AND WRITING

1. Work in groups of three. Write a questionnaire to find out about other people's shopping habits. You can use some of the questions in *Listening and Speaking* activity 1 but try to add at least five more questions.

2. Each member of the group should go around the class and interview different people using your questionnaire. Write down their replies.

3. In your groups, share the answers you got and use the information to write a report on other students' shopping habits.

Do you think anyone you interviewed was "born to shop"?

35 | *Trends*

Future continuous and future perfect

READING AND SPEAKING

1. Work in pairs. You're going to read an article called *Growing Trends* which is about life in the future. Here are the topic sentences taken from four of the paragraphs. Discuss what you think each paragraph will say.

1. In the 21st century we will almost certainly be living in a warmer world.
2. In the 21st century most families will be using computers in their homes to do a wide variety of tasks.
3. By the 21st century a population explosion will have taken place in the developing world.
4. Statistics show that society is becoming more violent.

Now read the passage and check if you were correct.

2. Answer these questions and try to guess the meanings of the words and phrases in italic.

1. *…sketched in outline…* – Does this mean *described in detail* or *in general terms*?
2. *The vast bulk of the technology…* – Is this likely to mean the *majority* or the *minority*?
3. *A population explosion…* – Is this likely to mean an *increase* or a *decrease*?
4. *…will have stabilized…* – Does this mean it *will have continued to change* or *will have stopped changing*?

3. Here are some suggestions to help you survive in the 21st century. Match each suggestion with one of the predictions in the text.

1. Don't fear technology or become a slave to it. It's more important to learn what technology can do for you than to understand how it is done.
2. Do your best to conserve energy, in your home and when you travel.
3. Buy sun-hats and sunscreen and teach children to keep out of the sun.
4. Start talks with neighbors about hiring private security guards.
5. Take out a private pension plan so that you are not dependent on the government when you are older.
6. Travel as much as you can now. With decreasing fuel supplies it may not be possible when you are older.

4. Work in pairs and discuss what you think about these suggestions. Are there any that you don't agree with? Now work with another pair and compare your ideas.

Growing Trends

What will our world be like in the next century? Scientists today are analyzing statistics that show how the world has changed in previous years and using them to try to predict the future. They want to know what sort of jobs we will be doing, what technology we will be using in our daily lives, what kind of homes we will be living in, and what our world will look like in the 21st century.

We have sketched in outline some of the growing trends and the scientists' predictions below.

The environment In the 21st century we will almost certainly be living in a warmer world. The world will continue to use fossil fuels which release carbon dioxide, the main cause of global warming.

Damage done to the ozone layer by man-made chemicals will mean that our children will have an increased risk of developing skin cancer.

We will be living in a world with less energy available and we will be forced to reduce our energy consumption.

Technology In the 21st century most families will be using computers in their homes to do a wide variety of tasks. The vast bulk of the technology we will be using a generation from now already exists in some form. One out of three American households has a personal computer today—some 32 million in all. In 25 years computers will be a million times faster than they are today and will work in a way that resembles the human brain. They will have become easier to use, but anyone who has not learned how to use the new technology will be seriously disadvantaged, particularly in the field of employment.

Population By the 21st century a population explosion will have taken place in the developing world. In developed countries, the size of the population will have stabilized but the proportion of older people will have increased dramatically and there will be problems associated with care of the elderly and increasing pressure on the medical services. It may no longer be possible for the government to provide Social Security for everybody.

Society Statistics show that society is becoming more violent. Seventy-seven percent of Americans said that they worry about becoming victims of violent crimes; the murder rate has climbed 20% since 1985. The number of people under the age of 18 arrested for carrying a weapon has jumped 106% in the last ten years. This trend will almost certainly continue. Rising crime will be one of the main problems that people in the 21st century will have to deal with.

GRAMMAR

> Future continuous and future perfect
>
> **You use the future continuous:**
> **– to talk about something which will be in progress at a particular time in the future.**
> *We **will** almost certainly **be living** in a warmer world.*
> **– to talk about something which is already planned or is part of a routine.**
> *In the 21st century most families **will be using** computers in their homes.*
> **– to ask politely about someone's plans.**
> ***Will you be taking** care of the older members of your family?*
> **You use the future perfect to talk about something which will be completed by a specific time in the future.**
> *The proportion of older people **will have increased** dramatically.*

1. Look at the examples of the future continuous and future perfect in the text. How do you form these tenses?

2. Complete these sentences with a future continuous or future perfect form of the verb in brackets.

 1. ____ you ____ (go) to the energy conference next week?
 2. This time next week I ____ (fly) to Taiwan.
 3. I can't give you the report on Sunday because I ____ (not finish) it by then.
 4. It's after six o'clock so he ____ (finish) work by now.
 5. He didn't sleep last night. If he doesn't sleep tonight, he ____ (not sleep) for two nights.
 6. When I am going to bed in New York, they ____ (get) up in Tokyo.

 1. Will you be going to the energy conference next week?

3. Use the information in the grammar box to describe the uses of the future continuous or future perfect in the sentences in 2.

4. Here are some growing trends in the United States. Work in pairs and make predictions.

 1. In 1996 one person in three uses a mobile phone.
 2. Ten million people in the United States now use telephone banking services.
 3. Forty-eight percent of people own the house they are living in.
 4. People today live on average two years longer than they did twenty years ago.
 5. People are spending 80% more money than they did in 1971.

 1. In the future more and more people will be using mobile phones.

WRITING AND SPEAKING

Work in groups of three or four. Are the trends in *Grammar* activity 4 similar in your country? Write some predictions about life in the future in your country. Try to use the future continuous and future perfect forms.

Now write ten pieces of advice to help you survive in the 21st century.

36 *For Better or Worse*

Future in the past

VOCABULARY AND LISTENING

1. Work in pairs. You are going to hear four old friends talking about what they were going to do when they left high school. Look at the words in the box and find the ones that are connected to *college life*.

> cheerleader homeless battered Peace Corps shelter custody pre-med
> sleazy major research reunion career picket fence scholarship alimony
> pharmaceutical

What do the other words mean?

2. 🔲 Listen to Alice, Ben, Corey, and Deb talking together. Find out where they are and what they are talking about.

3. Fill in the chart below about each person. What were their plans and what was the outcome?

Name	Plan	Outcome
Alice		
Ben		
Corey		
Deb		

4. 🔲 Listen again and check your answers to 2 and 3. Can you fill in any more details about each person?

5. Here are some expressions that the friends use. What do you think they mean? Can you rephrase them in a simpler way?

1. I was going to marry *Mr. Right*.
2. I was going to live *happily every after.*
3. *I'm keeping my head above water.*
4. I wanted it all—*the whole nine yards.*
5. *Boom! End of story.*
6. *Tell me about it!*

GRAMMAR

> **Future in the past**
> You can use *was/were going to* + infinitive to talk about something that was planned or promised for the future at some point in the past but which didn't happen.
> You **were going to change** the *world.*

1. Look at your answers to *Vocabulary and Listening* activity 3 and write sentences describing each person's plan that wasn't realized. Use a future in the past structure.

2. Match the two parts of these sentences.

1. Alice was going to marry Mr. Right, ...
2. Ben never said he was going to change the world, ...
3. Corey was going to play professional football, ...
4. Deb was going to study law, ...

a. he said he was going to try.
b. but she didn't because she thought the profession was too sleazy.
c. but she got divorced and had to put herself through night school.
d. but he injured his knee and couldn't play anymore.

3. Think of things you had planned to but didn't. Explain why you didn't do them.

SOUNDS

1. The letter *t* makes more than one sound in American English. Look at these words. Which ones contain the /t/ sound in American English? What other sound does the letter *t* make?

still   wanted   shelter   greatest   represented   settled
tell   practice   little   downtown   letter   waiting
different   written   quantity

2. 🔲 Listen and check. As you listen, say the words out loud.

WRITING

1. Look at these expressions often used in discussions and use them to complete the sentences below.

To express an opinion: *personally, in my opinion*
To contradict someone: *on the contrary, actually*
To express something obvious: *obviously, of course*
To make an assumption: *presumably, I suppose*
To express a wish for the future: *hopefully*
To describe an outcome: *eventually, as a result*
To sum up (very formal):   *in conclusion, to sum up*
To say how it appears: *apparently, evidently*
To express a happy outcome: *luckily, fortunately*

1. It took many years but ____ they got to the moon.
2. He had a white coat on so ____ he was a scientist.
3. ____, I think the next century will be very interesting.
4. ____ , in the future life will be better for everyone.
5. He said class sizes would get smaller. ____, I said, they'll get bigger.
6. He lost his job, but ____, found another one immediately.

2. Work in pairs. Choose either Ben, Corey, or Deb from the *Vocabulary and Listening*. Write a short summary of what he or she was planning to do and why it didn't happen.

Start by saying what the person was going to do.
Alice was going to get married to Mr. Right.

Continue the paragraph with extra information and examples.
She was going to have kids and live in a pretty little house with a white picket fence.

Begin a new paragraph with a topic sentence presenting an opposite view.
However, things didn't turn out quite as she planned. She had kids, but she was divorced by the age of twenty-five.

Continue the paragraph with extra information.
Unfortunately, she found herself with no money, no education, and no house.

Finish the summary with a new paragraph, starting with a topic sentence which states your conclusion.
But in my opinion, things turned out well for Alice in the end.

State your reasons.
Eventually, she succeeded in getting an education, she now has a job she loves, and she has two beautiful children.

37 Davy Crockett

Passive constructions with *say*, *believe*

Davy Crockett is the most famous of America's early frontier men and women. Born in Tennessee in 1786, Davy was the son of settlers, and learned early on how to survive in this rugged "New World" by hunting, trapping, and clearing the land. Davy was elected to Congress by his home state in 1827, and quickly became a popular folk figure. After his death in 1836 at the Alamo—fighting for Texas' independence from Mexico—many exaggerated stories, or "tall tales," were invented about Davy's strength and abilities.

It is said that Davy Crockett could carry thunder in his fists and throw lightning from his fingers. That's the same Davy who liked to shout, "I'm half horse, half alligator, and a bit of snapping turtle!" By the time Davy Crockett was eight years old, it is believed that he weighed 200 pounds with his shoes off, his feet clean, and his belly empty! No one could be said to be stronger, braver, or more cunning. One night, in the middle of a thunderstorm, Davy encountered the Big Eater of the Forest—the biggest, meanest, wildest panther this side of the Mississippi. Well, old Davy, who was believed to be half varmint himself, beat that darned beast in arm-to-claw combat, with nothing but a stick! He couldn't bring himself to kill the magnificent beast, however, so he tamed him, brought him home, and taught him how to rake the leaves!

Davy Crocket was considered to be a real-life inspiration for the new pioneers of America. Tall tales about him and others like him spurred these settlers to struggle against the very real hardships of the wild frontier. These stories also helped to create a new "American personality," which vigorously rejected the strict class-based European society in favor of the wits, determination, and confidence of the individual. For all their bravado and humor, tall tales such as those about Davy Crockett illustrate the struggle of the individual against nature, as well as the wary respect for the dangers of nature, that are part of the American character today.

READING

1. Work in pairs. You are going to read a passage about Davy Crockett, the "king of the wild frontier." Have you ever heard of this folk hero? Write four or five questions which you would like the passage to answer. Use the illustration to help you.

2. Read the passage and choose the best title.

1. The Big Eater of the Forest
2. Tall Tales
3. Davy Crockett: An Inspiring Folk Hero
4. Davy and the Panther

3. Look at these adjectives. Which of them describe Davy Crockett? Explain why you think so using examples from the passage.

strong   lonely   confident   brave
insecure   timid   intelligent   happy
humorous   cruel   kind-hearted

strong – the passage says he could carry thunder in his fists

4. Work in pairs. You are going to read some more tall tales about Davy Crockett.

Student A: Turn to Communication Activity 13 on page 104.

Student B: Turn to Communication Activity 19 on page 106.

Now retell your tall tale to your partner. Be sure to include all the exaggerations about Davy Crockett that you read in the tall tale. How are the tales similar? Do you find these tall tales inspiring?

GRAMMAR

> Passive constructions with *say, believe*
> **You can use the following passive constructions with *say, believe,* etc. to show that you're not sure of the truth of the statement or that you want to distance yourself from it.**
> *It* + **passive** + *that* **clause**
> **It is said that** *Davy Crockett could carry thunder in his fists.*
> **It is believed that** *he weighed 200 pounds by the time he was eight years old.*

1. Look at the sentences below. In which sentence is the speaker distanced from the information?

1. a Davy Crockett could throw lightning from his fingers.
   b. It is said that Davy Crockett could throw lightning from his fingers.
2. a. Davy was half horse.
   b. Davy is said to have been half horse.

2. Underline the passive constructions in the passages in the Communication Activities. Add to the list of verbs in the grammar box that you can use with these passive constructions.

3. Rewrite the following sentences using *it* and a suitable passive construction.

1. When he was eight years old, he weighed 200 pounds.
2. Davy beat the Big Eater of the Forest with nothing but a stick.
3. He tamed the panther and taught him to rake the leaves.
4. Davy Crockett was as strong as a horse.
5. Tall tales inspired early Americans to survive in a rugged new land.
6. Davy was the strongest, bravest, and smartest person this side of the Mississippi.

1. It is said that when Davy was eight years old, he weighed 200 pounds.

SPEAKING

1. Work in pairs. Can you think of any well-known folk heroes or legends from your country? Are there any tall tales told about them? Talk about:

– who the person was
– if he or she really lived
– what he or she is famous for
– where the tall tale takes place
– what happened

2. Tell your story to the rest of the class. Has anyone heard of them before? Are any of the stories similar?

38 | *Folk Heroes and Legends*

Speculating about the past: *may have, might have, must have, can't have*

VOCABULARY AND LISTENING

1. You're going to hear three people talking about some American folk heroes.

Pecos Bill   Johnny Appleseed   Paul Bunyan

Each folk hero is famous for one of the following reasons.

He planted apple seeds over all of the northeast of the United States
He was raised by coyotes.
He was a lumberjack who had a blue ox named Babe.

Match the folk heroes with their pictures.

2. Look at the pictures and decide which of the folk heroes in 1 you think these words could be used to talk about.

orchard huge ax lasso cowboy rattlesnake lumberjack
wolf missionary coffeepot barefoot Texan snow
mountain lion trap cattle drive famous band friends
naked settlers

3. 🔲 Listen and find out what each folk hero is famous for.

4. 🔲 Work in pairs. Listen again and take notes about the folk heroes. Find answers to the following questions.

1. Why did Paul Bunyan sleep on a boat in a river when he was a baby?
2. Who was Paul Bunyan's friend?
3. Why was Pecos Bill raised by a band of coyotes?
4. What did Bill ride like a horse?
5. Why did Johnny Appleseed look strange?
6. Why did the wolf follow Johnny around?

5. Work in pairs. Decide which of the following statements are true and say why.

1. Paul Bunyan must have been strong.
2. Paul Bunyan can't have been as big as they say he was.
3. Johnny Appleseed must have been a vegetarian.
4. Pecos Bill can't have been adopted by coyotes when he was a baby.

GRAMMAR AND FUNCTIONS

> Speculating about the past: *may have, might have, must have, can't have*
>
> **You can use past modal verbs to speculate about the past and draw logical conclusions based on known facts.**
>
> **You can use *may have* or *might have* to talk about something which possibly happened or was true in the past.**
>
> **You use *must have* to talk about something which probably/certainly happened or was true in the past.**
>
> **You use *can't have* to talk about something which probably/certainly didn't happen or was not true in the past.**
>
> **You can also use the main verb in its continuous form with past modals.**

1. Look at these sentences and explain the difference between them. Which mean the same?

   a. Paul Bunyan may have been a real lumberjack.

   b. Paul Bunyan must have been a real lumberjack.

   c. Paul Bunyan might have been a real lumberjack.

   d. Paul Bunyan can't have been a real lumberjack.

2. Write sentences drawing conclusions about what *must have, might have,* or *can't have* happened.

   1. His car is wrecked.

   2. She's crying.

   3. He looks terrified.

   4. I'm sure I heard a strange noise outside.

   5. She seems tired.

   6. He's still laughing about the movie last night.

   1. His car is wrecked. He must have had an accident.

SOUNDS

1. Underline the words which are likely to be stressed in this dialogue.

  A That was Big Foot! That must have been Big Foot! It was only a few yards away! I saw it.

  B No way! You can't have. You must have imagined it!

  A There are its footprints! It must have been running pretty fast if you didn't see it! Where's your camera?

  B I'm out of film. Anyway, it could have been a bear.

  A But it must have been at least twenty feet tall!

  📼 Now listen and check.

2. Work in pairs and act out the dialogue.

WRITING

1. You are going to prepare a guide to folk heroes or legends in your country, or around the world. Working on your own, choose a legend or folk hero and write notes about him or her. Make sure you all choose different folk heroes or legends.

Big Foot—a big, hairy beast, lives in the woods.

2. Use your notes to write a paragraph about the legend.

Big Foot is said to be a big, hairy beast who lives in the woods.

3. Work in pairs. Give your partner the paragraph you wrote in 2 and read the paragraph he or she gives you. Read it and write questions concerning details which you would like to know more about.

Where are the woods that Big Foot lives in?

Then pass the notes and your questions back to your partner.

4. Rewrite your paragraph including the answers to the questions your partner asked in 3, if possible.

Big Foot is said to be a big, hairy beast who lives in the woods in the Pacific Northwest.

5. With the whole class, draw a rough map of the world or the country where your folk heroes or legends come from. Put your paragraph by that town or country.

39 Brand Image

Reported speech

SPEAKING AND LISTENING

1. This lesson is about advertising. First, check that you know what the word *brand* means.

2. Look at these well-known brand names. Which ones do you recognize? What type of product do you associate with each brand?

3. Think about brand names you know from your own and other countries. What values and qualities do they suggest?

4. You are going to hear someone talking about some brands and the image they present. First, look at the list of international brands. Which country do you associate them with?

☐ Mitsubishi ☐ Benetton ☐ Gillette
☐ Mercedes ☐ Chanel ☐ Nike
☐ Heinz ☐ Swatch ☐ Panasonic
☐ Sony ☐ Samsung ☐ Apple
☐ Rolex ☐ Kellogg's ☐ American Express

What type of product do you associate these brands with? Choose from the following.

drinks food personal care and pharmaceuticals cosmetics fashion
household products   high tech products   motor vehicles
leisure and cultural   credit and retail

5. 📼 Listen to someone talking about three brands. Put a number 1–3 by the brand name and the product in activity 4.

6. Work in pairs. Make notes on what the speaker mentioned about the following aspects of each brand:

– brand name – product
– image – appeal

7. Which of the following sentences did the speaker say?

1. "You shouldn't buy a Mercedes because it'll let you down."
2. "In the past, drivers of Mercedes Benz belonged to all social classes."
3. "Mercedes now only appeals to rich people."
4. "Benetton began their advertising campaign by wanting to shock people."
5. "Benetton appeals to the young consumers who feel they have accepted the world as it is."
6. "You could only buy Gillette products in America."
7. "Gillette is a luxury product."
8. "Gillette has always had the same image."

8. 📼 Listen again and check your answers to 5, 6, and 7. Are there any details you can add to your notes?

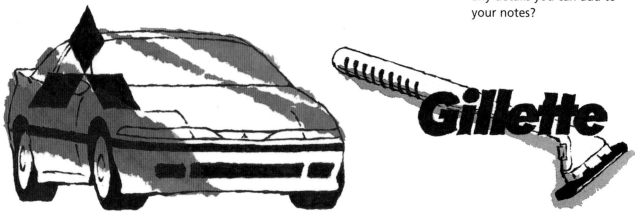

GRAMMAR

> **Reported speech**
>
> **When you put direct speech into reported speech, you usually change:**
> – the tense of the verb.
> – adverbs of time and place.
> – the pronouns, unless the speaker is talking about him/herself.
> **You don't usually make these changes:**
> – when the tense of the main reporting verb is in the present tense.
> – if the statement is still true at the time of reporting.
> – if the direct speech contains the modals *may, might, could, should, ought to.*

1. Correct the statements in *Speaking and Listening* activity 7.

She said that you should buy a Mercedes because it won't let you down.

2. Rewrite this passage changing the direct speech to reported speech.

A woman went into town to do some shopping. A man was standing outside the supermarket handing out small cups of a new soft drink. He said, "It'll be the best thing you've ever tasted." She tried it. "It tastes horrible," she said. "I don't like it much either," he said. She laughed and went into the supermarket. At the cheese counter the woman couldn't decide whether to buy Cheddar or Swiss. "Which cheese do you like best?" she asked the clerk. "I think you should buy the Swiss," the clerk said. "I had some last week and it was delicious." Next the woman went to get some juice. She wanted orange juice but they only had pineapple left. She asked another clerk, "Where can I find the orange juice?" But the clerk replied, "We are sold out. We'll be getting some more tomorrow, but you'd better come early 'cause we're selling out quickly in this hot weather. Why don't you try some of that refreshing new soft drink they are advertising outside the store?"

SOUNDS

Do these verbs suggest a loud, soft, or neutral voice? What would the speaker's mood be?

stammer   laugh   whisper   groan   sing   shout

 Now listen to the following sentences. Which words can you use to describe the way the speaker speaks?

1. I want to go home.
2. I think this is a beautiful country.
3. I can't go on like this.
4. What an amazing place!
5. Oh, what a beautiful morning!
6. I said I agree with you!

VOCABULARY AND LISTENING

1. Work in pairs. You're going to hear radio ads for five of the following products:

– perfume   – a car dealership – life insurance
– a diet program   – a vacation
– a concert   – a movie

Think of words which you may hear in each ad.

2. Listen and number the products in 1 as you hear the ad.

3. Which of the following words did you hear in each ad?

> mysterious   popular   luxurious   fast   powerful
> dependable   action-packed   exotic   great   romantic
> spectacular   amazing   reliable   personalized   tasty
> moving

 Listen again and check.

4. In which ads for products are you likely to hear the other words in 3?

5. Think of words you might use in ads for:

– an airline   – shampoo – a camera
– a computer   – dishwashing liquid

40 The Real Thing?

Reporting verbs

SPEAKING

Work in groups of three or four and discuss your answers to these questions.

1. What are the best and the worst ads in your country at the moment?
2. Where do you see or hear them?
3. Are there any restraints on advertisements in your country?
4. What do you think advertisers should or shouldn't do?

READING

1. You're going to read a passage about global advertising. First, look at these key sentences from the passage. Write the questions which these sentences answer.

1. The idea behind the advertising is that we really are part of a global village.
2. Corporations such as Coca-Cola want to be seen as worldly, altruistic giants.
3. Coca-Cola's advertising agencies have been able to promote the drink with messages so simple that they can be posted around the world.
4. Simplicity is the key; they are easy to understand, easy to translate.

2. Read the passage and choose the best summary.

1. Coca-Cola is one of a number of companies which are involved in global advertising.
2. The main advantage of global advertising is that you spend more money on a single advertisement.
3. Global advertising is about creating a single, simple message which can be used to promote a product around the world.

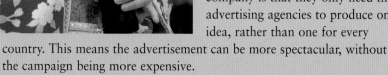

I'd Like to Teach the World to Sell

Telephone Coca-Cola and, while you wait to be put through, the corporation's "It's the Real Thing" jingle crackles down the line. "It's the Real Thing" is a global message first used by Coca-Cola in the 1940s; its meaning is clear (do not be fooled by lesser imitators) and it is inescapable. It translates perfectly well into Roman, Arabic, Cyrillic script, and most other languages and stands for an instantly recognizable product in Brussels, Baltimore, Bali, or Bangkok.

This is the advertising technique now being taken up by more and more companies and advertising agencies from Sprint to Sony as their products reach out around the world. Huge resources are being poured into single advertising campaigns.

The idea behind the advertising is that we really are part of a global village: we all want the same things, we all have access to them and we all respond to the same imagery. Coca-Cola sells itself as democratic, international, and liberating.

The sub-text might be that corporations such as Coca-Cola want to be seen as worldly, altruistic giants, linking the people of the world in one warm and smiling embrace—all the better to sell them things. An added bonus for the company is that they only need their advertising agencies to produce one idea, rather than one for every country. This means the advertisement can be more spectacular, without the campaign being more expensive.

Coca-Cola was the first company to break into global advertising. The most memorable of these early international ads was "I'd like to teach the world to sing... Coca-Cola... the real thing," made in 1971 and reshot in 1989. It featured a crowd of young people, ostensibly from all corners of the world, learning to sing the words "Coca-Cola" in perfect harmony while smiling through even more perfect white teeth.

By making just one key, desirable, and homogeneous product, Coca-Cola's advertising agencies have been able to promote the drink with messages so simple that they can be posted around the world without causing confusion, upset, or censure.

Simplicity is the key; they are easy to understand, easy to translate, and, after being repeated enough times, become synonymous with the product.

Adapted from an article by Jonathan Glancey from *The Independent*

3. Look at these sentences from the passage. Decide who or what the word in italics refers to.

1. ...*its* meaning is clear...
2. *This* is the advertising technique now being taken up...
3. ...we all have access to *them*.
4. An added bonus for the company is that they only need *their* advertising agencies...
5. *This* means the advertisement itself can be more spectacular...

4. The passage contains a mixture of main ideas and examples. Look at the first and last sentences of each paragraph. Do they express a main idea or an example?

LISTENING AND VOCABULARY

1. Here are some sentences from a dialogue between a customer and a sales clerk. Decide who says each sentence. Write C or SC after each sentence.

- ☐ Can I help you, ma'am?
- ☐ Let me see. Oh yes. We have had some problems with this brand. Would you like me to replace it with a similar model?
- ☐ You know, I think you should check what you sell more carefully.
- ☐ What seems to be the trouble?
- ☐ Well, the salesperson said it was waterproof, but when I wore it in the swimming pool it just filled with water.
- ☐ Yes, I bought this watch here last week and I've been having a few problems with it.
- ☐ Thank you.
- ☐ Of course. We can do that for you Do you have your receipt?
- ☐ Actually, I'd rather have my money back.
- ☐ Yes, here it is.
- ☐ Yes. I'm very sorry about that.

2. Match the sentences above with a suitable reporting verb from the list below.

agree	explain	complain	apologize	thank	warn
offer	insist	promise	suggest	argue	point out
admit	ask				

3. 📼 Listen and number the sentences in the order you hear them.

Now work in pairs and act out the dialogue.

GRAMMAR

> Reporting verbs
>
> **You can often use a reporting verb to describe the general sense of what someone thinks or says. The main patterns for these verbs are:**
> **– verb + *to* + infinitive**
> *He decided to ask for his money back.*
> **– verb + object + *to* + infinitive**
> *He asked her to replace it.*
> **– verb + (*that*) + clause**
> *She admitted that there had been some problems.*
> **– verb + object + (*that*) + clause**
> *He told her that he had got the receipt.*
> **– verb + object(s)**
> *He thanked her.*

1. Look at the reporting verbs in the vocabulary box in *Listening and Vocabulary* activity 2. What pattern does each verb follow? Write sentences showing how they are used.

2. Rewrite the sentences in *Listening and Vocabulary* activity 1 using suitable reporting verbs.

3. Choose four or five verbs from the vocabulary box and write similar sentences, leaving out the verb. When you're ready, show your sentences to another student. Does he or she know which verbs you left out?

WRITING AND SPEAKING

1. Work in pairs. Look at the advertising claims below. What do you think the products are? Choose one (or write your own) and use it to write a dialogue between a customer and the person who sold him or her the product.

LEARN WHILE YOU SLEEP

LOSE TWENTY POUNDS IN A WEEK

TEACH YOUR DOG TO SPEAK

ENGLISH BY MICROWAVE

SPEAK A LANGUAGE OF YOUR CHOICE FLUENTLY IN THREE WEEKS

2. Perform your dialogue for the rest of the class.

Fluency **5** *Beyond Words*

Saying what you mean

SPEAKING AND LISTENING

1. Work in pairs and discuss your answers to the questions.

1. Look at some coins or bank notes from your country. Who or what is shown on them? What values do they represent?

2. What product, manufactured in your country, is famous around the world? Describe its features and decide what kind of person is likely to buy it, or would like to buy it.

3. Design a stamp which shows people, places, objects, or symbols which represent the spirit and the values of your home town.

4. Which of the following values are important in your culture?

   individual rights collective responsibility equality
   harmony assertiveness loyalty patriotism honesty
   freedom of speech age education liberty

   Can you think of examples of how these values affect your behavior in certain situations?

5. What words do you associate with the following?
   politics police home money religion childhood

6. What do you associate with the following colors?
   black white green yellow blue red

7. Choose five prestigious jobs in your country and five unprestigious jobs.

2. 📻 Listen to Joe answering some of the questions in 1. Put a check (✓) by the questions he answers.

3. Work in pairs and make notes about what Joe said. Try to include as much detail as possible.

📻 Now listen again and check.

4. Look at these gestures. What do they mean in your language?

5. 📻 Listen to Joe saying what the gestures mean to an American. Write the number of the gesture by the meaning.

Do you mean me? ☐   Someone is calling you. ☐

Come here. ☐   Take it easy. ☐

Good luck. ☐   Be quiet! ☐

6. Work in pairs and check your answers to 5.
📼 Now listen again and check.

7. What gestures do you use to express the following ideas?

Don't know.   Go straight.   Sit down.
Telephone!   Naughty.   Delicious!   Nasty!
Give me patience.
I can't look.   I beg you.   No.   Yes.

8. Work in pairs. How do you feel when someone …

– looks you in the eye?
– stands a long way away from you?
– touches your head?
– remains silent?
– speaks loudly?

FUNCTIONS

> #### Saying what you mean
> **There are some common expressions in English which may be used differently when translated into other languages, or have no equivalent.**
>
> *We must have lunch.* Between two friends leaving each other, this is not an invitation, but a vague promise for a future meeting. There are many vague promises like this.
>
> *Of course!* This means that something is obvious, and is not an emphatic *Yes, I agree with you.*
>
> *Really?* When someone replies to something you say with this, it doesn't mean they don't believe you. It means something like "That's very interesting!" You don't reply with *Really!*
>
> *Excuse me.* You say this when you would like someone to let you pass, or when you've sneezed or coughed.
>
> *Pardon?* This means I didn't hear what you said, please repeat it.
>
> *Bon appetit!* In English there is no single expression to use as you start eating a meal. "Enjoy your meal" would only be suitable from a waiter.
>
> *Don't you understand what I'm saying?* If someone ask you a negative question, or uses a negative tag, a *yes* answer means *Yes, I do understand you* and a *no* answer means *No, I don't understand you.*

1. Work in pairs and answer the questions in your language.

1. Your teacher asks you a question and then says "You don't know the answer, do you?" This is true. So what do you say honestly?

2. Today is Friday. Someone says "It isn't Friday already, is it?" What do you say?

3. You go with a friend to a very nice restaurant. Your friend says "This is a very nice restaurant!" How do you agree with him?

4. Someone says "Come by if you're ever in the neighborhood." What do you reply?

5. You say to someone "The traffic was awful this morning." She replies "Really?" What do you say?

6. What do you say when you start a meal in your country?

7. Someone says something you can't quite hear. What do you say?

8. You're on a bus and it's very crowded. You'd like to get off. What do you say?

2. Answer the questions in 1 in English.

READING AND WRITING

1. Here are some well-known proverbs or sayings in English. Read them and find out if there are any which are similar to proverbs and sayings in your language.

"Time is money."
"You can't have your cake and eat it, too."
"The less said the better."
"Where there's a will, there's a way."
"His bark is worse than his bite."
"When in Rome, do as the Romans do."
"An apple a day keeps the doctor away."
"Look before you leap."
"Let sleeping dogs lie."
"Every cloud has a silver lining."
"Strike while the iron is hot."
"A stitch in time saves nine."
"Beggars can't be choosers."
"Love your neighbor."
"Don't count your chickens before they hatch."

2. Work in pairs. Discuss what the proverbs mean. What cultural values do the proverbs represent?

3. Think of five or six well-known phrases or sayings in your language. Translate them into English. Do you think they represent important values in your culture?

Progress Check **33–40**

VOCABULARY

1. Remember that it's more important to recognize what idioms mean than to use them yourself. People use them in informal situations, often to create a personal and sometimes exaggerated impression of what they are describing.

There are many ways of categorizing idioms. Here are some idioms:

– to describe personal qualities or behavior.
to have a heart of gold   to be as tough as nails   to go the whole nine yards to be quick off the mark

– to describe feelings.
to be on cloud nine   to be down in the dumps   to be beat to be at death's door

– to describe problems or reactions to situations.
to be between a rock and a hard place   to sweep things under the rug to see the light at the end of the tunnel

– to talk about communication.
to talk down to someone   to get to the point   to speak your mind to talk up a storm

Look at these sentences and decide which of the above categories each idiom belongs to.

1. He never remembers anything.
   He has a mind like a sieve.
2. She came up behind him quietly and said "Boo!"
   She frightened the life out of him.
3. Your children are well-behaved.
   They are as good as gold.
4. He was really angry. He was as mad as a hornet.
5. I think I'll take a back seat and let him do all the work.
6. You have got to get your act together and organize your work better.
7. I won't beat about the bush. I'll tell you what I really think.
8. She's very long-winded. She always uses ten words where two will do.

You may like to use these categories when you note down new idioms.

2. There are many words which have very informal or slang equivalents.

children – kids   advertisement – ad   television – TV   dollar – buck

It may be useful to note down if a word is informal or slang. Use your dictionary to find out what these words mean:

So long!   pal   OJ   cops   buddy

GRAMMAR

1. What are the countable equivalents of the following words?

grass   furniture   luggage information   advice   luck clothing   smoke   sugar news   lightning

a blade of grass

2. Choose the correct word.

A Can I withdraw *some/several* cash, please.
B Yes, sir, how *much/many* do you need?
A Thirty dollars.
B There you are, sir. Are you interested in our new savings account? It offers *much/many* more interest than usual.
A At the end of the month, I've only got *a few/a little* money left. How *much/many* do I need to open the account?
B Five hundred dollars. And you can take it out at *any/some* time.
A Five hundred dollars! I don't have five hundred cents!

3. Complete the sentences with a future continuous or future perfect form of the verb in parentheses.

1. This time tomorrow, I ____ (be) in a meeting in New York.
2. I can't give you back your book when I see you because I ____ (finish) it by then.
3. ____ (take) a train or a plane tomorrow?
4. It's after eight o'clock, so he ____ (leave) for work by now.
5. While we're having our lunch here, they ____ (have) breakfast in Washington.
6. We ____ (be) married for twenty years next March.

4. Complete the sentences with *must have* or *can't have* and a suitable form of the verb in brackets.

1. Her eyes are red. She ____ (cry).
2. She never goes out. She ____ (go out) tonight.
3. There's no answer. They ____ (go out).
4. It wasn't true. He ____ (tell) a lie.
5. He looks brown. He ____ (be) on vacation.
6. They looked bored. The movie ____ (be) very good.

5. Rewrite these sentences with *It* and a suitable passive construction.

1. People say that carrots help you see in the dark.
2. People think that Oprah Winfrey is the richest woman in show business.
3. People believe that smoking is bad for you.
4. People claim that computers will run our lives in the future.
5. People know that certain people have more bad luck than others.
6. People expect that a cure for cancer will be discovered.

It is said that carrots help you see in the dark.

6. Rewrite the sentences in 5 with a subject + passive construction, where possible.

Carrots are said to help you see in the dark.

7. Rewrite the main idea of these sentences in reported speech, using one of these reporting verbs.

admit   beg   complain   promise   suggest   threaten

1. "Go away, or I'll call the police," he said.
2. "Why don't you go home early?" she said.
3. "Oh, Jane, please come with me," he said.
4. "I'll be there on time, I really will," she said.
5. "You never buy me flowers," he said.
6. "Well yes, I guess I have been pretty thoughtless," she said.

SOUNDS

1. Homophones are words which sound the same but have different meanings and spellings. Which of the following words are NOT homophones?

1. right   write
2. weather   whether
3. aloud   allowed
4. waist   waste
5. where   were
6. raise   rays
7. team   tame
8. their   there

🔊 Listen and check. As you listen, say the words out loud.

2. Homographs are words which have the same spelling but a different sound. How do you pronounce the words in italics in these sentences?

1. I *read* a newspaper every day.
   I *read* The New York Times yesterday.
2. We *live* in Seattle.
   There's *live* music at the bar tonight.
3. There's a north *wind* today.
   I've got to *wind* up the clock.
4. I like to wear a *bow* tie.
   The Japanese usually *bow* when they greet each other.

🔊 Listen and check. As you listen, say the sentences out loud. You may need to keep a special record of homophones and homographs.

SPEAKING

1. Work in groups of three or four. Imagine you're going to live in a foreign country for a long period of time. Decide:

– which country you're going to.
– how long you'll be staying there.
– what you'll take with you.
– what you'll do there.
– what you'll enjoy most.
– what you'll find most difficult.

2. Work with someone from another group, and make notes about what their group decided. Tell them what your group decided. Try to use reported speech and reporting verbs.

3. Write a brief description of what your partner in 2 told you about his or her group.

Communication Activities

1 *Lesson 6*

Functions, activity 4

Student A: Criticize the following behavior and habits and listen to Student B's response. If Student B disagrees, add another criticism to justify your viewpoint. Use the expressions in the functions box.

1. Pete spends all his time reading detective novels. He never talks to people at home because he's always reading. He never goes out and has very few friends.

2. Linda starts work at seven o'clock in the morning. She usually finishes at around eight o'clock at night. Sometimes she doesn't come home until ten o'clock. She often brings work home and works at the weekends as well.

3. Joan never throws anything away. Her kitchen is full of old newspapers, empty bottles, plastic containers, and old grocery sacks. Joan says they will come in handy one day.

Now listen to Student B criticizing someone. If you think the person's behavior is unreasonable, agree with Student B. If not, disagree and justify your viewpoint.

Use the expressions in the functions box.

Now turn back to page 13.

2 *Fluency 3*

Functions, activity 2

Student A: Take turns making and responding to compliments. Use the expressions in the functions box. Make compliments on:

– how well Student B speaks English.

– Student B's clothes

– Student B's handwriting

Now turn back to page 58.

3 *Lesson 23*

Reading and Listening, activity 1

Add up your scores using the following table. Then look at the profiles below.

1.	a. 2	b. 1	c. 3	
2.	a. 2	b. 2	c. 1	
3.	a. 3	b. 2	c. 1	d. 0
4.	a. 1	b. 2	c. 3	
5.	a. 2	b. 2		
6.	a. 0	b. 2		
7.	a. 1	b. 2		
8.	a. 3	b. 2	c. 1	
9.	a. 0	b. 1	c. 2	d. 3
10.	a 2	b. 3	c. 1	d. 3
11.	a. 1	b. 1	c. 1	d. 0 e. 0
12.	a. 0	b. 3		

25 – 30 points

You are a true gourmet. You are adventurous in your eating habits and not afraid to try something new. You appreciate good food and if you opened your own restaurant you would probably be successful.

15 – 25 points

You are quite conservative in your eating habits, but you know what you like and you enjoy your food. If you tried eating a few different things, you might be pleasantly surprised.

0 – 15 points

You don't mind very much what you eat as long as there is plenty of it. However, you feel safest with foods you know. Why not try something different for a change? If you try something new, you may find that you like it.

Now turn back to page 54.

4 *Lesson 34*

Listening and Speaking, activity 2

Student A: 🔲 Listen to Jorge talking about his shopping habits.

Make notes about what he says.
Turn back to page 85 and fill in the chart as you listen.

5 *Lesson 9*

Speaking and Writing, activity 1

Student A: Read this biography of Lisa St. Aubin de Terán. There is some information missing. Ask Student B questions to find the missing information and fill in the gaps.

Lisa St. Aubin de Terán was born in (1) _____ in 1953. She left school at the age of sixteen and got married to a Venezuelan. They traveled in Italy for (3) _____ and then returned to his family home in the Andes. During her seven years in South America she managed her husband's sugar plantation, and she based her first novel, *Keepers of the House* (1983), on this experience. During this period she had a daughter. She is the author of (5) _____ novels, and has also written a volume of poetry, a collection of short stories, and a book of memoirs. She left Venezuela and returned to live in England with her daughter. She then married her second husband in (7) _____, bought a house in Italy and lived there for three years. She returned from Italy in 1993 to live in (9) _____ again. She's now working on her next novel.

Now turn back to page 23.

6 *Lesson 18*

Listening, activity 3

Student A: 🔲 Listen to Ben Philips talking about his experiences teaching in the Sudan.
Make notes about what he says about:

– school subjects
– the classroom
– length of classes
– amusing incidents

Now turn back to page 44.

7 *Lesson 30*

Reading and Writing, activity 5

Student A: Dictate these sentences to Student B. Write down the sentences Student B dictates.

1. A woman was doing her Christmas shopping and after buying the last present she went to have a cup of coffee in a department store café.

2. _____
   _____
   _____
   _____

3. She told the department store security what had happened, but she didn't really expect to see her possessions again.

4. _____
   _____
   _____
   _____

5. She was delighted by the news and hurried to the store.

6. _____
   _____
   _____
   _____

7. The disappointed shopper went home and as she opened her front door, she suddenly realized that it was the thief who had spoken to her on the phone.

8. _____
   _____
   _____
   _____

Now turn back to page 73.

Lesson 4

8 **Listening, activity 2**

Student A: 🔲 Listen to Mrs. Davies and Pete talking about social customs.

Find out:

– what Mrs. Davies thinks about children's behavior in the past.
– what Pete says about family decision-making today.
– what Mrs. Davies thinks about manners today.

Now turn back to page 9.

9 *Lesson 34*

Listening and Speaking, activity 2

Student B: 📼 Listen to Nanthapa talking about her shopping habits.

Make notes about what she says.
Turn back to page 85 and fill in the chart as you listen.

10 *Progress Check 1–8*

Sounds, activity 4

Rewrite the story using the key words on your piece of paper to help you.

Now turn back to page 21.

11 *Lesson 20*

Reading and Writing, activity 3

Write a letter to a newspaper giving your opinion about the judgment. Here are some arguments for and against the judgment.
In favor of the judgment: Phillips was unarmed; Lewis committed a crime by shooting at Phillips; if you can shoot burglars, you can shoot anyone, even young boys stealing from an apple tree.

Against the judgment: Lewis acted in self-defense; he is an elderly man, who may have been very frightened; people who are injured while they are committing crimes deserve all they get; the law treats criminals too leniently.

Now turn back to page 49.

Lesson 30

12 **Reading and Writing, activity 3**

...the reason he had raised his clipboard was to take a pen from the sideclip.

Now turn back to page 72.

13 *Lesson 37*

Reading, activity 4

Student A: Read the following tall tale about Davy Crockett and then retell it to your partner.

It is said that Davy Crockett, king of the wild frontier, found himself suffering with a mighty toothache one fall morning as he was out hunting with his rifle, Betsy. Well that tooth just kept bothering him till he thought he could stand it no longer. It is believed that just then Davy heard a great roaring behind him like a huge clap of thunder. Feeling mean and ornery as thunder himself, he decided to investigate. The sound was coming from inside a big old hollow tree, so Davy climbed up that tree like a squirrel and then he fell in head first! He landed on a huge, soft smelly old she-bear who must have roared that roar moments before to clean out her snoring tubes! Well Davy wasn't going to stay stuck down in that tree with that bear all winter, so he pulled out his knife and gave her a little poke. It is said that the she-bear was ready to eat him alive when she got woken up—till she saw that Davy Crockett was the one poking her. Then she turned tail and headed up and out of that tree as fast as she could. Well, that was fine by Davy who grabbed on with both hands and bit down on that bear's tail with his teeth. That bear got them both out of that tree and didn't stop running till she got to Texas. It is said that Davy let go long before Texas, of course. But that bite he'd taken out of that bear's tail completely cured his toothache and he went about telling everybody about the new cure. In fact, down in Tennessee it is still claimed that a bite of a bear's tail is the very best cure for toothache.

Now turn back to page 91.

14 *Fluency 3*

Functions, activity 6

Student A: Act out the following dialogues with Student B.

1. You've invited Student B for dinner. Offer him or her a drink and then invite him or her to come to the table. Offer him or her something to eat.

2. You're visiting Student B. Accept something to drink, and agree to go into the backyard, but you don't want to sit in the sun. Make a compliment about how the backyard looks.

Now turn back to page 59.

15 *Lesson 9*

Speaking and Writing, activity 1

Student B: Read this biography of Lisa St. Aubin de Terán. There is some information missing. Ask Student A questions to find the missing information and fill in the gaps.

Lisa St. Aubin de Terán was born in London in (2) _____. She left school at the age of sixteen and got married to a Venezuelan. They traveled in Italy for two years and then returned to his family home in the Andes. During her (4) _____ years in South America she managed her husband's sugar plantation, and she based her first novel, *Keepers of the House* (1983), on this experience. During this period she had a daughter. She is the author of seven novels, and has written a volume of poetry, a (6) _____, and a book of memoirs. She left Venezuela and returned to live in England with her daughter. She then married her second husband in 1990, bought a house in (8) _____ and lived there for three years. She returned from Italy in 1993 to live in England again. She's now working on (10) _____.

Now turn back to page 23.

16 *Lesson 18*

Listening, activity 3

Student B: 🔲 Listen to Ben Philips talking about his experiences teaching in the Sudan.
Makes notes on what he says about:
– students
– equipment
– exams
– embarrassing incidents

Now turn back to page 44.

17 *Lesson 30*

Reading and Writing, activity 5

Student B: Write down the sentences Student A dictates to you. Dictate these sentences to Student A.

1. _____
   _____
   _____
   _____

2. Minutes later, she suddenly realized that someone had taken her bag, with her purse, check book, front door keys, everything.

3. _____
   _____
   _____
   _____

4. So she was pleased when the department store called her later that day and told her they had found her bag and she could pick it up right away.

5. _____
   _____
   _____
   _____

6. But no one there knew what the woman was talking about.

7. _____
   _____
   _____
   _____

8. While she was out, he had burglarized her house and had taken everything.

Now turn back to page 73.

18 *Lesson 32*

Vocabulary and Listening, activity 4

Student B: 🔲 Listen and find the answers to these questions.
– When did Steve first hear Mahler's ninth symphony?
– What does Jessica like about "I'm Still Alive"?
– How many times has Jessica read her favorite book?
– Does Steve read a lot?

Now turn back to page 77.

19 *Lesson 37*

Reading, activity 4

Student B: Read the following tall tale about Davy Crockett and then retell it to your partner.

It is believed that one cold January morning Davy Crockett saved the earth from certain destruction. It is reported to have happened like this: One winter's night it got so cold in Tennessee that the sun couldn't rise in the morning. When Davy noticed that the sun was not rising on time, he decided to light his pipe and go and investigate. He tried to strike a little fire by slamming his fists together as he usually did, but found the fire froze faster than he could collect it. So he ran out towards where the sun should have already appeared. It is thought that he ran a hundred miles to the top of Sunrise Hill before he figured out what the matter was. It seems that it had gotten so cold that the earth had actually frozen on its axis and the sun had frozen between two pieces of ice. So, it is alleged, Davy took some hot bear oil that he always kept in his pocket for emergencies and reached up and poured it all over the sun. Then he gave those pieces of ice a couple of kicks till he'd kicked the sun loose. The sun woke up and smiled bright, warm light down on Davy, who lit his pipe with a ray of sunshine. It is well known that he carried a piece of sunshine around in his pocket for years after that.

Now turn back to page 91.

20

Lesson 6

Functions, activity 4

Student B: Listen to Student A criticizing someone. If you think the person's behavior is unreasonable, agree with Student A. If not, disagree and justify your viewpoint.

Use the expressions in the functions box.

Now criticize the following behavior and habits and listen to Student A's response. If Student A disagrees, add another criticism to justify your viewpoint.

1. When Martin gets the check in a restaurant, he always demands a menu and then goes through the check item by item with a pocket calculator. If there is anything wrong, he questions the waiter in a loud voice. His friends find this very embarrassing.

2. Bill is obsessively neat and spends his time cleaning, vacuuming, and doing the dishes. As soon as you put down your coffee cup, he takes it to the kitchen to wash it. His friends feel very uncomfortable in his home and would like him to be more relaxed.

3. Anna keeps rabbits. She has about fifty of them. Some live in the house and some in the backyard. The neighbors are often angry because the rabbits in the backyard escape and eat all the vegetables in their gardens. Anna has plans to buy at least twenty more rabbits.

Now turn back to page 13.

21 *Lesson 32*

Vocabulary and Listening, activity 4

Student A: 🔊 Listen and find the answers to these questions.

– Why doesn't Jessica like classical music?
– What does Steve think of Pearl Jam's music?
– Has Steve seen the movie of "The Remains of the Day"?
– Has Jessica read "The Chosen"?

Now turn back to page 77.

22 *Lesson 4*

Listening, activity 2

Student C: 🔊 Listen to Mrs. Davies and Pete talking about social customs.

Find out:

– who was served first at meals in Mrs. Davies's household.
– at what age Pete thinks people should get married.
– what Mrs. Davies says about where young people lived before they got married.

Now turn back to page 9.

23 *Lesson 22*

Speaking and Listening, activity 6

All the inventions were real, with patents applied for.

Now turn back to page 52.

24 *Fluency 3*

Functions, activity 2

Student B: Take turns making and responding to compliments. Use the expressions in the functions box. Make compliments on:

– how good Student A's pronunciation is.

– Student A's shoes.

– Student A's handwriting

Now turn back to page 58.

25 *Lesson 4*

Listening, activity 2

Student B: 🔲 Listen to Mrs. Davies and Pete talking about social customs.

Find out:

– what Pete thinks about discipline today.

– at what age girls got married when Mrs. Davies was young.

– what Pete thinks about relations between friends and neighbors today.

Now turn back to page 9.

26 *Fluency 3*

Functions, activity 6

Student B: Act out the following dialogues with Student A.

1. You've been invited by Student A for dinner. Accept a drink, and ask if you can wash your hands before you sit down. Admire the view from the dining room. Accept something to eat.

2. Student A has come over to see you. Offer him or her something to drink and invite him or her to come into the backyard, and sit down. Ask him or her to sit by the swimming pool.

Now turn back to page 59.

27 *Fluency 4*

Listening and Speaking, activity 4

Student A: 🔲 Listen again and make notes on what the speaker said about:

– business hours

– social life at work

– office layout

Now turn back to page 78.

28 *Fluency 4*

Listening and Speaking, activity 4

Student B: 🔲 Listen again and make notes on what the speaker said about:

– giving gifts

– greeting colleagues

– retirement age

Now turn back to page 78.

Grammar Review

CONTENTS

Present simple

Use

You use the present simple:

- to talk about a general truth, such as a fact or a state. (See Lesson 5.)
  Soccer games attract both the rich and poor of Mexican society.

- to talk about something that is regular, such as routines, customs, and habits.
  At noon on Sundays, thousands of Mexicans go to watch soccer games.

- to talk about events in a story or a commentary on a game.
  ... after 10 minutes, Las Chivas scores a beautifully simple goal.

- to criticize behavior with *just.*
  He just watches movies all day.

Present continuous

Use

You use the present continuous:

- to talk about an action which is happening at the moment or an action or state which is temporary. (See Lesson 5.)
  Today, Club America is playing at home against Las Chivas.
  I am living in Seoul at the moment.

- to give background information.
  Before kickoff, the Las Chivas fans are shouting at the Club America fans.
  As we walk into the stadium, the band is playing and the crowd is cheering.

- to criticize behavior with *always.*
  He's always watching football on television.

You don't usually use these verbs in the continuous form.
believe feel hate hear know like love smell sound taste understand want

Past simple

Use

You use the past simple:

- to talk about a past action or event that is finished. (See Lesson 11.)
  I went to Chicago yesterday.

Pronunciation of past simple endings

/t/ *finished   liked   walked*
/d/ *continued   lived   stayed*
/ɪd/ *decided   started   visited*

Future simple *(will)*

Use
You use the future simple:

- to talk about decisions you make at the moment of speaking. (See Lesson 8.)
  I'll give you the money right now.

- to make an offer. (See Lesson 8.)
  I'll get the tickets.

- to make a prediction about the future. (See Lesson 8.)
  We'll have a great time together.

- to make a promise, threat, or give a warning. (See Lesson 8.)
  If you won't be quiet, I'll call the waiter.

- to make a request. (See Lesson 8.)
  Will you ask them to be quiet?

- to make an invitation. (See Lesson 8.)
  Will/Won't you join us?

- to refuse something. (See Lesson 8.)
  No, I won't be quiet.

Remember that you can also use the future simple:

- to talk about things you are not sure will happen with *perhaps* and *It's possible/probable that…* (See Lesson 8.)
  It's possible that I'll be late tomorrow.

Present perfect simple

Form
You form the present perfect with *has/have* + past participle. You use the contracted form in spoken and informal written English.

Past participles

All regular and some irregular verbs have past participles which are the same as their past simple form.
Regular: *move – moved,   finish – finished,   visit – visited*
Irregular: *leave – left,   find – found,   buy – bought*

Some irregular verbs have past participles which are not the same as the past simple form.

go – went – gone	*be – was/were – been*
drink – drank – drunk	*ring – rang – rung*

Been and *gone*

He's been to the United States. (= He's been there and he's back here now.)
He's gone to the United States. (= He's still there.)

Use
You use the present perfect simple:

- to talk about an action which happened at some time in the past. We are not interested in when the action took place, but in the experience. You often use *ever* in questions and *never* in negative statements. (See Lesson 10.)
  I have made other great railway journeys.
  (At some time in my life, we don't know when.)
  Have you ever been to Brazil?
  I've never been to Brazil.

  Remember that if you ask for and give more information about these experiences, actions, or states, such as *when, how, why,* and *how long,* you use the past simple.
  When did you travel to Brazil?   Three years ago.

- when the action is finished, to say what has been completed in a period of time, often in reply to *how much/many.* (See Lesson 10.)
  Lisa has written several novels.

- to talk about a past action which has a result in the present, such as a change. You often use *just.*
  I have just arrived in Brazil.

You can use:

- *already* with the present perfect to suggest *by now* or *sooner than expected.* It's often used for emphasis and goes at the end of the clause.
  Should I pick up the tickets?
  No, I've picked them up already.

  You can put *already* between the auxiliary and the past participle.
  I've already picked up the tickets.

- *yet* with the present perfect in questions and negatives. You use it to talk about an action which is expected. (See Lesson 10.)
  Have you booked your flight yet?
  No, I haven't booked my flight yet.

  You usually put *yet* at the end of the sentence.

  Note: In American English, the past simple is often used instead of the present perfect with *yet* and *already.*

  Did you pick up the tickets yet?
  I already picked them up.

- *still* to emphasize an action which is continuing.
  I'm still waiting to hear from the travel agent.

  You usually put *still* before the main verb, but after *be* or an auxiliary verb. In negatives it goes before the auxiliary.
  He still goes to college.   *He is still in college.*
  He still hasn't gone to college.

Present perfect continuous

Form
You form the present perfect continuous tense with *has/have been + -ing.* You usually use the contracted form in spoken and informal English.

Use
You use the present perfect continuous:

- to talk about an action which began in the past, continues up to the present, may or may not continue into the future, and to say how long something has been in progress. You use it to talk about how long something has been happening. (See Lesson 10.)
  I have been waiting for the train for two hours.

  You use *since* to say when the action or event began.
  I've been living in Brazil since 1990.

- to talk about actions and events which have been in progress up to the recent past that show the present results of past activity. (See Lesson 10.)
  What's Mary been doing?
  She's been washing her car.
  (The car is now clean. She may be wet.)

  We can sometimes use the present perfect simple or continuous with little difference in meaning. However, as with all continuous tenses, the speaker is usually focusing on activity in progress when using the continuous form.

Past continuous

Form
You form the past continuous with *was/were +* present participle. You use the contracted form in spoken and informal written English.

Use
You use the past continuous:

- to talk about something that was in progress at a specific time in the past. (See Lesson 11.)
  I was working at the hospital three years ago.

- to talk about something that was in progress at a specific time in the past, or when something else happened. You join the parts of the sentence with *when* and *while.*
  The doctor was driving in the hospital grounds when he met Nurse Coxall.

  The verb in the *while* clause is usually in the past continuous.
  While the doctor was driving in the hospital grounds, he met Nurse Coxall.

- to talk about an activity that was in progress when interrupted by something else.
  The nurse was talking to the doctor when I knocked on the door.

  Remember that you use *when* + past simple to describe two things which happened one after the other.
  I called my mother when I heard the good news.

You don't usually use these verbs in the continuous form.
believe feel hear know like see smell sound taste think understand want

Future in the past

You can use *was/were going to* + infinitive to talk about something that was planned or promised for the future at some point in the past. To express this idea, we use similar structures to the ones we normally use to talk about the future, but we change the verb forms. Instead of *am/is/are going to,* we use *was/were going to.* It is usually used when the plans or promises didn't happen. (See Lesson 36.)
You were going to change the world, but you didn't.

Past perfect simple

Form
You form the past perfect with *had* + past participle. You use the contracted form in spoken and informal written English. (See Lesson 11.)

Use
You use the past perfect simple:

- to talk about an action in the past which happened before another action in the past. The second action is often in the past simple. (See Lesson 10.)
  Although we arrived on time, the doctor had already left.

- in reported speech or thoughts after verbs like *said, told, asked, thought.* (See Lesson 40.)
  "These products have been highly recommended."
  He told me that these products had been highly recommended.

- with *when*, *after*, *because*, and *until* for the first of two actions.
  After they had promoted the product, the sales rose steadily.

  You can use two past simple tenses if you think the sequence of actions is clear.
  After they promoted the product, the sales rose steadily.

Past perfect continuous

Form
You form the past perfect continuous with *had been* + present participle. You use the contracted form in spoken and informal written English. (See Lesson 11.)

Use
You use the past perfect continuous:

- when you want to focus on an earlier past action which was in progress up to or near a time in the past rather than the completed event.
  You often use it with *for* and *since*.
  Nurse Coxall had been running Ward 4 for many years.
  I had been working at the hospital since I graduated.

Future continuous

Form
You form the future continuous with *will be* + present participle. You use the contracted form in spoken and informal written English. (See Lesson 35.)

Use
You use the future continuous:

- to talk about something which will be in progress at a particular time in the future.
  Scientists say we will be living in a warmer world in the next century.

- to talk about something which is already planned or is part of a routine.
  We will be having another exam next week.

- to ask politely about someone's plans.
  Will you be staying for the next few days?

Future perfect

Form
You form the future perfect with *will have* + past participle. You use the contracted form in spoken and informal written English.

Use
You use the future perfect:

- to talk about something which will be finished by a specific time in the future. (See Lesson 35.)
  By the year 2000, the proportion of older people will have increased dramatically.

Questions

Asking questions

You form questions in the following ways:

- without a question word and with an auxiliary verb. The word order is auxiliary + subject + verb. (See Lesson 1.)
  Have you ever studied another foreign language?

- when a verb has no auxiliary, you use the auxiliary *do* in the question, followed by an infinitive without *to*.
  Do you write down every new word you come across?

You don't use *do* in questions with modal verbs or the verb *be*.
Can you guess what a word means from the context?
Are you looking forward to working in groups?

You can use *who*, *what*, or *where* and other question words to ask about the object of the sentence.
What did you study last year?
I studied English. (= *English* is the object of the sentence.)

You can use *who*, *what*, or *where* and other question words to ask about the subject of the sentence. You don't use *do* or *did*.
What helps you the most, your textbook or your dictionary?
My dictionary helps me the most. (= *My dictionary* is the subject.)

You can form more indirect, polite questions with one of the following question phrases.
Would you mind helping me with this activity?
Could you pass me my dictionary?
I wonder if you could tell me what these words mean?

Negative questions

You often use negative questions when you expect the answer *yes*. For this reason, they are often used in invitations and exclamations. (See Lesson 2.)
Won't you stay a little longer?
Aren't you worried about the cost?
You can also use negative questions to express the idea of criticism.
Hasn't Mary contacted you yet?
Aren't you supposed to be working today?

Imperative questions

You use imperative questions to give an order or to encourage someone to do something. (See Lesson 2.)
Take out the garbage, will you?
Give me a hand with this couch, will you?

Reply questions

You often reply to a statement by making a short question, containing just the auxiliary verb and the personal pronoun. Reply questions do not ask for information. They express interest, contrast, or surprise, depending upon the intonation. (See Lesson 2.)
It takes three hours by train.   Does it? I didn't know that.

Tag questions

Tag questions turn a statement into a question. (See Lesson 2.)

Tags after affirmative statements

If the statement is affirmative, you use a negative tag.
You speak Chinese, don't you?
It is usual to give short answers to tag questions.
You speak Chinese, don't you? Yes, I do./No, I don't.

Tags after negative statements

If the statement is negative, you use an affirmative tag.
You haven't forgotten that too, have you?
Yes. (= Yes, I have forgotten it.)
No.(= No, I haven't forgotten it.)

To ask a real question, the intonation rises on the tag. To show you expect agreement, the intonation falls on the tag. You often use tag questions to show friendliness or to make conversation.

Verbs patterns

Verbs of sensation

See, hear, feel, watch, listen to, and *notice* are verbs of sensation.
You can use an object + *-ing* when you only feel, see, or hear part of an action and the action continues over a period of time. (See Lesson 16.)
I heard a child crying.
I felt someone squeezing my hand.

You can use an object + infinitive without *to* when you feel, see, or hear the whole action and the action is now finished.
I felt someone grasp my hand.
I saw someone enter the bathroom.

Remember + noun/*-ing*

You can use *remember* + noun/*-ing* to talk about a memory. (See Lesson 9.)
I remember meeting you last year.
Do you remember the first time we met?

When the subject of the memory is different from the subject of the sentence, you put a noun or a pronoun between *remember* and the *-ing* form.
I remember my mother reading bedtime stories every night.
I remember her reading bedtime stories every night.

Noun/adjective + *to* + infinitive

You can use *to* + infinitive after certain nouns and pronouns, usually to describe purpose. (See Lesson 22.)
Where are the keys to lock this door?

You can use *to* + infinitive after these adjectives.
pleased disappointed surprised difficult easy

I was surprised to see Mary at the party.
It's difficult to concentrate when there is a lot of noise.

You can use *of* (someone) + *to* + infinitive after these adjectives.
nice kind silly careless good wrong clever stupid generous

It was stupid of Pete to forget the tickets.
It was generous of the company to give us a bonus.

You can use *for* + object + *to* + infinitive after these adjectives.
easy common important essential (un)usual (un)necessary normal rare

It's rare for men to wear a hat these days.

You can use *for* + *-ing* to describe what something is used for.
It's a thing for brushing your hair.
It's a device for shaving.

Clauses of purpose

You use *to/in order to* to describe the purpose of an action when the subject of the main clause and the purpose clause are the same. They can be followed by a present tense with a future meaning. (See Lesson 21.)
I'll get up early tomorrow to miss the traffic.

In order to makes a clause of purpose sound more formal.
We'll write to our attorney in order to confirm the arrangements.

In negative sentences, you have to say *in order not to*.
In order not to disrupt the conference, I left without saying goodbye.
I'm going to leave now in order not to miss the bus.

You use *so (that)*:

● when the subject of the main clause and the purpose clause are different.
I'll give you my address so that you can send me a postcard.

● when the purpose is negative.
I'll give you my address so that you don't get lost.

● with *can* and *could*.
We arrived at the airport early, so that the children could watch the planes.

Modal verbs

The following verbs are modal verbs.
can could may might must should will would

Form
Modal verbs:

● have the same form for all persons.
I may see you tomorrow.
She could call you next week.

● don't take the auxiliary *do* in questions and negatives.
Can you give him the tickets?
You must not smoke in the library.

● take an infinitive without *to*.
I'll come as soon as I can.
I should phone her tonight.

Use
You use *must*:

● to talk about something you are obliged to do. The obligation usually comes from the speaker and can express a moral obligation. (See Lesson 19.)
You must call me as soon as you arrive.

You often use it for strong advice or safety instructions. (See Lesson 19.)

You must fasten your seatbelt.

Have to has more or less the same meaning as *must* but the obligation usually comes from someone else. You often use it to talk about rules. (See Lesson 19.)
I have to work from 9:00 A.M. until 5:00 P.M. every day.
You have to drive on the right in the United States.

You can often use *have got to* instead of *have to*. (See Lesson 19.)
I've got to work from 8:30 A.M. to 5:00 P.M. this week.

But you use *have to* for things which happen regularly, especially with an adverb or adverbial phrases of frequency.
We have to buy a car license every year.

You use *can't* and *must not*:

● to talk about what is not possible to do or what you're not allowed to do. (See Lesson 19.)
You can't learn English in six weeks.
You must not smoke in the classroom.

You can only use *must*, *must not*, and *have got to* to talk about the present and future. Here is how you talk about obligation in the past.

Present	must	have to	have got to	must not
Past	had to	had to	had to	couldn't or wasn't/weren't allowed to

You use *must have*:

● to talk about something that probably or certainly happened in the past. (See Lesson 38.)
I don't have my keys. I must have left them at home.

You use *can't have*:

● to talk about something which probably or certainly didn't happen in the past.
I can't have left my keys at home, because I know I put them in my pocket.

You use *should* and *shouldn't*:

● to say what is right or wrong or express the opinion of the speaker. (See Lesson 20.)
I don't think the government should increase taxes.

● to give less strong advice.
You don't look well, you should stay in bed.

You use *should have* and *shouldn't have*:

● to describe actions in the past which were wrong. (See Lesson 30.)
He should have stayed in bed, but he didn't.
He shouldn't have gotten up, but he did.

● to express regret or criticism about actions in the past. (See Lesson 30.)
I should have called the store to check that the call was genuine.
I shouldn't have left the house.

Ought to have/ought not to have has a similar meaning to *should have/shouldn't have* to express criticism.

You use *may have* or *might have*:

● to talk about something which possibly happened in the past. (See Lesson 38.)
John wasn't at work yesterday. He might have been sick, or he may have been on vacation.

Don't need to/didn't need to

You use *don't need to* + infinitive to say either what isn't necessary to do or what you don't have to do. (See Lesson 20.)
You don't need to/needn't carry identification, but it's a good idea. (= It isn't necessary to carry identification.)

You use *didn't need to* + infinitive to say that something was unnecessary. We don't know if the person did it or not.
He didn't need to phone the police. (= It wasn't necessary to phone the police, we don't know if he did or not.)

Zero conditional

Form
You form the zero conditional with *if/whenever* + present simple, followed by present simple or imperative. *If* means the same as *whenever.* (See Lesson 23.)

Use
You use a zero conditional to talk about general truths, habits, or routines.
If you heat ice, it melts.
Whenever I go to the gym, I always have a shower.

You separate the two clauses with a comma.
The *if* clause can go at the beginning or end of the sentence.

First conditional

Form
You form the first conditional with *if* + present simple or present continuous, followed by *will* + infinitive. (See Lesson 23.)
If I go to the post office, I'll mail the letter for you.
If I'm driving by the post office, I'll mail the letter for you.

Use
You use the first conditional to talk about a likely situation and to describe its result. You talk about the likely situation with *if* + present simple. You describe the result with *will* or *won't.*
If I'm working late tonight, I'll go out and buy a sandwich.

When the *if* clause is at the end of the sentence, no comma is necessary.
I'll mail the letter for you if I go to the post office.
You often use the contracted form in speech and informal writing. The *if* clause can go at the beginning or end of the sentence.

Second conditional

Form
You form the second conditional with *if* + past simple or past continuous, followed by *would* + infinitive. (See Lesson 23.)
If I knew her name, I'd tell you.

Use
You use the second conditional:

● to talk about an unlikely or imaginary situation and to describe its result. You talk about the imaginary or unlikely situation with *if* + past simple. You describe the result with *would/wouldn't.* (See Lesson 23.)
If I won a lot of money, I'd travel around the world.

● to give advice.
If I were you, I'd see a doctor.

You often use the contracted form in speech and informal writing. The *if* clause can go at the beginning or end of the sentence. When the *if* clause is at the end, no comma is necessary.
I'd see a doctor if I were you.

Third conditional

Form
You form the third conditional with *if* + past perfect, followed by *would have* + past participle. (See Lesson 23.)
If Pete had seen me at the party, he would have spoken to me.

Use

You use the third conditional to talk about an imaginary or unlikely situation in the past and to describe its result. You talk about the imaginary or unlikely situation with *if* + past perfect. You describe the result with *would have/ wouldn't have*. (See Lesson 15.)
I wouldn't have met Pete if I hadn't gone to the party.
You can use *may have, might have,* or *could have* if the result is not certain.
If he had pulled out his knife, I could have been injured.

You often use the contracted form in speech and informal writing. The *if* clause can go at the beginning or end of the sentence. When the *if* clause is at the end, no comma is necessary.

If and *when*

You use *if* in zero and first conditional sentences for actions and events which are not certain to happen.
If a waiter suggests water, I ask for bottled.
If I go out tonight, I'll have dinner early.

You use *when* in zero and first conditional sentences for actions and events which are certain to happen.
When I drive to work, I always listen to the radio.
When we go out tonight, we'll have dinner in a nice restaurant.

Unless, even if, as long as/provided (that), or/otherwise

You can use *unless, even if, as long as/provided (that)* with zero and first conditional sentences to talk about likely situations and their results.

You can use *unless* to mean *if ... not.* (See Lesson 24.)
It is dangerous to swim in the sea, unless you are a good swimmer.
(= It is dangerous to swim in the sea, if you're not a good swimmer.)

You use *even if* to emphasize *if* or to express a contrast or to give some surprising information. Compare:
If they offer me the job, I won't accept it.
Even if they offer me the job, I won't accept it.

You use *as long as* and *provided (that)* to mean *on condition that.*
I'm sure you'll get the job as long as you prepare for the interview.
You can come and stay tomorrow provided (that) you call me first.

You can also use the expressions with second conditional sentences, when you talk about an unlikely situation and its result.

You can follow an instruction/advice with *or* or *otherwise* + clause to describe the result if you don't follow the instruction/advice.
You'd better take your sunscreen on vacation or you might get a sunburn.
Make sure you take an umbrella, otherwise you'll get wet.

Phrasal verbs

Phrasal verbs are verbs with a particle. They cannot necessarily be understood by knowing what the individual parts mean. Sometimes the meaning is obvious because the meaning of the verb plus particle can easily be figured out. In other words, the meaning is literal. (See Lesson 32.)
I looked up at the beautiful, blue sky.

Sometimes the meaning is not obvious because the meaning of the verb plus particle cannot be figured out. In other words, it is non-literal.
I looked up the word in my dictionary.

There are four types of phrasal verbs.

Type 1 These do not take an object.
My car has broken down.

Type 2 These take an object. The noun object goes before or after the particle.
It's cold. You'll have to put on your coat.
or *It's cold. You'll have to put your coat on.*
The pronoun object must go before the particle.
You'll have to put it on.

Type 3 These also take an object. The noun and the pronoun object go after the particle.
I drove into the wall.
I drove into it.

Type 4 These have two particles and take an object. The noun and the pronoun object go after the particle.
I get along with my parents.
I get along with them.

It is usual to use phrasal verbs, especially in spoken English. But it's usually possible to replace them with another verb or verbal phrase.
You'll have to put on your coat because the weather is cold.
You'll have to wear your coat because the weather is cold.

Used to and *would* + infinitive

Remember that you use *used to* and *would* + infinitive to talk about past habits and routines which are now finished. You often use it to contrast past routine with present state. (See Lesson 18.)

Every summer we used to go to the coast for our summer vacation. Now we go to the country.
We would meet the same people at the beach every year.

You can also use *used to* to talk about past states, but not *would*.
I used to like ice cream when I was a child.

Be/get used to + noun/-ing

Be used to + noun/-ing has quite a different meaning from *used to* + infinitive. If someone is used to something it means it is no longer strange, but they have become accustomed to it. (See Lesson 18.)
I've lived in New York for three years now, so I am used to the busy traffic.
The weather in the mountains can be dangerous, if you are not used to it.

You can use *get used to* to mean *become used to*. This expresses the idea that something was difficult or unusual before, but is no longer so.
I am getting used to the cold climate in this country.
I've gotten used to the spicy food, although it seemed strange at first.

Describing a sequence of events

Before and after

You can use *before* and *after* + -ing to describe a sequence of two events which both have the same subject. (See Lesson 12.)
After graduating, he moved to London.

You can use *when, as,* and *while* to describe two events which happen at the same time. The second verb is often in the past simple and is used for the event which interrupts the longer action. (See Lesson 12.)
When she was working in hospitals abroad, the terrible conditions made her angry.

Restrictive relative clauses

You can identify people, things, and places with a relative clause beginning with *who, that, which, where,* or *whose*. The information in the restrictive relative clause is important for the sense of the sentence and gives essential information about the subject or object of the sentence.
(See Lesson 27.)

You use *who* or *that* to define people:
– as a subject pronoun.
The man who called me earlier was my husband.
In this sentence *who* refers to the subject = *the man*.

– as an object pronoun.

The most interesting speaker who we met was Dr. Harada.

In this sentence *who* refers to the object = *Dr. Harada*.

You can leave out *who/that* when referring to the object of the relative clause.

You can use a participial clause instead of a relative clause if the noun or pronoun is the subject of the clause. You use a present participle to replace the relative pronoun + a present or past tense in a restrictive relative clause.
The family who lives next door is very friendly.
(= The family living next door is very friendly.)

You use *which* or *that* to identify things:
– as a subject pronoun.
There's a large garage which is attached to the house.
– as an object pronoun.
This is the book which/that we're using in class.

You can leave out *which/that* when it is the object of the relative clause.
This is the book we're using in class.

You use a past participle to replace the relative pronoun + *be* in passive sentences in a defining relative clause.
Any house (which is) situated on the beach is in danger from storms.

You use *where* to define places.
The house where my parents live is near the city center.
If you leave out *where*, you have to add a preposition.
The house my parents live in is near the city center.

You use *when* for times. You can usually leave out *when* in a restrictive relative clause.
The time when I get up is usually around 8 o'clock.
The time I get up is usually around 8 o'clock.

Nonrestrictive relative clauses

You use a nonrestrictive relative clause *who, which,* or *where* to give extra information about the subject or object of a sentence. Relative pronouns cannot be left out of nonrestrictive relative clauses. Commas are necessary around nonrestrictive relative clauses when written, and pauses when spoken. (See Lesson 27.)

You use *who* for people.
Barbara Kingsolver, who has written many books, is one of my favorite authors.

You use *which* for things. You cannot use *that* in nonrestrictive relative clauses.
I gave him a glass of water, which he drank immediately.

You can use *which* to refer back to the whole sentence.
My car is at the garage, which means I will take the bus to work.

It is also possible, but not common, to use a participial clause instead of a nonrestrictive relative clause if the noun or pronoun is the subject of the clause.
The people, who were working so hard, are now going to have a relaxing vacation.
(=The people, working so hard, are now going to have a relaxing vacation.)

Participial clauses

Participle clauses are often used in stories to describe background information. They focus on the action by leaving out nouns, pronouns, auxiliary verbs, and conjunctions. This often creates a more dramatic effect. (See Lesson 15.)

Use

You can use a participial clause:

● when two actions happen at the same time. You use it for one of the actions.
I sat in the chair watching television.

● as a "reduced" relative clause.
I used to walk to the bus stop with the elderly gentleman living near us.
(= I used to walk to the bus stop with the elderly gentleman who lived near us.)

● when one action happens immediately after another action. You use it for the first action.
Walking to the chair, he sat down.

● when an action happens in the middle of a longer action. You use it for the longer action.
Thinking this was another guest, I said good evening.

● to say why something happens.
Not wanting to contradict him, I said nothing.

When it is important to show that one action has finished before another action begins, you use the perfect participle.
Having told my mother the news, I then called my sister.

I wish and *if only*

You can express:

● regret about a present state with *wish* + past simple or past continuous.
I wish she spent more time with me. (See Lesson 6.)
I wish I knew what I was going to do. (See Lesson 30.)

● regret about the past with *wish* + past perfect.
I wish I hadn't acted so badly. (See Lesson 30.)

● a wish with *could* + infinitive.
I wish I could travel more. (See Lesson 30.)

You can use *if only* if the feeling is stronger.
If only it were more exciting. (See Lesson 6.)
If only I had called the store.
(See Lesson 30.)

You can use *I wish ... would* to express a wish about the future if you think the wish is *not likely* to happen.
I wish you would help me wash my car tomorrow.
(= I know you are not going to help me.)

You can use *I hope* + present simple to express a wish about the future if you think the wish *is likely* to happen.
I hope you help me wash my car tomorrow.
(= I think you probably will help me.)

The passive

You form the passive with the different tenses of
be + past participle.
Present simple passive: *Japanese is spoken here.*
Past simple passive: *The man was told to fix the television.*
Present continuous passive: *The house is being painted.*
Past continuous passive: *He was being taken to the hospital.*
Present perfect passive: *The child has been sent home.*
Future passive: *It is an industry which will be encouraged.*
Modal passive: *I might be given a pay raise this year.*

Use

You can use the passive:

● when you do not know who or what does the action. (See Lesson 25.)
The cable TV is connected to our phone.

● when you are not interested in who or what does something. (See Lesson 25.)
All the electrical appliances were shut down.

● when you want to take away the focus of personal responsibility and to give an "official" tone. (See Lesson 25.)
We have been told that the problem will be fixed as soon as possible.

We sometimes begin a passive sentence with the known information and end the sentence with the new information. You can use a passive infinitive as the subject of a sentence for emphasis.
To be contacted by e-mail is not very sociable.
Usually, however, the sentence begins with "it."
It is not very sociable to be contacted by e-mail.

You can use a passive infinitive without *to* after modal verbs.
The Internet should be controlled by the government.

You can use a passive gerund:

● as the subject of a sentence.
Being connected to an e-mail system is very useful.

- as the object of a sentence.
  Most people like being contacted by e-mail.

- with a preposition.
  People are afraid of being controlled by the government.

By and *with*

You use *by* to say who or what is responsible for
an action.
The basement has been flooded by the washing machine.

You use *with* to talk about the instrument which is used to
perform the action.
The lights were turned on with the car phone.

You also use *with* to talk about materials or ingredients.
The bedroom windows are covered with ice.

Passive constructions with *say, believe,* etc.

You can use the following passive constructions with
say, believe, etc. to show that you're not sure of the truth of
the statement or that you want to distance yourself from it.
(See Lesson 37.)
You can use *it* + passive + *that* clause.
It is believed that the government will reduce taxes.

You can use subject + passive + *to* + infinitive when the
belief is referring to an earlier action.
The government is said to have reduced taxes.

You use these constructions in a formal style.
Here are some of the verbs you use them with:
*consider expect know report say understand think
allege claim acknowledge*

The indefinite and definite article

Here are some rules for the use of articles. (See Lesson 4.)

You use *a/an:*

- when you refer to a singular, countable noun when the
  listener/reader does not know exactly who or what is
  being referred to or when you talk about something for
  the first time.
  There's a red car parked outside our house.
  I watched a very good movie last night.

You use *the:*

- with singular and plural nouns when the listener and
  speaker both know who or what is being referred to.
  (See Lesson 4.)
  The red car outside our house belongs to our neighbors.
  Did you like the movie we watched last night?

- if there is only one of something.
  The moon was shining very brightly last night.
  I traveled around the world last year.

- before certain public places.
  I went to the theater with my sister.
  Can you take this letter to the post office?

- before some geographical areas.
  Boston is on the Atlantic Coast.
  I visited the Painted Desert while I was on vacation.
  Have you ever been to the Bahamas?

You don't use any article:

- with plural, abstract, or uncountable nouns when you talk
  about something in general. (See Lesson 4.)
  Teachers are pretty well paid today.
  I used to drink coffee, but now I drink tea.

- before the names of most countries, towns, and streets.
  I lived in Brazil for five years.
  The flight from L.A. to Portland took about three hours.
  We walked up Pike Street toward Westlake Mall.

Countable and uncountable nouns

Countable nouns are the names of things which you can
count. They have both singular and plural forms.
(See Lesson 33.)
This dress is very expensive.
These dresses are very expensive.

Uncountable nouns cannot be counted and always take
singular verbs.
The weather is very good today.
I think tea is a better drink than coffee.

Some nouns can be both countable and uncountable
depending on the way they are used.
I like wine.
Burgundy and claret are wines from California.
The glass in the window is broken.
Can I have a glass of water?

Some countable nouns are seen more as a mass than a
collection of separate elements.
bean(s), spice(s)

Sometimes a word is uncountable in English and countable
in other languages. For example, *information*
is uncountable in English but countable in many
other languages.

Quantity words

You can use the following expressions of quantity:
(See Lesson 34.)

● with countable nouns.
a few   few   many   both (of)   several
neither (of)   a couple (of)
I only have a few dollars in my wallet.
I know several people who like eating fish for breakfast.

● with uncountable nouns.
very little   not much   a little   less   much
a great deal of
I have very little money left in my wallet.
I hope we pay less tax with the next government.

● with both countable and uncountable nouns.
some   any   no   none   hardly any   half   all   a lot of
lots of   (not) enough   more   most
Could you lend me some money?
I'm sorry, but I have hardly any cash in my wallet.

Some is common in affirmative clauses, and *any* is common in questions and negatives. But you use *some* in questions if you expect, or want to encourage, the answer *yes*.
Would you like some more coffee?
You can use *any* when you mean it doesn't matter which.
You can get a loan from any major bank.

Adjectives

When there is more than one adjective, you usually put *opinion* adjectives before *fact* adjectives. (See Lesson 13.)
She was wearing a beautiful, new dress.

You can sometimes use a noun as an adjective before another noun.
car door   cassette box

Nouns used as adjectives do not have a plural form. You put a hyphen between the two parts of the noun clause.
The train journey takes two hours.
It is a two-hour train journey.

You can turn a participle + adverb phrase into a compound adjective. You put a hyphen between the participle and the adverb.
The landscape was whitened with snow.
It was a snow-whitened landscape.

When you want to create a word picture of the way something looks you can use a simile – comparing one thing with another.
The mist drew back like a set of theater curtains.
The river was so far below us it looked like an old shoelace.

Reported speech

Reported statements

You report what people said by using
said (that) + clause.
When you put direct speech into reported speech, you usually change:
– the tense of the verb.
– adverbs of time and place.
– the pronouns, unless the speaker is talking about him/herself.

You don't usually make these changes:
– when the tense of the main reporting verb is in the present tense.
– if the statement is still true at the time of reporting.
– when the direct speech contains a modal verb, such as *may, might, could, should, ought to*. (See Lesson 39.)

Reporting verbs

You can often use a reporting verb to describe the general sense of what someone thinks or says.

Reporting verbs include:
advise   admit   argue   boast   claim   complain   confessed
explain   insist   maintain   offer   point out   promise
recommend   say   suggest   tell   threaten   warn   wonder

There are several patterns for these verbs. (See Lesson 40.)

Pattern	**Verbs**
1. verb + *to* + infinitive	*agree ask decide hope promise refuse* *He decided to go home.*
2. verb + object + *to* + infinitive	*advise ask encourage persuade remind warn* *She persuaded him to take the job.*
3. verb + *(that)* clause	*agree decide explain hope promise suggest warn* *She explained that she had lost her purse.*
4. verb + object + *(that)* clause	*advise tell warn* *He told the man that he was driving too fast.*
5. verb + object	*accept refuse introduce* *She accepted the invitation.*
6. verb + 2 objects	*introduce offer* *She offered her a cup of coffee.*

Tapescripts

Lesson 2 **Sounds and Speaking, activity 2**

PAT You speak French, don't you?

DON Yes. In fact, I speak French and Chinese.

PAT Chinese! You didn't learn Chinese at school, did you?

DON Yes, when I was seventeen. I took Chinese for a couple of years.

PAT You've never visited China, have you?

DON No. In fact I've almost forgotten Chinese. It's easy to forget a language if you don't practice.

PAT And what about your French? You haven't forgotten that, too, have you?

DON No, I practiced when I was in Canada.

PAT I've got an idea. I'd love to go to Montreal, wouldn't you?

DON For the weekend?

PAT Well, why not? It's only a few hours from the border, isn't it?

DON Is it? Yeah, I guess it is. But aren't you worried about the cost?

PAT No, it'll be fun. And you'll have plenty of opportunities to speak French, won't you?

Lesson 2 **Listening, activity 2**

Conversation 1

Q Hello, Hannah.

HANNAH Hi.

Q Um...can you tell us how many languages you speak and what they are?

HANNAH Yes, uh... I speak three languages. English, French, and Japanese.

Q Good, how interesting. How did you learn them?

HANNAH Um... well, I was brought up in Montreal and you had to learn French, um... when you were in school. And Japanese I chose to learn, I thought it would be, you know, useful to learn it.

Q Right. And, um... do you still remember it from school?

HANNAH Well, not really. I've forgotten most of it now because it was really a long time ago. Um ...

Q What was the most difficult thing about learning it?

HANNAH Well, I was very embarrassed when we had to speak Japanese in front of the rest of the class, you know. The terrible pronunciations and things. Also, I think listening, the listening comprehension was very difficult because it was always so fast...

Q Oh, yes. Everyone says that!

HANNAH Yeah. Difficult to keep up, you know.

Q What do you think the most useful thing to do is?

HANNAH Well, I think the grammatical system is the most useful because if you learn about grammar in another language you can relate it to your own native language and I think that's very helpful.

Q Do you mean structure and everything?

HANNAH Yes.

Q Thanks very much.

Conversation 2

Q Mike.

MIKE Hi.

Q How many languages do you speak and, er... what are they?

MIKE Well, I speak English and I speak Spanish.

Q Uh-huh. And how did you learn them?

MIKE Um... I was living in Ecuador. Actually, uh... more my parents ... moved to Ecuador and so I had to learn to speak Spanish or I couldn't speak to anybody.

Q Right. Where did you learn? At school?

MIKE Uh-huh. I went to school and I had to speak Spanish in class, er... but I always spoke English at home.

Q Right. What was the most difficult aspect of learning a foreign language?

MIKE Oh, I suppose getting it perfect. I mean, even now I ... I make mistakes all the time and ... and Spanish-speaking people would laugh at me...

Q Hmm ...

MIKE But they seem to understand what I'm trying to say most of the time.

Q Right. What do you think the best way to learn a language is?

MIKE I think to go to a country that speaks that language and then you have to throw yourself in and learn how to speak it. Um...I think it's probably a lot easier to learn a language when you're young.

Q Yes. I'd agree with that.

MIKE And you are maybe less afraid of making mistakes.

Q Hmm...

Conversation 3

Q Janet.

JANET Hello.

Q Hi. Can you tell us how many languages you speak and, er... which ones they are?

JANET Um... well, I speak English, which is my native language, and Spanish.

Q Oh right. And how did you learn Spanish?

JANET Well, really by listening to cassettes in my car and watching videos at home and then, um... well, I got a weekly magazine for about two years.

Q So you are pretty much self-taught. Was it difficult?

JANET Um... well I've got to say when I meet real live Spanish-speakers I find it pretty difficult, yeah.

Q What did you think the most important aspect would be?

JANET Oh, definitely to have a very good grounding in grammar.

Q Uh-huh.

JANET And also I always used a dictionary if I didn't understand a word, too.

Q Right. Um... did you... how did you feel about the self-study method? Was that the one you used?

JANET Oh gee, well, it fit in with my professional life. It's a very lonely way of doing things, the self-study um... but like I say, it fitted in with my life as a doctor.

Q Oh, right. Thanks very much.

Lesson 3 **Vocabulary and Speaking, activity 2**

JANE You must be Jim Dennis.

JIM Yes, that's right, but call me Jim.

JANE Sure, Jim, good to meet you. Welcome to the company! My name's Jane and I'm going to show you around the office.

JIM Hello, Jane. Thanks a lot.

JANE I'll introduce you to everyone. Let's go and meet your boss. Ah, there she is. Sylvia, this is Jim Dennis, it's his first day. Jim, this is Dr. Sylvia Crewe.

JIM How do you do, doctor.

SYLVIA Call me Sylvia, Jim. Everyone calls me Sylvia. Welcome to the company.

JIM Thank you, Sylvia.

Lesson 4 **Listening, activity 2**

Q Mary.

MRS. DAVIES Yes?

Q I hope you don't mind my calling you Mary.

MRS. DAVIES Well, most people do call me Mrs. Davies ...

Q Oh, of course. A generational difference, you know, the customs have changed so much in the U.S. over the last fifty years, haven't they?

MRS. DAVIES Yes, they certainly have.

Q Do you think children behave very differently now?

MRS. DAVIES From my day, yes, I do, because children in my day were supposed to be seen and not heard. And the discipline, it was very strict. Everyone wanted their children to learn to be disciplined, to work hard, and to respect their elders.

Q I see. And what do you think, Pete, as a member of a younger generation? Do you think children behave very differently now?

PETE Yes, I think they do. Um... there is less discipline now. I mean, sometimes discipline is a problem nowadays, and then you definitely... well, they're definitely not meant to be seen and not heard. They're a vocal part of family life, aren't they? So, things have changed.

Q Hmm. And the whole family structure has changed, hasn't it? Who was the head of the family in your day, Mrs. Davies?

MRS. DAVIES Oh, it was always the father! Um... I mean, he was even served first at dinner, uh... he was the one that made all the big decisions in the family.

Q Ah, yes.

MRS. DAVIES Hmm.

Q And Pete, do you think that's still the same in today's world?

PETE Not to the same extent, no, and I mean in a lot of families, in our family, we all make decisions together. It's not like the father is the lord and master which I think is how he was treated. It's more democratic, I think. It's... it's more equally shared.

Q Hmm. And I guess, Mrs. Davies, that people's ideas about marriage have changed a lot too, haven't they? Did people get married at a different age when you were young?

MRS. DAVIES Um..., well, yes, yes, they did indeed. And certainly the girls felt if they weren't married by the time they were twenty-one or twenty-two they were old maids! Absolutely.

Q Do you know any twenty-one-year-olds who feel like old maids, Pete?

PETE No, not at all. People wait a lot longer now. Maybe because they live longer, I don't know. You've got a longer life so lots of people don't get married until they're in their thirties. But, I guess, some people still get married young. And then get divorced!

Q Uh-huh.

PETE Yeah.

Q That's a big difference.

PETE Mmm.

Q Have manners changed a lot? People address each other differently, don't they?

MRS. DAVIES Oh, yes, certainly. I mean, you'd always call people, you know, Mister and use his last name or Mrs. and use her last name. You wouldn't use their first names, I mean unless it was a family member or a friend. And your neighbors, I mean, no, you wouldn't call them by their first names like you just called me Mary!

Q Sorry about that! How about you, Pete?

PETE Well, nowadays you do use first names, most of the time. But with older people, no. I mean I'd call them Mister or Mrs. something until they said call me Bob, or whatever.

Q And who do you call Sir or Ma'am?

PETE Oh, you know, strangers ...

Q A lawyer or maybe a police officer?

PETE Yeah. But most people you can usually call by their first name.

Q And I suppose families used to live together longer too, didn't they? When you were young, Mrs. Davies, were parents, and grandparents, and children all living together in the same house, or is that a myth?

MRS. DAVIES Yes, yes. No, no, no. Usually, they certainly did. They probably left home when they got married and established a family of their own, but usually they would stay in the same house, yes.

Q Now, Pete, how would you like to live with your grandmother?

PETE No, well, I love to visit my granma, but we... people generally leave home, I mean, when they go to college. That's when I left home. Um... and even women, I mean, there's no... there's no hard and fast rule that women stay at home until they marry now; they usually go and live in an apartment somewhere and leave the family nest.

Q Yes, that's true.

Lesson 6 **Speaking and Listening, activity 2**

DAVE My dad took me to my first game when I was... oh, I can't have been more than about five. And I still support the same team...

JANE Now I go every day before work and sometimes on weekends, too, and it's great. I meet my friends, have a long workout and then a shower and a drink, and I like the feeling I have of, you know, really being in shape.

SARAH I just wanted to go back a little way, like maybe... a hundred years or so, to when my family first immigrated to this country from England. But the more I did it, the more interested I became. Now, I'd like to go back in the family just as far as I possibly can.

TIM Oh, they're wonderful! You get these huge insects or giant vegetables or whatever moving around the town and everyone takes it so seriously. And it doesn't matter that the special effects are lousy, it's nothing like what we can do today—that's part of the charm!

Lesson 6 **Speaking and Listening, activity 3**

DAVE Well my girlfriend says I'm obsessed. She's always complaining that I spend every Saturday either at a game, or watching it on TV. I don't think I'm obsessed. I only watch football about, well, maybe three times a week. Football's great, so exciting. And it's awesome now that they play weekday games and on Sundays too. I've loved football ever since I was a kid; my dad took me to my first game when I was... oh, I can't have been more than about five. And I still support the same team: the Dallas Cowboys. They're the greatest!

JANE I suppose you could say I'm obsessed. It all started about five years ago when I fell off my bicycle and broke my leg. I had to stay in the hospital for ages and I couldn't move and people kept bringing me chocolates and stuff and I got really fat. When finally they let me out of the hospital I still couldn't do much for about six months and I felt just awful. When my leg was better, I started going to the gym to get back into shape. It took months of hard work but it was really worth it and after I got in shape again, well, I just kept going. Now I go every day before work and sometimes on weekends, too, and it's great. I meet my friends, have a long workout and then a shower and a drink, and I like the feeling I have of, you know, really being in shape.

SARAH Well, I've always loved history and visiting old country houses. And then one day I decided to find out about my family history. So I began looking up old records and finding out who my ancestors were and what kind of lives they had. It started about three years ago when my sister had a baby. At first I just wanted to go back a little way, like maybe... a hundred years or so to when my family first immigrated to this country from England. But the more I did it, the more interested I became. Now, I'd like to go back in the family just as far as I possibly can. I'm stuck around the 16th century, but there are some records in a church in Leeds in England that I think might help me. So I'm going there next summer to try to find out more. Some of my family think I'm crazy, but I don't care. I just want to know everything I can and I'm determined to find out as much as possible.

TIM With me it's old B movies. You know those old movies they produced in the fifties to play alongside the big movies. They were always about, you know, like giant ants taking over the world and aliens landing from outer space and causing strange things to happen to people in small-town America. Oh, they're wonderful! You get these huge insects or giant vegetables or whatever moving around the town and everyone takes it so seriously. And it doesn't matter that the special effects are lousy, it's nothing like what we can do today—that's part of the charm. I got hooked on B movies when I was a teenager. Now I collect them on video. They still put them on TV but usually in the middle of the night. My friends can't understand what I see in them, but for me they're just the greatest thing ever. *Revenge of the Killer Potatoes*, that's my favorite.

Lesson 6   Speaking and Listening, activity 6

WOMAN 1 Dave and his football? Oh, it's definitely an obsession. You know he even watches it on TV when he's seen it live—you know when he's actually been to the game! I can't understand it. It's boring. All they do is throw a ball around. I wish he spent more time with me. But no, it's football, football, football with him!

MAN 1 Oh, I couldn't agree more. But, well, you know I worry about Jane. All that exercise! It can't be good for you to do it so often. I mean, she goes to the gym every day! If only she'd do something different too—at least on the weekend! I think you can overdo it if you're not careful.

WOMAN 1 Oh, I disagree. I think she's in really great shape. She looks terrific! I just wish I could be that disciplined.

WOMAN 2 Oh, so do I. But what about Tim! Those movies are such a strange thing to be obsessed with. I mean, they're so old and the acting is so bad! He's always watching them. If only he were interested in something more normal. But Tim thinks they're wonderful.

MAN 2 Yes! He's absolutely right. They *are* the best things on TV.

MAN 1 Well, I try to get involved in Sarah's interests but I just can't get excited about history. I wish it were more exciting. I just can't see the point of digging up the past.

Lesson 7   Vocabulary and Listening, activity 2

Conversation 1

WOMAN Good morning, Museum of Modern Art, may I help you?
MAN Yes, can you tell me what time you open?
WOMAN We open at ten Monday through Saturday and at noon on Sunday.
MAN OK, and what time do you close?
WOMAN We're open until seven every evening, except on Fridays when we stay open until ten.
MAN OK, thank you very much.

Conversation 2

WOMAN Good evening, East Coast Grill.
MAN Hi, yeah, I'd like to make a reservation for tomorrow night.
WOMAN Sure, for how many people?
MAN Six.
WOMAN So, a table for six on Friday June 7th. OK, we can do that. What time do you want it for?
MAN Make it eight o'clock.
WOMAN Eight o'clock. And your name is?
MAN Stein.
WOMAN OK, Mr. Stein, we'll see you tomorrow at eight. Bye.
MAN Thanks, bye.

Conversation 3

WOMAN Good morning, this is Nordstrom's, can I help you?
MAN Yes, could you tell me if you have a travel agency in the store?
WOMAN Yes, sir, we do.
MAN OK, and does it do flight and hotel bookings for Asia?
WOMAN You tell them where you want to go, and they'll get you there, sir.
MAN Good, I'll try and get down there tonight. You're open until nine, aren't you?
WOMAN That's right.
MAN Thanks. Bye.

Conversation 4

WOMAN Hello. Could I speak to the manager, please?
MAN Could I ask what it's about?
WOMAN The music last night went on way too long, and I want to speak to the manager about it.
MAN I'm really sorry that it bothered you, ma'am.
WOMAN I thought the club closed at two.
MAN It usually closes at two, but not last night. And tonight it's going to stay open until four.
WOMAN So it's going to be just the same tonight?
MAN That's right, ma'am.
WOMAN Great! That's great!

Conversation 5

MAN Can I have two tickets for the concert tonight?
WOMAN Yes, sir. Where would you like to sit?
MAN Oh, not too far back.
WOMAN How about in row D?
MAN Sure, that'll be fine.
WOMAN It starts at seven thirty. How would you like to pay?
MAN I'll pay by Visa. Can you tell me what time it finishes tonight?
WOMAN About ten thirty.
MAN OK. My card number is ...

Lesson 7 **Listening and Speaking, activity 1**

GARY Well, I guess we'd better plan an itinerary.

ANGELA I guess so. We really need to impress him.

GARY OK. Um… well I guess we'd better start at breakfast. How about breakfast in Harvard Square?

ANGELA Great. I love that place.

GARY At eight o'clock?

ANGELA Yeah. Eight o'clock's great.

GARY OK. Good. Good. And that should take us what, half an hour or so… then from say eight thirty to eleven we can take him sight-seeing. In Cambridge?

ANGELA Well, why don't we start at nine? I think we should allow a little bit longer for breakfast. You know what it's like.

GARY OK, a relaxed start to the day…

ANGELA Yeah.

GARY …and then we'll just rush through Cambridge. It's just a bunch of universities, anyway. OK…

ANGELA Mmm….

GARY …and then so noon-time we can find ourselves up on Beacon Hill. Maybe have a little stroll around there?

ANGELA Perfect. That sounds great.

GARY OK, yeah. Which should take us right through to my favorite part of the day …

ANGELA Lunch … at the Union Oyster Bar!

GARY The Union Oyster Bar!

ANGELA Yeah, come on.

GARY I've never been there.

ANGELA Oh, it's fantastic. You'll love it.

GARY Are you sure he likes oysters?

ANGELA Oh, I'm sure he will. It really has a wonderful atmosphere.

GARY OK. Oysters at what, say, one o'clock?

ANGELA Perfect!

GARY Excellent. So what, we need another hour for lunch, then we can walk along Commonwealth Avenue.

ANGELA Well, shouldn't we have an hour and a half for lunch, and say start again at two thirty?

GARY Well, I guess so. I don't want him to think we're lazy or anything, though.

ANGELA Well, it's just that I hate pushing things and things always take longer than you think.

GARY And you don't want to go walking on a bellyful of oysters.

ANGELA No, you don't!

GARY OK. Well, that'll take us all the way down to Back Bay, where we can do some shopping, say, around what, three?

ANGELA Oh, that's wonderful!

GARY Yeah?

ANGELA Yeah, no, that sounds great.

GARY That'll take the afternoon. Then in the evening, how about drinks? At … where?

ANGELA The Hyatt Regency.

GARY Good idea.

ANGELA OK. And let's say seven thirty?

GARY Well, let's make it seven.

ANGELA I don't know, I think…

GARY How much shopping?

ANGELA … well I can shop till I drop, so please can we say seven thirty?

GARY OK!

ANGELA OK.

GARY You got it. But then let's not drink for long. I'd say let's go for dinner at … where? Joseph's Aquarium?

ANGELA Yes. That's a great idea.

GARY Eight P.M. I'll reserve a table.

ANGELA Oh, again, I don't know if… um…. I think we should say eight thirty to give us an hour for drinks before dinner.

GARY OK.

ANGELA OK.

GARY Whatever you say.

ANGELA Great.

GARY So then let's finish the evening at, um … Quincy Market.

ANGELA Oh, perfect. That's a really good idea.

GARY At what, ten o'clock?

ANGELA Yes, ten sounds wonderful.

GARY Uh-huh.

ANGELA I think he's really going to be impressed with all that.

GARY Yes. It's a great idea.

Fluency 1 **Listening and Speaking, activity 3**

WOMAN Good morning.

MAN Good morning. What can I do for you?

WOMAN I'd like to pay this bill, please.

MAN Sure.

WOMAN Here you are.

MAN I'll need your signature. Could you sign here, please?

WOMAN There! Is that OK now?

MAN Yes, thank you.

MAN Here's your receipt. Thank you very much, miss. Have a nice day.

WOMAN Thanks. Bye!

MAN Bye. See you later.

Fluency 1 **Listening and Speaking, activity 6**

Q OK, Sharon, now we're talking about what you would say in certain situations, about how you'd respond. So tell me, what do you say when someone opens the door for you?

SHARON Oh, when someone opens the door for me, I actually like that.

Q You like it when they open the door for you…

SHARON I do, especially if I'm carrying packages or something. I, I think that's really sweet, for someone to open the door. I say, "thank you."

Q OK, so that's how you respond, you say "thank you" when somebody opens the door for you.

SHARON Yes, call me old-fashioned, but I still like it, especially when a man opens the door for me.

Q All right. So, we don't think you're too old-fashioned. All right, so now then, let's think about, um, now what, how do you respond or what do you do, say, if one of your neighbors brings in your laundry when it starts to rain?

SHARON Oh, my gosh, that would be so thoughtful, if a neighbor brought in my laundry when it started to rain. Oh, my! I would probably say "thank you" at the time and then bake them some cookies or something, because that's a very sweet thing.

Q OK, so now then, maybe you're on the street. You see a friend, you need to write something down. What if they lend you a pen? How would you, how would you respond?

SHARON Well, everyone's lending pens all the time, so if a friend lent me a pen, that's really not a big deal. I would probably just say "thanks" and I might even forget to return it!

Q Here's an embarrassing one. What would you say to your neighbor if you broke their window playing baseball?

SHARON Oh, no!

Q You'd say "Oh, no!"?

SHARON Actually, I would say "Oh, no!" to myself and then I would apologize to the neighbor profusely. I would just keep apologizing and keep apologizing, probably every time I saw that neighbor, I would apologize, and of course I'd pay for the window.

Q Wait a minute. Now stop. Imagine for a second I'm the neighbor. Tell me exactly what you'd say.

SHARON I am so so so sorry. I did it. I broke your window. I'm a terrible baseball player. Please forgive me. And please let me pay for the window.

Q I think that's abject enough. OK, so let's see. Hmm. Here's another situation. What are you going to tell a sales clerk who gives you exactly what you want to buy?

SHARON Well, that would be great. I'd say "Thank you, here's the money."

Q That seems good enough—thank you, here's the money. Um, yeah, that seems pretty straightforward.

SHARON You know, so often you get things you don't want to buy, if they brought me what I really wanted to buy, I'd be thrilled. It would save me time and I'd say "Thank you, here's my money."

Q All right. So, now tell me, tell me how you buy a bus ticket.

SHARON How I buy a bus ticket?

Q Yeah. Imagine I'm the, I'm the guy at the bus station and you need to buy a ticket. Tell me.

SHARON OK. I would say, "I need a round-trip ticket to wherever I'm going and how much is that?" And "Here's the money, thank you."

Q You need a round-trip ticket to where? Where are you going?

SHARON Oh, gosh! Where should I go? —New Jersey!

Q You need a round-trip ticket to New Jersey. All right, uh, that's a dollar fifty.

SHARON Thank you so much.

Q Ah. Tell me, um, here's another thing... Imagine that you're at a dinner party and I'm the host, and you're about to leave the dinner party.

SHARON Oh, I would say "Thank you so much, we had a wonderful time."

Q You'd say "Thank you so much, we had a wonderful time." Now imagine for a second that the food was terrible and the conversation was boring.

SHARON I would still say "I had a wonderful time and the food was delicious" because I think it's polite.

Q So what happens when you bump into someone you don't know—you literally run into them?

SHARON Oh, I would apologize. I'd say "I'm so sorry!"

Q So, you'd apologize. What if they like dropped things?

SHARON Oh, of course, I would help them pick them up. Then I'd just say, "I'm very sorry. I didn't mean to bump into you."

Q All right. So let's move on and, um, you're in a coffee shop...

SHARON OK.

Q And someone serves you a cup of coffee.

SHARON I would say "Thank you very much." I love coffee, so I'd be happy.

Q You're thanking people all the time! Would you ask for anything else—cream, sugar or...?

SHARON Skim milk, if they have it.

Q OK, um, it really sounds like in almost all of these situations that you're just unfailingly polite.

SHARON Well, my parents raised me well. What can I say?

Q Well, to use your own words, Sharon, "thank you very much!"

SHARON You're welcome!

Q It's been a pleasure. Bye.

SHARON Thanks.

Lesson 10 Listening, activity 2

Speaker 1
New York for me. I visited the East Coast four years ago but didn't quite get to New York, but I'd love to go there. I'd like to spend time in the city that supposedly never sleeps, that has such a... a vibrancy and is about four gears higher in... kind of pace of life than here. I think I'd really like that.

Speaker 2
I suppose to jump out of an airplane, preferably with a parachute, but I also wouldn't mind if I didn't do it because I'm so apprehensive, if not frightened of doing it. But I would like to, yes, yes, I would like to.

Speaker 3
Germaine Greer. I think she's intelligent, and, uh... academically pretty brilliant. And she has a great sense of humor. Her book *The Female Eunuch*, uh... is a book that actually changed... changed me in a big way back in the 1970s. I like the way she's not afraid to say the first thing that comes into her head, even if it's wrong sometimes. Um... and she seems to have a very positive and joyous approach to life.

Speaker 4
It was, um... in a beach hut on Koh Samui in Thailand and I was there with my boyfriend and we were young and in love and we were staying in this little hut which was only about twenty feet from the sea. And we could just run out into the sea first thing in the morning and we just lived on fish and fruit and it was wonderful.

Speaker 5
Plastering? Yeah, I know it sounds dumb, but I didn't think I could do it. There was a great big wall that had to have all this old plaster taken off and a whole lot of new plaster and skimming done. And I didn't think I could do it, but I did, and I felt really good about it.

Lesson 11 Listening, activity 3

Part 1
Nurse Coxall had been running Ward 4 for many years. Her pride and joy was her own little office, scrupulously clean, its walls glistening with fresh white paint. She sat at her desk, her eyes unseeing. Who was this new doctor, anyway? Some silly kid fresh from medical school? What right had he to interfere in the running of her ward?

She had met him yesterday. He had driven into the hospital grounds and almost run over her. There were plenty of speed bumps to slow people down. Besides, almost everybody who worked at the hospital knew she walked through the grounds at that time of day.

"Are you all right?" he had said, getting out of his car. "I wasn't paying attention." He seemed embarrassed. "Um, ma'am, I'm really sorry."

She couldn't help smiling. "That's all right, Mr.—" she paused politely.

"Doctor—Dr. Green. I've just arrived, as you can see," he grinned. "I'm taking over Ward 4."

Nurse Coxall noticeably stiffened. "Ward 4?" she echoed.

"Look, hop in, and I'll drive you where you're going."

They sat in silence and soon were climbing the dingy staircase leading to Nurse Coxall's little apartment. Once inside, she took off her coat. "Sit down, Doctor, I'll make some coffee."

Sitting and drinking the coffee, Dr. Green explained that he had always been interested in psychiatric work and when he had finished his studies, he had applied for this post in one of the country's largest psychiatric hospitals. He had not expected to get the job, but he did, and without an interview.

He told her of the great changes and new ideas he hoped he would introduce. "For instance," he said, "the nurse on Ward 4 has been working there for ten years. She must have lost her identity to some extent. Her patients must be more like children to her than sick people." He leaned forward. "You know, Nurse, she is in danger of illness herself. Tomorrow, when I begin my work, I intend to move that nurse to a different ward. She may not realize it at the time, but the change will do her good."

Nurse Coxall listened, a faint pink flush tinging her ears.

Lesson 11 **Listening, activity 5**

Part 2

The day had arrived. She looked around her office. She was going to be removed from this, her home, and placed among strangers.

"No!" she screamed, and her fist came heavily down upon the desk, scattering pens into sudden life.

Nurse Coxall's mind began to work. Now it raced. Nobody knows he is coming here except me. He said he was going to stay at a hotel last night and was coming straight to the ward this morning, before reporting to the Personnel Office. He had no white coat or identity badge yet.

A diabolical smile drew back the corners of her thin straight mouth. "There is only one thing to do," she muttered, and rose and went to the door.

"Nurse," she called, "a new patient is expected this morning, a Mr. Green. When he arrives, bring him straight to my office." She looked down at the empty report paper she held in her hand. "It says here that he is paranoid and greatly confused; he thinks he's a doctor. Humor him, Nurse. I'll prepare a strong sedative."

Going to the cupboard, Nurse Coxall took down a syringe and filled it with a cool orange liquid. She then took an empty file from a cabinet and began to prepare a written report on Mr. Green.

She sighed. The ward was full of men, all confused, all insisting they were doctors. No one was ever going to take her ward and office away from her. No one.

Lesson 14 **Listening and Speaking, activity 2**

Q So, Kathy and Terry, I want to ask you a few questions about going on vacation, something most of us look forward to! Kathy, what's your idea of paradise? What's the best vacation you can imagine?

KATHY Oh, I think it would be a sandy beach with blue sky, warm water, ... and no people.

Q No people? How are you going to manage that, a desert island?

KATHY Not at all. I once spent a week with some friends at a house in Hawaii. It had access to a beautiful, private cove with no people at all. The only way to get to the beach was from the house, or by boat. It was really great.

Q And what about your idea of a vacation nightmare? What kind of trip would you hate?

KATHY Um, probably a vacation on a boat. I get really seasick. I found that out when I took a cruise in the Caribbean with some friends. The days in port, sightseeing, shopping, and swimming were great, but the nights on the ship were pure torture.

Q How awful! What about you, Terry? Would that be a nightmare for you, too?

TERRY No way! I love being on the water. My vacation nightmare is staying in a big city. Last year my wife and I had the chance to travel in Asia. The countryside was beautiful, the people were wonderful, but I felt claustrophobic every time we spent more than one night in a big city. All the people on the trains made me feel like I was in a can of sardines!

Q So what kind of vacation do you enjoy? What would be paradise for you?

TERRY Definitely a vacation in Costa Rica. I love the sun and the beach and the quiet there ... and the people, the people are so friendly. Even shopping is a pleasure. The shopkeepers really make you feel special.

Q So what's your favorite vacation activity? Lying on the beach?

TERRY No. I mean, I like lying on the beach, but probably my favorite thing is scuba diving. I first learned to dive in 1989 when I visited Costa Rica—oh, and eating too. I love to try new food when I'm on vacation.

Q What about you, Kathy?

KATHY My favorite activities? Oh, reading. I love to catch up on my reading when I'm on vacation.

Q And are there any things that you always take with you when you leave home?

KATHY Mmm, yeah. I always take my favorite hat and a good book. I have to have my hat for keeping the sun off my face and out of my eyes, and like I said, I love to read on vacation, so I always have books.

TERRY I always take my Walkman. I like to listen to my own music on the plane. It makes the time on the airplane pass more quickly.

Q Hmm. What about company? Who would be your ideal companion for your perfect vacation?

TERRY Definitely my wife.

KATHY Well, my husband and kids. But ... well, I would like there to be some kind of entertainment for the kids, you know, some special activities just for them or something, because if it's going to be a vacation for me, I want some time to spend by myself or with just my husband for a change.

Q I can relate to that. And what about things you miss when you are away from home? What do you miss the most?

KATHY Well. don't laugh, but I miss my soap opera. I'm kind of addicted to my hour a day. I don't usually tell people that, though.

Q Our little secret. How about you, Terry? Is there anything you miss?

TERRY Yeah. I really miss my dog. I've been living with him longer than my wife, and I kind of worry about him when we're gone.

Lesson 16 **Listening, activity 2**

Part 1

LINDA Hey, you won't believe what happened to me! What? Well, one Christmas skiing vacation when I was in high school, right, I went with my best friend, my mom and dad, and my older sister to this old inn in Utah ... in the mountains. It was really beautiful, you know, but, well, like, really isolated and sort of spooky. You know, like it reminded me of the kind of really nice, quiet place that ends up being a setting for a horror movie. So, anyway, I was sharing a room with my best friend, Cynthia. We were staying in this little room at the top of this old ... this old tower, sort of like next to the inn. It was kind of dark in there and kind of cold and there was no TV or anything, so we liked to hang out down in the TV room on the main floor by the desk. Well, one time we got to talking with this old housekeeper, you know, she cleaned the room and stuff. She was really cool, like friendly and smart and she'd been there forever ... anyway, Cynthia was telling my sister that she'd heard a man with a deep voice singing, "I'm Dreaming of a White Christmas" in the middle of the night. My sister just laughed at her, you know, she told her ... she said she was completely out to lunch. But, you know what, the housekeeper heard Cynthia telling her and she told us later that Bing Crosby used to stay at the inn all the time!

MAN/WOMAN No way! Really? It's like one of those urban legends or something ...

LINDA No, really. Honest! And Cyn said it sounded exactly like Bing! And anyway, we asked the guy at the front desk and he checked in his old books and stuff and said that Bing Crosby had stayed there at Christmas with his family in 1942, the same year the song came out!

MAN I can't believe that!

WOMAN No way!

Lesson 16 **Listening, activity 4**

Part 2

LINDA Yeah ... well, something else happened, too, that you're never going to believe! In the same place!

WOMAN Don't tell me ... you saw Marilyn Monroe!

MAN No, no, no, ... Elvis!

LINDA Yeah! Ha! I wish! No, no ... Anyway, one night we went to sleep and ... um ... this is still in that old tower next to the inn, right. Anyway, in the middle of the night, Cyn and I woke up at exactly the same time 'cause there was this really strong smell of smoke in our room. I mean, we smelled smoke! So, of course, you know, we ran out of there and we got my sister up.

WOMAN Did you see a fire?

LINDA No! We just ran out of there, straight to, straight out of there to my sister's room who ... who just hates to get woken up, you know. She didn't believe us of course and she was mad, but she got up and she came with us, but ... no fire! I mean there was no fire! Nothing! So then she was really mad and she went back to bed, but we woke up twice more that night smelling smoke.

MAN Didn't anyone come up?

LINDA Come up? No, they all thought we were making it up! Anyway, so the next morning, right, my big sister told everyone about what happened and everybody thought it was hilarious because there wasn't any fire. But another guy staying at the inn said he'd smelled it, too ... but he was just pulling our legs, you know, he thought it was funny. They all just sat there cracking up.

MAN Your parents, too?

LINDA Yeah. And ... um ... anyway, that cool old housekeeper came up to us later and she said she'd heard us talking about it ... how we'd smelled the smoke and all. And she looked kind of spooked about it, you know, sort of pale.

ALL Why?

LINDA Well, what she told us was that where we were staying, in that old tower, that it had burned down one night about twenty years before that. Yeah. And that a young girl, the daughter of the old owners of the inn, had died in the fire. Yeah! She slept in the same bedroom we were sleeping in! And that was the exact same date that we smelled the smoke ... on the anniversary of her death in that old tower!

Fluency 2 **Listening and Speaking, activity 4**

STUDENT Uh, excuse me?

ROSEANNE Yes?

STUDENT Hello! Um, I'm filling out a questionnaire about family life in the United States ... and I was wondering, could you help me with answering a few questions?

ROSEANNE Well, I can try!

STUDENT Oh, good. Um, first of all, who is head of the household in your family?

ROSEANNE Well, in my family, my husband and I share that responsibility. That's our...

STUDENT So both of you are heads of the household?

ROSEANNE Yes. We both earn income and so we both contribute financially to the household and then we both also take responsibility for it.

STUDENT I see. So both the mother and the father share the responsibilities of the household, uh...

ROSEANNE In my family, in, that's the way we do it.

STUDENT I see. And, um, what is the typical family like in your country? Are you the typical family?

ROSEANNE In a way, yes. My family is typical. I mean, in my opinion, we seem typical—that there's a husband and a wife and two children—a boy and a girl.

STUDENT Oh, I see. And, um, in the typical family, which is about four people, right?

ROSEANNE Right.

STUDENT Mother, father, two kids, um, do you have the grandparents living with you?

ROSEANNE Well, not in my case. My parents, uh, don't live with us. They're retired. They live in another part of the country. And I think that's typical of many of my friends—that they don't live close to their parents.

STUDENT So grandparents usually live, uh, separate from their children.

ROSEANNE If they're still living. I mean, that's just, you're asking me...that's just my family.

STUDENT Ah, I see. And, um, uh, in raising your children, when do parents stop their financial support of their children?

ROSEANNE Well, I think that most people should stop supporting their children when they, uh, graduate from college.

STUDENT So, they should, uh, stop supporting them when they have, uh, finished school?

ROSEANNE Yes, uh, I would think that that should be the way it would happen. Um, that children start earning money while they're going to school usually—they have summer jobs and things like that—to get them ready for that experience.

STUDENT So, children start supporting themselves when they are maybe when they are teenagers, and they are still in school. And their parents still, their parents still support them, but the children help out.

ROSEANNE Right. Exactly!

STUDENT I see. OK. And, uh, does the whole family discuss important decisions?

ROSEANNE Um, yes, in our family. Uh, the whole family would, uh, although we tend to discuss the decisions that are affecting each child individually with that child.

STUDENT Uh-huh, I see. So you usually, if it has to do with one child, you discuss it with him only or her only.

ROSEANNE Right. Like my daughter's going to college and so we'll discuss with her what college and how much the college costs and when she's going to visit. And her younger brother isn't very interested in that.

STUDENT Oh, I see.

ROSEANNE So he doesn't want to be part of the discussion.

STUDENT So if that child is not included, uh, in the subject, then he will not be included in the discussing of that decision.

ROSEANNE Unless he wants to be. We're pretty loose about it.

STUDENT But if it's a decision regarding the whole family, then would everyone...

ROSEANNE Then everyone I think should be allowed to discuss it and be involved in the decision.
STUDENT I see. OK. Um, do children ask their parents' approval of the person they wish to marry?
ROSEANNE Uh, children in this country ask their parents who they can marry? No! No! I think it's nice when the family does approve, but they don't have to get permission and they rarely ask it.
STUDENT So they do not get permission from their parents to marry someone.
ROSEANNE No, they usually announce it to their parents!
STUDENT They announce it—oh, so they just tell you that they are going to marry this person. Oh!
ROSEANNE Exactly.
STUDENT And, um, if you have a financial problem, uh, would you expect your family to help?
ROSEANNE Yes, I would think my family should help. I would help my children. That's what I think parents want to do—they want to help their children.
STUDENT So... Ah, I see. OK. And, um, do you look after relatives who cannot look after themselves?
ROSEANNE Well, in my family we do. We follow that tradition. I think that younger people should do that. And so we do.
STUDENT So you look after your older people who cannot look after themselves.
ROSEANNE Right.
STUDENT I see. OK. And, uh, do grandparents help to look after their grandchildren?
ROSEANNE Um, I think in my family, in our situation, um, my parents don't live close to us. They would like to, but they don't live close.
STUDENT So your grandpa...so your parents do not look after your children. The grandparents in your family do not help out in watching the children.
ROSEANNE No, because our families don't live close to each other.
STUDENT I see. They're far away from each other, so it's not possible.
ROSEANNE Right.
STUDENT I see. OK. Thank you very much for helping me to fill out this questionnaire.
ROSEANNE Oh, you're welcome. I hope you do well with it!
STUDENT Thank you. Bye-bye.
ROSEANNE Bye-bye.

Fluency 2 **Functions, activity 4**

MAN I think it's ridiculous for sons and daughters to ask their parents who they can marry.
WOMAN Well, I'm not so sure. Wouldn't you say that their parents could help them make a suitable choice?
MAN Maybe, but frankly, I think that if you're old enough to get married, you're old enough to choose for yourself.
WOMAN Well, you have a point there, but it makes me sad to see people who marry so young and then realize they've made the wrong choice.
MAN No way! It doesn't matter if you make a mistake once or twice, does it?
WOMAN Well, yes, if there are children involved.

Progress Check Lessons 9—16
Listening and Speaking, activity 1

I was a nurse in a Chicago hospital going on the night shift at 8 **P.M.** I went up to my floor and began to check all the patients. Suddenly I heard a man's footsteps coming down the hall and I saw a man in a chauffeur's uniform who said, "I have come for my wife." I told him to go down to the Admissions Office to ask where he should

go, although I knew no patient would be allowed to go home at that time of night.
Later I was talking to a doctor friend who said she'd been with a woman patient who was dying. An ambulance had brought her in that morning, unconscious. The police were trying to find her husband, who was a chauffeur.
I told her about the chauffeur I had seen, and she went to ask about the matter at the Admissions Office. But she came back and said that no one had been there asking about their wife. And the security guard, standing in full view of the elevators said he hadn't seen anyone in a chauffeur's uniform.
The next day, my friend told me that she'd found out about the unknown woman who had died in the night. The woman's husband was the chauffeur for a rich family. Early on the previous morning he had set out on a long journey with his employers. But they had been involved in an accident and the chauffeur was killed.
When he left home that morning his wife seemed fine and was looking forward to spending a day with a friend. The friend had come by to pick her up, and she was surprised when no one answered the doorbell. She looked through the letterbox and saw the poor woman lying on the floor of the hall. She called the police and an ambulance took the chauffeur's wife to the hospital, where she failed to recover consciousness and died that night.
At this stage no one knew where her husband was. The police hadn't been able to contact him. They also didn't know that he had died in a car accident five hours before his wife died in the hospital.
It became clear to me that the man in the chauffeur's uniform I'd spoken to had in fact been dead for some time.

Lesson 18 **Listening, activity 3**

Q So, you spent some time in Africa as a teacher. Where were you?
BEN I spent about a year in the Sudan. I was in the Peace Corps.
Q And, and, when was that?
BEN About ten years ago.
Q And how long did you stay?
BEN I stayed for two years.
Q Oh, and you enjoyed it ... you had a good time?
BEN Yes, uh ... it was a real experience for me. Just after college.
Q So you were what, twenty-one, twenty-two when you went there?
BEN Yeah.
Q Great. And, and what subjects did you use to teach there?
BEN I taught English and some literature ... American literature, like, you know, *Tom Sawyer* and *To Kill a Mockingbird*. That sort of thing.
Q And did they just do English and literature in English? Or did they do other subjects as well?
BEN Yes, that was all I taught. All the other subjects were in Arabic.
Q I see. And what was a typical day like, I mean, how would you start your day when you were there as a teacher?
BEN Well, um, I lived in town, and the school was about two miles out of town. We'd start in a café, about seven in the morning having coffee. Walk to school, um ... along the Nile, I taught in a town by the Nile ... teach a couple of classes then have breakfast at school ...
Q How long were your classes, how long did they last?
BEN Um ... about forty minutes. Sometimes they were double classes. About forty minutes ...

Q So you taught two classes, then you used to have a break ...

BEN We used to have breakfast with the staff, um ... then two more classes, another break, two more classes and then we'd stop at around one ... one o'clock.

Q Wow! So you used to teach six classes a day?

BEN That's right.

Q And how many students did you have in the class?

BEN Well, the classes were large, because there was a shortage of teachers, really, so anything from forty-five to seventy, in a class.

Q Wow, that's huge! And what was the classroom like?

BEN Well, the classrooms were OK, there were enough desks and chairs, but not enough books for all the students, um ... the windows, without glass in them, and blackboards that were so old—they had holes in them.

Q So, the equipment wasn't really...

BEN There really wasn't any equipment, no, blackboards or chalk.

Q Blackboards and chalk ... And, uh, were you used to this kind of lack of equipment? When you began teaching?

BEN I knew what to expect, but um ... I was trained as a teacher with equipment you'd find in a classroom here, overhead projectors and so on ... but that was OK.

Q Yes, yes, I guess, after a year you got used to using no equipment, not having overhead projectors ...

BEN For a start, there wasn't any electricity during the day. And we had to get used to adapting what we wanted to teach, how we wanted to work with the class ...

Q So you had classes that used to be about forty minutes long. Were there any exams at the end of the semester or ...?

BEN Yes, every class had exams at the end of the year, and the last year had national exams to take, um ... which were pretty tough.

Q Hmm ... Hmm ... And was there anything that, um, happened that you ... you were embarrassed about or that you found amusing ...were there any amusing incidents?

BEN Well, it was very interesting working and living in a different culture. I learned a lot there, but, yes, one time ... the staff used to have breakfast together as staff, and you eat with your hands, so it was quite important that you wash your hands. Um ... the first time ... the first day at school, I remember washing my hands in the water, the bowl of water was actually the drinking water ...

Q Oh!

BEN And, uh, well, luckily, everybody laughed.

Q Phew! ... People are very kind to visitors in a foreign culture, aren't they? Thank you.

Lesson 20 **Vocabulary and Listening, activity 3**

WOMAN Something that really intrigues me is the difference between the American legal system and the British legal system. For instance, in the United States are you innocent until you're proven guilty, or the other way round?

MAN Here, you're innocent until proven guilty, like in Britain, right?

WOMAN Right. What about if you're convicted of drug dealing? Are you always sent to prison or is there sometimes just a fine?

MAN Well, if you just have a little bit of something, you know, then you'll get a fine ... a big fine! But if you have enough to sell, then, yeah, then you get ... well, then you go to prison.

WOMAN Right. And weapons? Is it an offense to carry a weapon, like a gun or a knife?

MAN Oh, no! That's OK. You have to have a license to carry a concealed gun. And you're supposed to have a gun permit, but ... no ... Otherwise, no.

WOMAN Wow! It's so incredibly different, isn't it? And if the police arrest you, are you allowed to call a lawyer?

MAN When you're arrested, they read you your rights. Then, yes, as soon as you get to the station, you're given the option to call a lawyer. Obviously you don't have to, but I think it's a good idea.

WOMAN Absolutely. And if the police suspect you of a crime, is it legal to remain silent when they question you?

MAN You do, yes, you do have the right to remain silent, because if you say anything then they could use that against you, like, in court.

WOMAN Right. OK. And how about if you're charged with a crime? Do you always go into custody while you wait for a trial?

MAN That depends. If it's serious, then yeah. Or you might have to get bail. But if it's not serious, they might just release you while you wait ... wait for your trial.

WOMAN Right. OK. What about if you confess to a crime? Do you always get a lighter sentence?

MAN No. Well, yes ... I mean you do get some plea bargaining. If you confess to a crime, you might get a lighter sentence. It depends on the seriousness of the crime.

WOMAN Oh, right. And how about, are there any crimes which you can be executed for?

MAN Er... yes. Like in Texas, yeah. In lots of states. It takes a long time with, you know, appeals and things, but yeah.

WOMAN See again, that's a huge difference because ...

MAN Absolutely. Absolutely. It was illegal for a while, but ... Yeah, now states get to choose. It's mostly for murder, you know. And now they use a ... the electric chair or lethal injection to ... you know.

WOMAN Oh, wow. And is there always a trial by jury for serious crimes?

MAN Yes. Minor crimes go to Municipal Court, but um ... Superior Court, yeah ... with a jury for serious crimes.

WOMAN Wow. And who is the person who decides on a sentence? Is it the jury or is it the judge?

MAN Um... usually in most crimes the jury will give a decision on whether they're guilty or innocent, but it's usually the judge who does the sentencing, saying how long it is and what term, and so on.

WOMAN It's amazing. You know, there's just so many differences between the two systems.

MAN Really?

WOMAN Yeah.

MAN How interesting.

Lesson 22 **Speaking and Listening, activity 2**

WOMAN These are amazing inventions. But these illustrations here, now this first one, what's this?

MAN That first one is a baby patting device designed by Thomas V. Zelenka in California in 1968. At night it's difficult for the parents to stay awake and to help the baby fall asleep. And, so Mr. Zelenka designed this device to do it for them.

WOMAN Oh, I see.

MAN Um ... the possible disadvantage is that it could actually harm the baby.

WOMAN How?

MAN Well, if the baby moved around and the patter patted it on the head, it could injure it. Another problem is that it's powered by electricity.

WOMAN What's wrong with that?

MAN   Well, you should never have electricity in a baby's bedroom.

WOMAN   Oh. Right. And this second one, a saluting device?

MAN   Yep. It's to raise your hat when you meet someone in the street and your hands are full. When your hands are full it's impossible to raise your hat. Of course, it's always important to greet people politely. But nobody raises their hat these days.

WOMAN   Yes, that's true, that's true. And who wears hats like that anymore?

MAN   It's an old-fashioned device.

WOMAN   And what about this next one, this kitchen fork?

MAN   It's a fork hook, really, designed in 1919, for picking up a hot pan. When you're boiling something it's sometimes difficult to lift the pan without burning your hands.

WOMAN   I know, but what about eating with it?

MAN   It's way too big and dangerous to eat with!

WOMAN   Oh, wow! And then we have a knife mirror?

MAN   Yes, the knife mirror, which was designed in 1908, is to let you look at your teeth and inspect them after eating to see if you've got any bits of food stuck in your teeth. After a meal we're often surprised to find a bit of food stuck in our teeth.

WOMAN   Right. I know what you mean!

MAN   But it would be unusual for you to clean it off at the table.

WOMAN   Yes. And I find this amazing ... this grapefruit shield.

MAN   The grapefruit shield was to protect you from the juice when you cut into a grapefruit.

WOMAN   Neat idea.

MAN   It sometimes squirts out all over the place. When eating grapefruit, it's essential for you to avoid getting the juice in your eyes because grapefruit juice can sting. But it might be easier for you to cut the grapefruit into pieces, don't you think? The strange thing about this invention is the shield, if you look at it, is on the wrong side.

WOMAN   Oh, look at that!

Lesson 23 **Reading and Listening, activity 3**

JOSIE   It's nice here, isn't it?

PHIL   Yes. It's great. I really like it.

JOSIE   It's pretty busy.

PHIL   Yes.

JOSIE   Have you ever been here before?

PHIL   No, no. I heard it was good, though.

JOSIE   Right.

PHIL   I heard the main thing about the place was how great the food is. You know, it's the one thing I'm willing to pay for—if the food's, you know, good quality, that's the most important thing.

JOSIE   So ... this place is expensive?

PHIL   Yeah, but I also like the way the food is served. The appearance of the food is gorgeous. You know, it really looks like the chef's taken a lot of time to prepare it and I think that's important.

JOSIE   I don't really care that much about how it looks, I guess.

PHIL   Really?

JOSIE   No, I don't. I like the price to be good. You know, I think it's a shame to spend a lot of money in restaurants, really. But I think for me, what's important when I go out for dinner is the company. And I think you can have really good meals, it doesn't really matter what the food is like. If you've got good company, with your family or your friends, that's the important thing. It's the atmosphere, isn't it?

PHIL   Well, yeah, I know. But I think if I go out for a meal, you can always have that at home or at a party. If I go out for a meal, the most important thing is the food for me.

JOSIE   Yeah. So, do you try lots of different things ... or...?

PHIL   Yes. I love it. Especially anything I haven't had before or if it's kind of exotic and I can't pronounce it, that's the best thing! That's ideal. I really like to experiment, especially with new tastes.

JOSIE   Oh, really? Oh, you're way more adventurous than I am! I couldn't even ... I could never try anything that I couldn't pronounce. I'm very conservative, I guess.

PHIL   Really?

JOSIE   Yes, I'm afraid so.

PHIL   So you like quick things, simple things?

JOSIE   Yeah, well...

PHIL   For me a quick meal's a sandwich.

JOSIE   Oh, really?

PHIL   That's the quickest thing, yes.

JOSIE   Oh, a sandwich is lunch for me. I mean ...

PHIL   Really?

JOSIE   I don't like hamburgers or fast food. No, it makes me feel a little sick.

PHIL   Right.

JOSIE   But do you think ... would you ever give anything up?

PHIL   What do you mean?

JOSIE   Well, is there any food that you would give up? I'm thinking about giving up meat, for example. I could be a vegetarian.

PHIL   Yeah. Yeah.

JOSIE   But would you give anything up, like desserts, or something like that?

PHIL   I love desserts! I love desserts! Would I give anything up? I don't know, I mean I love fruit and I love bananas, they're my favorite.

JOSIE   Do you?

PHIL   I don't think I'd ever be able to give that up. I would be able to give up most things, but not fruit, because I just love the taste and the texture.

JOSIE   Yes, me too. I always like to finish a meal by eating an apple because it makes my mouth taste nice and fresh.

PHIL   Yes, it's great.

Lesson 23 **Sounds**

1. She's coming with us tonight. When you see her, you can ask her.

2. If we're late, start without us.

3. I'm going to the restaurant now. When I get there, I'll call her.

4. If it's a nice day tomorrow, we'll have a barbecue.

5. They may not be at home, but if they are, I'll invite them over.

Fluency 3 **Speaking and Listening, activity 3**

JOAN   Well, you've asked me what is a typical American home like? Hmm. I have to say, I don't know if there is any such thing as a typical American home. You know, they can be very different. But, if there were such a thing as an average American home, I would say that it would have all the modern conveniences, you know. It'd be about six or seven rooms, and it would have a television, of course, maybe a couple of televisions, and a couple of telephones, certainly. The kitchen would probably have a dishwasher, of course. And if they're lucky maybe even a clothes washer and a clothes dryer—or even a laundry room where they could separate out the doing the laundry from the kitchen. It may have a backyard with a nice garden, or maybe a front yard, depending on how the house is situated on the property. And it probably would have a garage, large enough for one car, and maybe some storage room in the garage.

Uh, it would either have carpeting or some rugs. Most American families like to put some rugs or carpeting down for warmth. If it's a really nice place, it would have central heating and a couple of air conditioners. Um, and of course no bathroom would be complete without a shower.

If it's a really nice place, it might have two levels, so there'd be an upstairs and a downstairs. But your average place would probably be on one floor, and maybe there'd be a basement or a family room downstairs. And of course, while I'm at it, if you live in a really nice house, you might have a fireplace in the living room. There's nothing I like better than the smell of a wood-burning fireplace.

You might also have a patio or a deck on which you would keep a barbecue and some lounge furniture for the nice weather. This sounds like such a nice house, I'd like to move into it myself!

Fluency 3 **Speaking and Listening, activity 5**

STUDENT Oh, excuse me?

JOAN Hi.

STUDENT Hi. I'm doing some interviews and I was wondering if you wouldn't mind answering some questions.

JOAN Oh, sure, sure! Fire away. Ask me anything you want.

STUDENT Um, I wanted to know about housing in the United States.

JOAN Oh, housing?

STUDENT Yes, and how you live. Would you prefer to own a new or an old house?

JOAN Oh, wow! An old house or a new house? That's an interesting question. you know, because in America they don't build houses like they used to, you know.

STUDENT Oh.

JOAN The old houses are so great! They are so strong and the walls are so sturdy...

STUDENT Oh, the old houses are much more sturdy than the...

JOAN Much stronger, and they have a lot of character and...

STUDENT What do you mean, they have a lot of character, the old houses?

JOAN Well, I guess I mean they, they have a unique quality. Each house has its own personality, you know. Like today, if you have a new house, they're all alike.

STUDENT So, old houses have more personality, they're more, they're more different than new houses.

JOAN Yes. But if I had to choose, I'd like to have an old house with new plumbing.

STUDENT Oh, new plumbing. So, oh, you want all new things in the old house?

JOAN Yeah. I'd want to be sure that the hot water always worked and that the toilet always flushed, you know. I'd want to have the best of an old house mixed with the best of a new house.

STUDENT Oh, so you would prefer to, uh, renovate. You'd buy an old house and you would renovate it. You would change...

JOAN Oh, I would love that.

STUDENT Um, how many rooms does a typical home have?

JOAN A typical home? Hmm. I wonder if there's any such thing as a typical home in America. It's all so different, you know, based on your income and how large your family is.

STUDENT So, if you have a big family, say, uh, five children, how many rooms would you have?

JOAN Oh, boy! Well, of course you'd have a kitchen and of course a bathroom and probably there'd be a master bedroom...

STUDENT A master bedroom?

JOAN For the mom and the dad. Or if it's a single parent home, there'd still be a master bedroom.

STUDENT So the head of the household will have, uh, the master bedroom.

JOAN That's right.

STUDENT Oh, OK.

JOAN And that'd probably be the biggest bedroom, and then the children would probably double up, you know, there'd be more than one child sleeping in the same bedroom.

STUDENT Oh!

JOAN So, maybe there'd be two bedrooms and two children would sleep in one bedroom and three children would sleep in the other.

STUDENT So there may be more than one child in each room.

JOAN Oh, definitely. Probably they'd share a room if they have a large family. And maybe there'd be a living room or a family room that also doubles as a bedroom. You know, sometimes in the living room you can have a couch that turns into a bed.

STUDENT So, um, how many rooms?

JOAN So, that'd be about five rooms. And then, if it's a nice house, maybe there'd also be a dining room; so that'd be six rooms.

STUDENT So maybe six rooms in a typical house. Um, what is more common for people in your age group—uh, do you rent apartments or do you own property, or do you still live with your parents?

JOAN Oh, no! I don't still live with my parents. I don't think anybody in my age group, you know, in the late 30s, early 40s age group; I don't think any of us live with our parents anymore.

STUDENT So no one ... who is 30 or 40 generally lives with their parents?

JOAN That would be pretty unusual in this country. Although sometimes students who have just graduated from college go back and live with their parents these days. But in my age group, people are starting to buy their first home now—and whether it be a condominium apartment or a house in the suburbs, this is the time when people...

STUDENT A condominium? Some people in your age group own a condominium?

JOAN Yeah. You know, a condominium would be where you'd buy an apartment in an apartment building and you'd negotiate a mortgage from a bank. You know, you'd get the bank to lend you money to pay for the monthly payments on the house.

STUDENT So a mortgage is a loan from a bank to buy a house.

JOAN That's right. Usually a very large loan!

STUDENT OK. Um, in the United States, do you often entertain guests at home?

JOAN Oh, yes, all the time. I love to entertain. Want to come over to my house for dinner?

STUDENT Yes! And when you do entertain in your home, which rooms do you usually use to entertain in?

JOAN Well, in my house, I usually make dinner because I love to cook, so I usually entertain in the dining room.

STUDENT Oh, in the dining room.

JOAN Yes. I cook the food in the kitchen and then bring it out into the dining room. And then after dinner, we move into the living room and sit around with coffee or a drink...

STUDENT I see. So you prepare the food in the kitchen.

JOAN That's right.

STUDENT And then you move to the dining room to eat it.

JOAN That's right. We sit around the big dining room table.

STUDENT Uh-huh. And then, after the dining room, you move to the living room.

JOAN Exactly.

STUDENT So, are there any rooms that the visitors are not allowed to go into? Or just do not want to go into?

JOAN Well, I don't have that many rooms! I only have about six rooms, so there's nothing too private about any of my rooms. But in some houses where people own their own business or work out of their home, perhaps the room that they use as an office might be off limits.

STUDENT So, when you entertain, do you, uh, go into the bedrooms with the guests? Do you ever...

JOAN Usually, if you're having a party, people put their coats on the bed in the bedroom. But they don't usually hang out and talk in the bedroom.

STUDENT Um, are there any particular customs that you have, uh, when you enter or you leave a home—for the guests?

JOAN Well, if people come to your house, of course, the polite thing to do is to wipe your feet before you come in.

STUDENT So guests may wipe their feet before they come into the house.

JOAN That's right. On a welcome mat in front of the door. And of course you'd shake hands and say hello or probably hug your guests hello.

STUDENT Uh-huh. I see.

JOAN And if you know them really well, you'd kiss them hello.

STUDENT Oh! OK.

JOAN And then you'd take their coat and their hat and hang it up for them.

STUDENT Oh, I see.

JOAN Sometimes, if you're a guest, you bring something to the host or the hostess, like a bottle of wine, or a dessert, or something to eat.

STUDENT So you may bring a gift to your host?

JOAN That's right.

STUDENT I see.

JOAN It's polite to bring a gift.

STUDENT And what would you do when you leave your host's home?

JOAN Again, you would, you would say goodbye, you would embrace, or hug, or shake hands, and, uh, you would thank them very much for having you over to their house...

STUDENT I see, so you would, uh, you would shake their hand and then you would thank them? And do you wipe your feet again?

JOAN No, you don't have to wipe your feet when you leave! Only when you enter.

STUDENT I see. Well, thank you very much. This has been very helpful to me.

JOAN You're welcome!

STUDENT Thank you for answering my questions.

JOAN It's my pleasure.

STUDENT Bye-bye.

JOAN Bye.

Fluency 3 **Functions, activity 4**

TED Hi! Come in. How are you?

BILLY I'm fine, thanks, how are you? I hope I'm not too early.

TED Not at all. Come on in and join us. Would you like a drink?

BILLY Yes, please. Could I have a Coke?

TED Sure. Ice?

BILLY That'll be fine. Do you have any lemon?

TED Uh-huh. Here you go.

BILLY Wow, this really is a beautiful place! What a great view!

TED Why, thank you. Here's your drink. Sit down. Make yourself at home.

BILLY Thank you. This is great. Is it OK to put it here on this table?

TED Go right ahead.

Progress Check Lessons 17—24
Listening and Writing, activity 1

MAN A man tried to smuggle four baby parrots, worth $8,000, from Brazil to the United States. When he got to the Miami airport, he took the birds from his suitcase and put them in his pants. When customs officers heard chirping noises coming from his pants, they searched him. He was fined $10,000.

WOMAN A man in Kansas claimed he had lost his court case over a trespassing dispute because the loud snoring of the judge's dog had distracted him from his own defense. The judge said the dog was guilty of nothing more than breathing noisily.

MAN A Montana ambulance crew who went to the wrong address took a healthy man fifty miles to the hospital. "I tried to protest," said the man, "but they said that from then on, they were making the decisions and that I had no say in it."

Lesson 26 **Vocabulary and Listening, activity 2**

RICH Anna, I wonder if you could help me understand what these different things are?

ANNA Sure.

RICH First of all, a CD-ROM. What's that?

ANNA A CD-ROM. OK. It's a way of keeping information on a disk, which then can be read by a computer.

RICH So you put it into the computer ...

ANNA Yes ...

RICH ... And then the computer reads it. I see. Right. Now, a fax. I know that that's a way you send or receive printed material on the phone line in an electronic form, but how does that differ from e-mail?

ANNA Well, e-mail, electronic mail, is a system which is used by computer users so messages can be sent from computer to computer, but a fax uses the telephone.

RICH Right.

ANNA And a fax machine.

RICH Right. I see. So it's like two computers talking to each other.

ANNA Right.

RICH I see.

ANNA But a fax isn't computer operated. It's using a fax machine and a phone line.

RICH The phone talking to the fax machine?

ANNA Right.

RICH Right. And what exactly is the Internet?

ANNA Right. Well, I suppose, you know, like with e-mail you've got computer to computer. It's a bit like that. It's a network that allows computer users from anywhere in the world to actually communicate with each other.

RICH Right.

ANNA You know, people usually pay a subscription to a company ...

RICH Yeah ...

ANNA And they go on-line.

RICH Right.

ANNA That's the term.

RICH So there's ... like ... loads of computers all talking to each other.

ANNA Right, yes.

RICH Oh right.

ANNA It's fascinating.

RICH And what exactly is satellite TV?

ANNA Well, it's a way of broadcasting television using a satellite that's up in space.

RICH Oh.

ANNA Rather than using, you know, a transmitter ...

RICH Like a transmitter on the ground?

ANNA Transmitters and aerials here on the ground are actually using a satellite up in space to pick up all the airwaves.

RICH So the signal's sent up to the satellite ...

ANNA Right, and then sent back down.

RICH I see. So what is cable TV, then?

ANNA Hmm. Well, that kind of works, I suppose, in the opposite way. It's a system, again of broadcasting television, but instead of having a satellite up in the air, you've got cables that run under the ground along maybe phone lines, that kind of thing. It gives viewers ... you know ... access to much more, many more channels.

RICH It's a physical connection ...

ANNA Yeah, that's right.

RICH ... from wherever they're sending the program to your television, so it's really one long cable.

ANNA Right.

RICH Oh, right.

Lesson 26 **Vocabulary and Listening, activity 5**

ANNA The thing is, Rich, CD-ROMs are actually much better than books.

RICH Why's that?

ANNA Well, you can store so much more information on the disks. I mean, not just stories, but you can have pictures from galleries, you can have, say, portraits from the Louvre in Paris or the Museum of Modern Art in New York, there's so much ...

RICH No, no, I disagree. I don't think anything will ever replace the book as a means of storing information in the way you actually look through a book to find it, and when it comes to art, there's no substitute for the real thing. Nothing will replace a visit to Paris or New York to see ...

ANNA Of course not, but you can have it in your own home, can't you?

RICH I know, but people are always saying that. Every few years something comes along and everybody says, "Oh, this is the wave of the future. This is going to replace..." I mean, a few years ago a friend convinced me that LPs and tapes were out, that CDs would replace them and that hasn't happened yet.

ANNA No.

RICH You see, there's nothing more convenient than a book, is there?

ANNA Well, I think you're a bit frightened of change. I mean ... I bet you've got a fax machine, haven't you, but actually e-mail is way better because it's much faster than a fax machine. And I bet you thought you'd never have anything as advanced as a fax machine, but look, you use it every day ...

RICH No, but yes, I use the fax, but I think e-mail is a very expensive form of sending letters because you've got to pay the subscription to the company and everything, whereas ...

ANNA Yeah, that's true.

RICH ...with a fax you're ... you're just paying for a simple phone call.

ANNA Well, I agree. And a fax is still a good way of sending visual information, such as drawings and diagrams. But, you know, a lot of people like to be... you know ... contacted by e-mail.

RICH Really?

ANNA Yeah. Oh yeah!

RICH I can't believe that!

ANNA It's quite a sociable thing, you know, because you can even ...

RICH I think it's even better to have a handwritten letter, don't you?

ANNA Well ...

RICH It sounds really impersonal to me.

ANNA Well, no ... not really, because you can be quite sociable, you know; you can talk to people, rather than ... you send something, somebody sends something back, you know, you can do one line here, one line there. It's great.

RICH No, I disagree. I don't think it's very sociable to be contacted by e-mail and be talking to a computer screen. I mean, it's like talking to a robot.

ANNA Well, I think it's good to be connected to e-mail, because it is a very spontaneous way of communicating with people all over the world.

RICH What about the Internet? I mean, you're a huge fan of that, now, aren't you?

ANNA Well, you're right, I am. I mean, I don't think it should be government controlled, because then, you know, you lose your freedom of speech, your ...

RICH Well ...

ANNA ... your rights, to say what you want to say ...

RICH I can see what you're saying, but I do believe there should be some control over the Internet, otherwise it could be used as a way of sending political propaganda, or pornography. There's a huge amount of pornography, and it goes to anyone with a computer. I think that's wrong.

ANNA Well, I agree with that. But there are a lot of people that are afraid of being censored by the government ...

RICH Well, people are being censored right now... And... in lots of different ways. Why do we only use the Internet as an argument there?

ANNA Well, I see your point, but what about TV then? What are your views on that? Because, you know, I think that if you can watch TV stations from anywhere in the world, then obviously it's going to help you to find out about other cultures. You know, being connected to cable and satellite TV is not as expensive as you might think these days.

RICH No, but if there's a lot of satellite television coming in and it's all in different languages, it's not much use because you won't understand it!

ANNA Yes, I suppose so. But you can still look at the pictures!

Lesson 28 **Vocabulary and Listening, activity 3**

Q I'm here in California and I'm interviewing Don Wright. He's a computer programmer and he lives in a very elegant ranch-style house here in Orange County, California. And this house is surrounded by vineyards, it's not far from the beach, which is located close to the town and which is used by most people at least once a day. Now, Don, tell me, what I'd like to know is, and what my listeners would like to know is, what's your attitude toward your possessions? Do you consider yourself to be a wealthy person?

DON Oh, I wouldn't call myself wealthy no, but I guess I'd have to say I'm pretty well off here. It's a nice place to live, don't you think?

Q Yes, I do.

DON And the family next door, well, I'd say they were quite wealthy. I mean, they've got vineyards and everything. But just because they're rich doesn't mean they're not friendly. They ... They're very friendly people, like most of the people in the neighborhood.

Q Oh, that's nice.

DON I mean, I don't feel particularly materialistic. I don't feel the need to have an expensive limousine parked in my driveway for instance, but I guess my lifestyle is fairly expensive. I'd like to have a house right down on the beach, but at the moment that's too expensive.

Q Is it? Right. And what are your leisure pursuits?

DON Well, I like to go surfing and I like rock-climbing and I like roller-blading, you know, that kind of thing.

Q Yeah?

DON And I like going camping, sometimes.

Q And … I mean, with all these things, with your camping and your rock-climbing, and everything, what about then your physical fitness? That's important, isn't it?

DON Absolutely. I feel like I can't even relax unless I feel fit. I think you'll find that's true of a lot of people in California. I like to go jogging every day, and so do my neighbors. You meet the whole neighborhood out before 8 A.M., running around in all the right gear!

Q Yeah.

DON It… it… means I can go into my working day feeling relaxed because my muscles have been worked.

Q Good, so you're not tense?

DON I'm not tense at all.

Q That's great! One of the things that seems to be sort of, um, a new thing, uh … certainly among almost everybody really, is a kind of feeling of spiritual development and mental development. I mean … how … What's your attitude toward that? Is it important?

DON It's very important. I used to, in my younger days, I used to live in a hippie community and um …

Q Oh, did you?

DON Yeah, and there was a change of attitude there toward mental and spiritual development and I find myself now turning to Buddhism and looking to the East, to the Eastern mysticism for a … for a way of life.

Q And does this affect your working pattern? Your work?

DON Well, I suppose it affects everything I do. It's a matter of being in tune with the world instead of fighting against it, I suppose. I'm a computer programmer and, um … and … my work is very important to my self-esteem, and so it's important to me that I, um, that I enjoy my work and that I'm not struggling against it.

Q Right.

DON And I find that the working environment here in California is fairly laid-back. Sometimes there's a little bit of stress at work, but, uh, I'd say everything goes pretty smoothly, as long as you're in the spiritual flow.

Q And what are your attitudes toward visitors, people who are not part of your immediate community?

DON Well, I really like the cosmopolitan …

Q …you do?

DON … aspects of California. I think you'll find if you talk to most of the people in the neighborhood, not many were actually born here. California's … is a place that all kinds of different backgrounds come to and there's a real … the area's really ethnically diverse and I find that particularly um … particularly pleasant as a place to live. I think you'll find very little racism in this area and I really hate racist attitudes.

Q Oh, yes, yes. So do I. Thank you very much, Don Wright.

Lesson 29 **Listening, activity 1**

JANET Well, I certainly had a lucky escape last summer. I'd been on vacation in Venezuela. I'd had a wonderful time, and for my last three days I'd traveled up to Curaçao, which is this wonderful tropical island off the coast. And, well, people had warned me that flights out of Curaçao were very unreliable, you know, they got cancelled all the time and that sort of thing. But the man in the airline office assured me that I definitely would get a plane on Thursday morning. You see I had to be in Caracas to get my flight back to Miami that night. Well, anyway, he said that cancellations were a thing of the past and that all their flights now left on time and there were no problems. Well, on Thursday morning I got up early, you know, to get to the airport in plenty of time, but there was no one there. No one at all—it was all closed up. It was seven in the morning and my flight was supposed to leave at eight thirty, so I was a little worried, but I thought, OK, keep calm, maybe somebody will come along soon. So I managed to stay calm … and at a quarter to eight a few people did come but they didn't know anything about an eight thirty flight. In the end at about half past *nine* someone from the airline company arrived but he just said he didn't know whether there would be a flight that day or not. I was really anxious by now because I just had to be in Caracas by ten o'clock in the evening or I would miss my flight home. No one seemed to have *any* idea what was going on. By twelve o'clock I got really frustrated because they wouldn't give me any information, and I didn't know what to do. There were no phones working and I didn't know who I could call for help anyway. Well, in the end, I sat at that miserable little airport for *eight hours*! A small plane did eventually come and I got to Caracas about thirty minutes too late. I was furious. I had to spend the night in Caracas and wait for a plane the following afternoon. But the next morning, I heard on the news that the plane I should have taken from Caracas to Miami had crashed. I was totally shocked. If I hadn't been delayed in Curaçao, I would have been on that plane. I would have been in the plane crash. It was a very lucky escape!

PAUL Well, I had a lucky escape just the other night. I was having a drink down at the bowling alley, when these two kids came in and they started a fight with another guy who was just sitting there, not causing any trouble or anything. Anyway, a couple of other guys and I tried to stop the fight, and we pulled the two punks off the man, but one of them managed to swing around and hit me in the face. I've still got a black eye. Well, in the end the police came and they arrested them. And I found out afterward that the one who had hit me had a knife in his pocket. So I suppose I was lucky that he didn't do more damage. If he'd pulled out his knife, I could have been in real trouble. But what really makes me furious is that I found out a couple of days later that the police just let them go. They didn't charge them or anything because they were only sixteen. I think that's disgraceful. They should have locked them up! In fact I'm going to call the police station to complain.

LISA I was involved in a really bad car crash a few months ago. In fact, I'm lucky to be alive. And if I hadn't been wearing my seat belt I wouldn't be alive today. I was driving down the road on my way home from work behind this big truck with a load of hay bales, you know a farm truck and the hay was piled up really high. I was thinking how nice it was that you still see country scenes like this, you know, farmers with loads of hay for their cattle driving down the road and … suddenly the truck swerved sharply to the left. I don't know if he was trying to avoid something on the road or what, but he swerved and the load of hay started to fall off the truck and there were all these bales of hay falling down on my car. And well, I braked as hard as I could, but I couldn't see where I was going because there was all this hay on the hood of my car, blocking the windshield. Well, I ran into the back of the truck and the whole front of my car was completely crushed in and I ended up in the hospital with broken bones. I think if I hadn't been wearing my seat belt and if I had been driving faster, I would have been killed for sure. I was extremely lucky.

Lesson 32 **Vocabulary and Listening, activity 4**

JESSICA What's your favorite piece of music, Steve?

STEVE Oh, that's a tough question! There are a lot of things I like. It's, it's hard to pick out just one.

JESSICA But if you were shipwrecked on an island and you could only have one piece of music, what would it be?

STEVE You mean something I could listen to again and again without getting tired of it?

JESSICA Yeah.

STEVE Well, you know, I think something classical. I mean, there are many songs that I like, you know, pop songs and so forth, but if I had to listen to it again and again, I might start to hate them. I think I would have to have something a bit longer like a symphony, then it would take a longer time to get bored with it. And I find that classical music does wonders for me. It's so relaxing. I listen to it and all my troubles just disappear.

JESSICA So which piece?

STEVE Probably Mahler's ninth symphony. I know it isn't a masterpiece, but it was played at the first classical concert I ever went to when I was a child, and I just fell in love with it. What about you?

JESSICA Well, I don't like classical music that much, especially dramatic orchestral stuff. I think it's too much—all those wailing violins and crashing cymbals. Personally, I prefer pop music. I'm a big fan of Pearl Jam. I think my favorite song right now is "I'm Still Alive." It's way cool!

STEVE Oh, I can't stand their music. It drives me crazy! Why do you like it so much?

JESSICA Oh, I don't know ... I just do. I like the lyrics and the beat, and, well, I like most of the songs that Pearl Jam do.

STEVE Do you have a favorite book?

JESSICA Oh, yes. I just love *The Remains of the Day* by Kazuo Ishiguro. I've read it five times. I can always find something new in it. Have you read it?

STEVE No, I haven't ... but I did see the movie. It was great.

JESSICA Oh, I haven't seen it yet. I'm really looking forward to it. So, do you read a lot?

STEVE No, not very much ... but I do have a favorite book— *Chosen* by Chaim Potok. It's fantastic. When I first read it, I just couldn't put it down.

JESSICA Oh, I've heard that's good, but I've never read it.

STEVE You really should—I'll lend it to you if you want.

JESSICA Oh, thanks!

Fluency 4 **Listening and Speaking, activity 3**

LEO My name is Leo. I'm a businessman in the U.S. And, uh, you've given me a list of statements about business practices in the U.S., in America, and, uh, I've, uh, been asked to tell you whether I perceive of them as being true or false. Uh, the first one you gave me: "Most people stay with the same company all their working lives." I'd have to say that's false. Uh, that might have been true in the first half of this century, uh, but lately—I think there have even been statistics about this—most professionals tend to change jobs four or five times over their professional lives, over, say, you know, thirty or forty years, so that's false.

The next statement you gave me: "You expect friends and relatives to help you get a good job." I'd have to say that's false. The word "expect", "you expect friends and relatives", that's, that's very strong language. I would say that's false. If they can lend some help to you to, to land a good position, that's appreciated, uh, but we don't really expect our, our families and our relatives to, to get us a good job.

The next statement you gave me: "It's very common to spend the evening with colleagues from work." That's false. I think that's much more common in Japan, where you're expected to, you know, have a couple of drinks and, and unwind and relax and maybe talk a little more business after hours with your working colleagues. No, in the U.S., um, you tend to go home to your family or to your own private life. There might occasionally be a drink with co-workers or perhaps with clients, or prospective clients—people you want to be doing regular business with—occasionally after hours, or with your co-workers to follow up on a project or a meeting that you've just had during the day, but, uh, it's not common to spend the evening with colleagues from work.

Your next statement: "It's important to greet all of your work colleagues when you arrive in the morning." Well, it's ... I'd say that's false. It's sort of common courtesy to at least, uh, mutter a hello and try to look cheerful, uh, to the people that you work with and maybe in your immediate department— the people that you work with every day, but, uh, you certainly don't have to go around to every office and every cubicle, every work area, and, and greet everyone hello and good morning. That's not expected at all.

The next statement here: "There's no place for social conversation during a business meeting." I'd have to say that's false. Um, but with this, uh, with this statement added to it, though, on my part. If, if someone's running late for a business meeting, uh, then it's perfectly natural to perhaps, uh, talk about one another's families, how your children are doing in soccer practice, how your wives are doing. But then once everyone is there, once all of the business associates are in attendance for the meeting, then social conversation would not be appropriate. Then you talk about business, you address the agenda, you might say, which means, uh, you talk about only what's intended and what's planned to be talked about during the meeting.

The next statement you have: "Businesspeople don't give gifts because they may be seen as bribes." Well, again, that's tricky. I'd have to say that that's, uh, that that's true. They don't give gifts because they might be seen as someone looking for a favor or, or a bribe. Uh, except during the holiday season, uh, from Thanksgiving in America which is late November on through the New Year, early January, it's in fact customary, uh, to give clients and prospects—people you want to do business with—a gift. Uh, perhaps as a show of appreciation for their business. And that's not seen as a bribe, or, um, as a bargaining for position with the person at all. It's, uh, it's considered a nice thing to do.

Your next statement: "If you leave your office door open it means you're ready to receive visitors." That's false. Uh, in America, you really have to have an appointment, uh, to do business or to have a meeting with someone who has their own office. If their door is open, it might be fine for other colleagues in the office to come in with a quick question or with information, or perhaps a visit from a secretary or, or an executive assistant, but certainly not someone outside the company. A visitor can't just drop by just because the person's door is open.

The next statement you gave me: "Business hours are from 9 A.M. to 5 P.M." That's true. Uh, executives, people that run companies and sometimes executive assistants or secretaries certainly stay longer. They might even come in earlier than nine in the morning, but normal business hours, uh, for, for, uh, customers to call, for instance, is nine to five.

Let's see, the next business practice statement you gave me ... oh, yes: "The most important people are in the center of an open-plan office. I'd have to say that's false. First of all, from "open-plan office," uh, I think what you mean is that there are no walls in the center of the area. Uh, you can put up portable walls and create cubicle space, uh, in the middle of the room. That's called an open-plan office. So the most important people, uh, they would be the CEOs—the chief executive officers—the people that really run the company. They would have windows. Uh, because they've earned them. It is considered, uh, delightful to have a window office, so they would be around the perimeter, or in other words, the edges of the open-plan office. And the last statement you gave me: "Most people retire at the age of fifty-five." That's definitely false. Most people in America work until the age of sixty-five. Uh, and perhaps on until they die. A lot of people in America never want to retire. They just want to keep on working.

Well, so I hope that helps clarify some of the business practices in the U.S. It's been nice talking to you.

Fluency 4 Listening and Speaking, activity 7

MAN Being a publisher must be very interesting.

WOMAN Well, yes, it can be, although it involves a lot of hard work.

MAN Oh, so tell me, what special qualities do you think you need to be a good publisher?

WOMAN Well, the first thing is you need to get along well with people.

MAN And I imagine you have to work well in a team.

WOMAN Oh, yes, that's certainly true. And you have to be calm and patient as well.

MAN Oh, I'm no good at staying calm, especially when I'm dealing with problems!

WOMAN Well, it takes a long time to learn how to deal with problems at work. And above all, you have to be able to concentrate for long periods of time.

MAN Oh, I am terrible at that. I just can't concentrate at all.

Lesson 34 Grammar, activity 1

WOMAN Can you lend me some money? I forgot to go to the bank.

MAN Well, I've only got a few dollars on me.

WOMAN Oh, darn. I need a lot. Don't worry. I'll go to the bank when I go shopping.

MAN If you're going shopping, can you get me a gallon of milk?

WOMAN What kind of milk?

MAN Any kind is OK. No, actually get one percent. Oh, and we need some cans of tomatoes. I'm making spaghetti tonight. We've got hardly any pasta. Could you get some pasta, too?

WOMAN Sure.

Lesson 34 Listening and Speaking, activity 2

Q Good morning. Do you have a few minutes to answer a questionnaire about shopping trends?

JORGE AND NANTHAPA Sure.

Q Thank you very much. First of all, can I ask your names and where you are from?

JORGE I'm Jorge and I come from Mexico.

NANTHAPA My name's Nanthapa and I'm from Thailand.

Q Great. Now can you tell me how often you go shopping? Jorge?

JORGE Well, in my country I suppose most people go shopping about two or three times a week. For food, I mean. We go to the supermarket and buy everything we need for every other day or so. There are a few things we might buy more frequently, like say bread, but on the whole I think about two or three times a week.

NANTHAPA Oh. In my country I think people go shopping every day because there are lots of markets and you, well, if you buy things at the market every day you know that they are really fresh.

Q I see. So that's a difference! What would you say you spend most money on?

JORGE Well, food of course. And personally I spend a lot of money on CDs. I really like music and I buy a lot of CDs. Also clothes. I spend a lot on clothes. I probably buy something every week.

NANTHAPA Yes, I think food and clothes for me too, really. But I don't buy clothes regularly—only when I see something I like.

Q And what about other things? Do you buy things for the home?

JORGE What do you mean?

Q Well, things like carpets, chairs, you know furniture and, well, pictures…

NANTHAPA I don't buy things like that very often.

JORGE I sometimes buy things for the home, but only every few months, not that often.

Q I see. Now which of the items you buy are necessities?

JORGE Well, food of course. That's definitely a necessity. Oh, and things like a newspaper and, uh, well, clothes. I think clothes are a necessity. Well, if you're buying them because you need them and not because you want something fashionable.

Q What about you Nanthapa?

NANTHAPA Necessities? Well, as Jorge said, food is a necessity. I'm not sure about a newspaper ... maybe clothes ... but really I think just food.

Q And how often do you buy presents for other people?

JORGE Oh, sometimes. If it's someone's birthday or at Christmas. But it has to be a special occasion.

NANTHAPA Well, I buy presents if I am going to someone's house. And sometimes I may buy something for a friend, just for fun because I know they will like it. So I guess I buy presents pretty often.

Q And what about paying for things you buy? Do you usually use cash or credit cards or checks? Which do you prefer?

NANTHAPA Oh, I always use cash.

JORGE It depends. For something big I would probably use a credit card. Otherwise I prefer cash.

Q Right. OK. What about borrowing money? Do you ever borrow money from friends or from a bank?

JORGE Not from a bank, no. And friends ... well, not very much. I might borrow a little money, you know, if I hadn't got enough for my bus fare or something like that. But not just because there's something expensive I want to buy. And I would never ask a friend to lend me a lot of money, no.

Q And you, Nanthapa, do you borrow money?

NANTHAPA No, I don't. I don't like to borrow money at all. If I want to buy something expensive then I wait until I have enough money to buy it.

Q So do you like to save money?

NANTHAPA Well, I try to save money, but it's very difficult. There are so many nice things I would like to buy; but if there's something special I want, then, yes, I'll save up for it. But then I'm saving to buy something in particular. Not saving to have lots of money in the bank. I'm no good at that!

JORGE Yes, I'm pretty much the same. I would really like to be able to save money and get interest on it, but usually I spend my money as soon as I've earned it.

Q Well, that's all the questions. Thank you both very much.

JORGE AND NANTHAPA That's OK. You're welcome. No problem.

Lesson 36 **Vocabulary and Listening, activity 2**

Part 1

ALICE So, here we all are again. After twenty years ... Boy, life sure has changed us, hasn't it? You think you know it all when you're eighteen, just out of high school, full of plans for the future. Everything's mapped out for you. I mean, here's me, Alice-the-cheerleader! All I ever wanted was to get married. That was my plan. You know the story, I was going to marry Mr. Right, have two kids in a pretty little house with a white picket fence and live happily ever after ...

BEN You look pretty happy to me!

ALICE Oh, sure, now I am. But first I got married to Mr. Wrong and had two beautiful kids, and was divorced by the age of twenty-five. No education, no money, and no house.

BEN So what did you do?

ALICE Well, I had always thought about going to college, you know, so I did. I put myself through night school, got a teacher's certificate, and now ... Well, I love teaching and I'm very happy with my job ... But I'm still looking for Mr. Right!

Part 2

ALICE What about you, Ben? What have you been doing these last twenty years? You know, I remember way back in high school, you always said you were going to change the world.

BEN No, no ... *You* always said I was going to change the world, not me. I only said I was going to try. Anyway, right after college I joined the Peace Corps. You knew that, right? I was in the Sudan for two years, teaching. That was the greatest thing ... the greatest thing. I learned so much there.

ALICE So what are you doing now?

BEN Oh, this and that. You know ... I'm keeping my head above water. I work downtown. I manage a shelter for battered women downtown. It's ... um ... hard. You wouldn't believe some of the stories I could tell. I guess you could say the world has changed me more than I've changed it. But it's worth it.

Part 3

COREY Well, no one can accuse me of wanting to change the world! Man, I just wanted to be rich and famous! I was going to play pro-ball ... the Dallas Cowboys. I wanted it all—the money, the fans, the Superbowl ring—the whole nine yards!

DEB That's right. You went to UCLA on a football scholarship, didn't you? I remember that. I remember reading about that somewhere. You got injured, right? Your knee, wasn't it?

COREY Yeah ... yeah. A quick end to my illustrious career! Boom! End of story. So then I actually had to do some studying. I got a law degree and now I do divorces. You know, seventy hours a week of custody battles and alimony. And I never got famous! But you know, Alice, I think I may have represented your Mr. Wrong.

ALICE That was you?

Part 4

DEB Me? Wow, I don't know. I mean, high school was such a long time ago. I never really had any plans, you know, beyond college. It took me so long to choose a major, my parents thought I'd never graduate. At first I was going to study anthropology, then law ... but that was too sleazy. Sorry, Corey!

COREY Very funny!

DEB So, I finally settled on pre-med 'cause one of the guys I was planning on going out with was going to be a doctor.

ALICE Good reason!

DEB Tell me about it! But I loved medicine. I loved it. It was great. So I dumped my boyfriend, got my degree, and then, and then ... went to med school, and ...

BEN Doctor Debra Fisher! Great!

DEB Yeah. But I'm not in practice. I do research for a pharmaceutical company. It's great. I'm doing cancer research.

ALICE Wow. That's great. You know ... I have had this pain in my back for a few months now. What do you think it could be? Do you think it could be sciatica?

Lesson 38 **Vocabulary and Listening, activity 3**

MAN Paul Bunyan was the hugest lumberjack that ever lived. So huge ... they say that when he was a baby he was too big to fit inside his house. So his father had to cut down trees and make him a boat and float him out on the river. When he grew up, his folks had to teach him not to step on the farmhouses or lean on any mountains or he'd crush the people in those parts. His folks also gave him his first ax. Well, Paul loved that! He could cut down forests like toothpicks. People say he could cut down a whole forest before lunch, and another one before dinner! Paul loved his life, but he was lonely—he needed a friend. One day when he was walking in the woods, in the deep of winter when it was so cold the snow was blue, Paul came upon a huge mountain that was almost as big as he was! Well, ol' Paul noticed the mountain was moving. First two huge horns appeared, then a head, then Paul could see the biggest ox ever, as blue as the snow he'd been under. Paul named him Babe and they became the best of friends. They took off to North Dakota and cut down every tree in the state so the farmers could farm. And after that they headed off to Alaska, and they just might be there still.

WOMAN Well, Pecos Bill, of course, Pecos Bill was the most famous cowboy that ever lived. He was the one that practically invented cowboying. Yes, sir. He was the youngest of fourteen brothers and sisters and when he was just born, his family decided to move farther west. Well ol' Bill fell out of their wagon while they were moving. Luckily, he was adopted by a pack of coyotes and raised like he was one of their own. He grew up wild and naked and didn't learn to speak any language but coyote. It wasn't till Bill ran into a Texan cowboy (who pointed out that Bill couldn't be a coyote 'cause he didn't have a tail) that Bill decided to try being a cowboy for a while. It wasn't long before Bill was surprised by a forty-foot rattlesnake that thought Bill looked like lunch. Well, Bill whipped that rattler around and decided he would make a good lasso. They say that was the first lasso ever invented! After that, he tamed a wild mountain lion and rode him for a horse. He soon met up with a band of cow hands, became their leader and invented a two-week cattle drive just for something to do. Yessirree, that Pecos Bill sure came a long way from living with those coyotes.

MAN Well, Johnny Appleseed is about the best darned thing that ever happened to this country, I reckon. He was an apple missionary. He went about spreading the good word of simple living and right thinking and helping all living creatures. Yes, sir, he had the radical idea that you ought to put back into life more than you got out of it. Well, Johnny decided the way he was going to do that was to wander around planting apple orchards all through the wilderness. "Seeds! Seeds! Apple seeds!" he'd call out to the settlers, who were amazed by this stranger.

Johnny Appleseed went about barefoot, with a tin coffeepot on his head and a sugar sack for a shirt. Johnny never hurt a living thing. It is said that he once put his campfire out when he noticed that mosquitoes were flying into it and getting hurt. He ate only nuts and gooseberries, talked to the animals, and sang to the birds. Why, they say he loosed a wolf from a farmer's trap one day, and that wolf was so grateful, he followed him around like a tame dog for the rest of his life.

People also say that Johnny Appleseed's ghost is still around today in those parts. They say that he's still there, looking after the orchards and taking care of the animals.

Lesson 39 Speaking and Listening, activity 5

MAN So tell me something about these brands and the image they project. What about Mercedes for example? What kind of image and appeal do they wish to convey to the consumer?

WOMAN Well, Mercedes is one of the world's best known brands for motor vehicles, of course, and Mercedes is famous for its image of excellent engineering, of safety of its cars, and of its German reliability, you know, you should buy a Mercedes because it won't let you down. Now, all this, you might think, could make it a very expensive product, designed to appeal to only the very rich, and it's true that in the past, drivers of Mercedes Benz cars belonged to the richest social class. But while it's true that a Mercedes is an expensive car, its appeal is much broader than you might imagine. It has what might be described as an *aspirational* appeal, which attracts people of all incomes and backgrounds. It's unlike most luxury cars, such as Rolls Royce, which deliberately set out to appeal to only a very small, select group of people, the aristocracy and the extremely rich. It's truly egalitarian in its image and appeal.

MAN How about Benetton?

WOMAN Benetton, yes. You could say that because of its controversial advertising campaigns, its image is better known than the product the brand represents. Well, Benetton is known for its fashion products, of course, and there's no question that the clothes are well-made, look very good, and are relatively cheap, with Italian style and flair. Benetton began its advertising campaign a few years ago with a multicultural, international image of its slogan, the United Colors of Benetton. But after a while, they decided the image they wanted to give its products was slightly different, somehow, slightly less ... how should I put it ... run of the mill. And now they set out to shock people with their advertising, while at the same time still stressing that the images all belong to the same kind of broad, all-embracing international community of fashion wear. And the appeal is very much to the young consumers, who feel different, who feel special, who feel they could change the world, or at least shake the world out of its complacency. It gives an interesting, exciting angle on what is frankly a rather uninteresting product.

MAN And what about Gillette? What image do they want to project?

WOMAN Well, in the beginning Gillette was as American as apple pie, but one of those products which not only everyone knew around the world, but everyone could actually buy around the world too, even if they didn't have much money. The product is of course personal care for men—razors, aftershave, shaving cream. And unlike say Mercedes and Benetton, the product is now not a luxury one but an essential, at least in those cultures where men shave every day. So we have an essential product used every day by men all around the world. Not much scope for any excitement in its image, you might think. Wrong. Gillette's image is one of freshness, of love of life. "Gillette—the best a man can get" is the slogan and its appeal is to every man, young at heart even if not in years. But recently, Gillette has slightly adapted this image so that it appeals to "today's" man, the "new man" if you like, who is in touch with his emotions, someone who takes his responsibilities as a father very seriously, since being a father is being part of this love of life I mentioned earlier.

So there are pictures of today's Gillette man tenderly holding his son in his arms, his son a member, presumably, of the next generation of Gillette users. Freshness, love of life, and fatherhood. That's what Gillette stands for.

Lesson 39 Vocabulary and Listening, activity 2

1 Classical music lovers are in for a real treat this week on Performance Today on WPBX, Public Radio. We'll be featuring the complete operatic works of Wolfgang Amadeus Mozart, starting tonight at eight o'clock with the ever-popular *Don Giovanni*. This is going to be a live broadcast from the San Francisco Opera, with Luciano Pavarotti in the lead role. Don't miss the magic and power of *Don Giovanni*, tonight at eight on WPBX.

2 Is it time for a dependable new car, truck, or utility vehicle? See the experts at Barton Beagle! Short on cash? See Barton Beagle! At Barton Beagle you will find a huge selection of new and used cars, trucks, 4-by-4s, and utility vehicles. Zero down on approved credit! Come in today and drive home in your dream vehicle! Stop in today at 1255 Madison Avenue, just across from the Northgate Mall. Barton Beagle—where we try harder for you!

3 **WOMAN** Would you like to lose ten pounds in ten days?
MAN Who wouldn't? Especially after the holidays!
WOMAN Well, you can! All you have to do is join Weightwatchers. They'll give you hundreds of dieting tips, menus, and serving suggestions. You'll learn how to take off the pounds and how to keep them off! And the first five pounds are FREE!
MAN You mean if I don't lose weight, I don't pay?
WOMAN That's right! But you will, and after that you get the monthly magazine for only $19.95 a year. Believe me, it's worth it!
MAN Hmm! Sounds great! How do I join?
WOMAN Just call Weightwatchers at 1-800-LBS-GONE. "One-eight hundred, pounds gone!" And the pounds will be gone!
MAN One-eight hundred, pounds gone! I'll call today!

4 Heat up the New Year with a hot getaway to Hawaii this January with Global Travel! Their New Year bargains will have you jumping out of the cold and onto a hot Hawaiian beach, so listen to this! Get away to spectacular Maui, Fridays in January, 6 nights, only $699! Imagine Maui in the Hawaiian Pacific, an exotic tropical wonderland where white powder beaches run into turquoise-colored waters. A playground with unbelievable sailing, swimming, snorkeling, golf, tennis, and more! Stop by your nearest Global Travel office today, or call 555-1234 for more details on these great vacation getaways!

5 Save hundreds or thousands of dollars on your life insurance! The company I'm talking about is Select-Quote. If you read the *Wall Street Journal*, *Kiplinger's*, or *Money*, you've seen their ads. Male non-smokers, 31 years old, $250,000 worth of life insurance for $220. If you're 36, $150,000 coverage for $165. At age 45, a half-a-million-dollar life policy is $695. Select-Quote saves you money because they continually compare the cost of the term life insurance policies of American's top-rated companies. Call Select-Quote today 1-800-932-5400, toll-free. They'll mail to you, without any obligation, a free, personalized price comparison of the five policies that get you the most life insurance for the least amount of money. Call Select-Quote today at 1-800-932-5400, and see how much you can really save on your life insurance!

Lesson 40 **Listening and Vocabulary, activity 3**

SALESPERSON Can I help you, ma'am?

CUSTOMER Yes, I bought this watch here last week and I've been having a few problems with it.

SALESPERSON What seems to be the trouble?

CUSTOMER Well, the salesperson said it was waterproof, but when I wore it in the swimming pool, it just filled with water.

SALESPERSON Let me see. Oh, yes. We have had some problems with this brand. Would you like me to replace it with a similar model?

CUSTOMER Actually, I'd rather have my money back.

SALESPERSON Of course. We can do that for you. Do you have your receipt?

CUSTOMER Yes, here it is.

SALESPERSON Thank you.

CUSTOMER You know, I think you should check what you sell more carefully.

SALESPERSON Yes, I'm very sorry about that.

Fluency 5 **Speaking and Listening, activity 2**

RICK Hi, Joe, my name is Rick. I'm doing a survey for my company about various things American.

JOE OK.

RICK Cultural ideas, uh, things about government, perceptions about politics maybe and, uh, we can start actually with what you're holding there—American money.

JOE Oh, yeah.

RICK I see it's a, it looks like a one dollar bill?

JOE Uh, yeah. This is a single, a dollar bill, um...

RICK It's the same thing—a single, a dollar bill?

JOE Yeah, yeah. That's what we call it, a single, a buck, you know.

RICK A buck, uh-huh. That's sort of slang, I guess.

JOE Yeah, I guess.

RICK Who's this person in the middle of the one dollar bill?

JOE Oh, this is George Washington. He's, you know, the first President of the United States.

RICK George Washington, the first President, uh-huh.

JOE Yeah.

RICK Uh-huh and it's a sort of greyish green color.

JOE Yeah, it's not the most attractive money in the world. It's a little greener on the other side.

RICK Yeah, it's much greener on the other side. It looks like it fits nicely into your wallet.

JOE Well, yeah, they make them that way.

RICK How convenient! And on the other side here, right in the middle, spelled out...

JOE In God We Trust.

RICK In God We Trust.

JOE Yeah, and then we've got an eagle over here, with, you know, some stuff in its claws ... I don't really know, I guess some wheat and some arrows.

RICK Mmm. Some wheat and some arrows, you say?

JOE Yeah. Yeah. I guess that's industry and, uh, and war, I don't know.

RICK Now what's this here, the, the, you have a coin as well.

JOE Oh, yeah. Well, I've got a nickel, uh, that's five cents.

RICK That's five cents.

JOE Yeah, yeah. That has Thomas Jefferson, I think.

RICK Thomas Jefferson. Was he also a president?

JOE Uh, he was, yeah, he was definitely president at some point, I don't know when. Sometime after George, I'm not sure.

RICK Uh-huh. This copper-colored coin is, is what?

JOE This is a penny. This is one cent. And this has Lincoln on it. Lincoln was, uh, Lincoln was president also.

RICK Well, about the United States. Can you tell me about some of the products that are manufactured in the U.S., in America, but they're exported, they're sent out, and they're famous around the world?

JOE Well, let's see. I guess the first thing that comes to mind would be Coca-Cola.

RICK Coca-Cola? Really?

JOE Yeah. The soft drink, yeah.

RICK Right.

JOE That's huge, I mean, that's everywhere. I mean, it's great, you know, it's, it's carbonated. It's got bubbles in it.

RICK It's bubbly and fizzy, right.

JOE Yeah, it's very sweet. You know they have a Diet Coke.

RICK It's a very popular drink.

JOE Oh, very popular.

RICK Mmm. And pretty much you can find Coca-Cola in any country, right?

JOE Yeah. They have it in Russia from what I understand, yeah.

RICK Wow, in Russia too! And, uh, so who would want to buy Coca-Cola? Pretty much anyone in the world?

JOE Yeah, I guess. I mean, I couldn't imagine anyone not liking it. I mean, I guess some people don't, but, but everybody drinks it.

RICK Besides Coca-Cola what are a few other products that we'd find, uh, anywhere in the world that are made in America?

JOE Gee, um, well, American movies...

RICK Movies? Really?

JOE Yeah.

RICK OK.

JOE That's a big industry and American movies are very popular all over the world.

RICK Hmm. So, they're, they're I guess dubbed or switched into the language of the country they're being sent to.

JOE Yeah, they dub them or they subtitle them, I guess.

RICK Uh-huh

RICK Getting back to work in America, and, uh, things to do. What would be five prestigious jobs; uh, jobs that are, when I say prestigious, meaning, uh, perhaps well-paying or...

JOE Or important jobs.

RICK Important jobs. Sure

JOE Um, well let's see—president of a bank.

RICK President of a bank.

JOE That's a pretty important job.

RICK OK. That's one.

JOE Uh, movie producer.

RICK Movie producer. That would be understandable since that's one of the leading exports, I guess.

JOE They make a lot of money too.

RICK OK, that's two. How about a third?

JOE Um, well ... politicians.

RICK Politicians is considered a prestigious job?

JOE Yeah, yeah, they're very important.

RICK OK, how about a fourth?

JOE Hmm, let's see, actors.

RICK Actors? A prestigious job?

JOE Sure, they make a lot of money.

RICK Uh-huh.

JOE A lot of money, you know, in the movies. Sure.

RICK How about a fifth important or, or prestigious job in, in America?

JOE Uh, I guess the chairman of a big company. They call them the CEO.

RICK CEO?

JOE Yeah.

RICK The chairman of a company. What does CEO stand for?

JOE That's, well, I think the chief executive officer.

RICK Great. That's five prestigious jobs. How about five, if you will, unprestigious jobs, or jobs that, uh, perhaps are looked down upon or not as important?

JOE Well, gee, I guess ... bus boy.

RICK Bus boy? OK.

JOE Yeah, the guys who take the plates away at restaurants.

RICK Oh, oh, OK. They take away your empty plates in a restaurant.

JOE Yeah, yeah. They don't make a lot of money.

RICK Right. How about another one?

JOE Uh, let's see ... a shoe salesman.

RICK A shoe salesman?

JOE Yeah.

RICK OK

JOE You know, the guy you buy your shoes from.

RICK OK, so we've got bus boy, shoe salesman. How about a third?

JOE Um, construction worker?

RICK Construction worker? It's considered not that prestigious, huh?

JOE Well, I guess they make some money, but, uh, I guess it's ... they're, they're considered to be pretty low class, on the whole.

RICK How about a fourth job?

JOE Uh, a plumber, I guess.

RICK A plumber? Works on the pipes?

JOE Yeah. Yeah. You know, if your sink gets clogged or your toilet backs up, you call a plumber.

RICK Sounds like sometimes, uh, important jobs can actually be considered unprestigious.

JOE Yeah, I guess so.

RICK OK. So, plumbers is the fourth one. How about one more not so prestigious job?

JOE Um, I guess a dog walker.

RICK A dog walker! OK. Uh, for people that are busy and don't have time to walk the dog.

JOE Yeah, yeah, you'll see guys walking down the street with twenty dogs.

RICK Wow! Oh, so instead of doing one at a time, they'll do twenty. They'll do a whole bunch of people's dogs.

JOE Yeah. And that's what they do for a living.

RICK Dog walker for a living. Wow, wow! That's sort of interesting, if unprestigious. That's it. Thanks for helping me with the survey.

JOE All right. Thanks a lot.

Fluency 5 **Speaking and Listening, activity 5**

JOE OK, well, let's see, I have a bunch of pictures here. Um, I guess you would say that they're universal signs. These are things that mean something that you don't really need words to express. I mean, they're, they're pictures that express something that everybody should know, I guess.

Um, let's see. There's a picture here of a guy pointing at his chest. That would mean, I guess, "Are you, are you asking me?" or "Do you mean me?" That's what, yeah, that's what that is. That's definitely something like that.

Um, here's a picture of a guy wiggling his forefinger, his, his index finger, uh, and that's, uh, let's see. That means "come here." Yeah, that means "come here," when you, when you pull your finger like that towards you, yeah, that means "come here."

Um, here we got a picture of a guy with his fingers crossed. Oh, OK. Your fingers crossed, that means, I guess, it means you want something to happen. You're hoping something will happen. It's, it's kind of a good luck gesture. Yeah, that's what that is.

Um ... hmm. Here's a picture of a guy with his little finger at his mouth and his thumb at his ear. Oh, well, this means you have a phone call. That's what that is—that means somebody's on the telephone and you're needed on the phone. That's what that means.

Um ... hmm. Now we've got someone waving their hand down. Oh, oh, OK. This means, uh, this means "take it easy" or "chill out." Yeah, that means, you know, "calm down" or just, you know, "tone it down a little." Yeah, that's definitely what that means.

And now we have a picture of someone with their finger on their lips. That's, that's easy. Everybody knows this. This means "be quiet." This means, you know, "shut up."

Macmillan Education
Between Towns Road, Oxford OX4 3PP, UK
A division of Macmillan Publishers Limited

Companies and representatives throughout the world

ISBN 0 435 29776 7

Text © Simon Greenall 1996
First published 1996
Design and illustration © Macmillan Publishers Limited 1998

Heinemann is a registered trademark of Reed Educational & Professional Publishing Limited

Author's Acknowledgements
I am very grateful to all the people who have contributed toward Move Up Advanced. Thank you so much to:
–   All the teachers I have worked with on seminars around the world, and the various people who have influenced my work.
–   Phyllis Dolgin for producing the tapes, and the actors for their voices.
–   The various schools who piloted the material.
–   Philip Kerr for his comments on the material, which are especially helpful and well-considered.
–   Helen O'Neill, Mike Sayer, Sue Bailey, and Elizabeth Fulco for their reports on the material. I have tried to respond to all their suggestions, and if I have not always been successful, then the fault is mine alone.
–   The Lake School, Sue Kay, and Ann Lee for allowing me to observe classes.
–   Simon Stafford for his usual skilful design.
–   Jacqueline Watson for tracking down some wonderful photos.
–   Helena Gomm for helping me out during a particularly busy period of writing.
–   Chris Hartley for his good faith in the Move Up project.
–   James Hunter and Bridget Green for their careful attention to detail and their creative contribution.
–   and last, but by no means least, Jill, Jack, Alex, and Grace.

Designed by Stafford & Stafford
Cover design by Stafford & Stafford

Illustrations by:
Adrian Barclay (Beehive Illustration), pp.46, 47, 72.
Hardlines pp.2, 5, 49.
Martin Sanders pp.20, 24/25, 26/27, 34, 39, 41, 43, 45, 48, 52/53, 60, 74/75, 79, 80, 82, 90, 94/95, 98, 100.
Simon Smith pp.3, 4, 12, 19, 59, 63, 72, 92, 93.

Commissioned photography by:
Chris Honeywell pp.54/55, 74, 76/77.

Acknowledgements
The authors and publishers would like to thank the following for their kind permission to reproduce material in this book:
BBC Worldwide Limited for an extract from the chapter "Santos to Santa Cruz" by Lisa St. Aubin de Terán from *Great Railway Journeys;* HarperCollins Inc. for an extract from *To Kill a Mockingbird* by Harper Lee; The Independent Newspaper Publishing plc for extracts from "I'd like to teach the world to sell" by Jonathan Glancey (*The Independent,* January 1993); "Growing Trends" by Paul Barker and Steve Connor (*The Independent on Sunday,* March 1995); The Observer for an extract from "Passion Play" by Beverley Glick; Vivienne Rae-Ellis for extracts from *True Ghost Stories of Our Own Time,* published by Faber and Faber Ltd; Random House UK Ltd on behalf of the Executors of the Estate of F. Scott Fitzgerald for an extract from *Tender is the Night,* published by The Bodley Head, and for an extract from *Beyond Belief* by Ron Lyon and Jenny Paschall, published by Stanley Paul and Company; Reed Consumer Books Ltd for an extract from *The Lost Continent* by Bill Bryson, published by Secker and Warburg; St. Martin's Press for an extract from *A Traveler's Guide to Latin American Customs and Manners* by Elizabeth Devine and Nancy Braganti; Times Newspapers Ltd for an extract from "Meals on Wheels" by Robin Young © Times Newspapers Ltd, 1994; Clive Anderson for illustrations from *Patent Nonsense,* published by Michael Joseph; H J Heinz Company Limited, Kellogg's Company of Great Britain Limited, Mitsubishi for use of their logos.

Photographs by: David Cannon/AllSport p.10; © BBC pp.22/23, 24; Nicholas Devore/Bruce Coleman p.36; Colorific p.66(b); Robert Harding Picture Library p.66(t); Hulton Deutsch p.70(t&b); Image Bank p.16(t), 32; Peter Newark's Western Americana p.51; The Photographer's Library pp.68/69; William Robinson p.56; Royal Army Medical College p.28; Matthew Sherrington p.44; Tony Stone Images pp.30/31, 33, 49, 83, 85, 89; Telegraph Colour Library p.64, 96; Zefa p.6, 15, 16(b), 86/87.

While every effort has been made to trace the owners of copyright material in this book, there have been some cases where the publishers have been unable to contact the owners. We should be grateful to hear from anyone who recognizes their copyright material and who is unacknowledged. We shall be pleased to make the necessary amendments in future editions of the book.

Printed in Thailand

2006   2005   2004   2003   2002
15   14   13   12   11   10   9   8   7